i-Ready Learning

MW01702658

Florida B.E.S.T. STANDARDS EDITION

Magnetic Reading™

GRADE 4

NOT FOR RESALE

ISBN 978-1-7280-5303-5

BTS24
15 14 13 12 11 10 9 8 7 6 25

Curriculum Associates

809537

Table of Contents

UNIT 2

Table of Contents (continued)

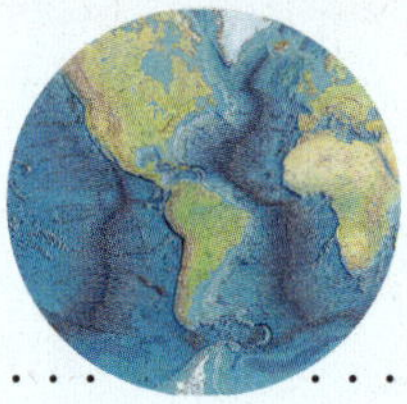

UNIT 3

UNIT 4

Traditions

Table of Contents (continued)

UNIT 6

Facing Challenges

Save
Save the Baobab tree

SESSION 1 TALK ABOUT THE TOPIC

Learning from Others

FOCUS QUESTION

What life lessons can we learn from others?

NOTICE AND WONDER

Look at the three stories you will read in this lesson. What do you notice? What do you wonder? Discuss your ideas with a partner.

THINK ABOUT LIFE LESSONS

The characters in these stories learn life lessons from challenges and get advice from others. Have you ever learned a life lesson from an experience or a person? Write notes and tell a partner about what you learned.

Memory	Lesson Learned

I remember ___.

The lesson I learned was ___.

from *Black Brother, Black Brother*
by Jewell Parker Rhodes

from *President of the Whole Fifth Grade*
by Sherri Winston

The Trouble with Talent
by Lee Lewis

from

Black Brother, Black Brother

by Jewell Parker Rhodes

Donte Ellison has been having a tough time at school. To feel more confident, he decides to learn fencing. Donte has just lost his first fencing match, or bout. As teammates and families start heading home, his coach gets permission from Donte's parents to take him to a doughnut shop to talk.

éclair = a cream-filled dessert with chocolate icing

1 "Get an old-fashioned. One with sprinkles. What about a chocolate **éclair**?"

2 In the pink-and-green shop, smelling of sizzling dough, I get all three. The éclair oozes like mud. Sprinkles look like glittery bugs; even the sugar tastes bitter.

3 Drinking black coffee, Coach watches me.

4 "Sorry I lost," I say, eyes cast down.

5 "I'm not worried about you, Donte. I'm proud of you."

6 My finger brushes sugar off the old-fashioned.

7 "I'm especially proud of how you rallied your team."

8 "Losing is still losing."

9 "Donte, it's not just about the bout. It's about leadership, giving respect. Patience and control."

10 I lift my gaze. "You're not mad?"

11 "Of course not. We're celebrating."

12 "I thought I was in trouble."

Stop & Discuss

How is Donte feeling at the doughnut shop?

Donte is feeling ___ because ___.

I can tell because ___.

13 “Not at all.” He leans against the table, his hands folded. “What’d you feel, Donte? When you were fencing?” Coach is urgent, intent like he’s holding his breath until I answer.

14 “It was the best.” I exhale. “The speed, the flick of the **foil**. The rush inside my head.”

foil = light, flexible sword used in fencing

15 “You felt alive?”

16 “Yeah. Like being on a huge screen in high-def. Everything clear, crisp. Even so fast, beyond fast. I knew moves before they happened. I can’t explain. Even though I was losing, it felt good.”

17 Coach’s hands smack the table. “I know exactly what you mean. I felt the same way.”

18 “You did?”

19 “I felt unstoppable when I fenced. Today, you reminded me of me. Yet, still without question, you. Watching your focus, your joy, I knew you were born to fence.”

20 Coach’s face is eager, happy. Crazy, he glows. He pats my hand. I feel the warmth, the bond between us.

21 Coach knows what’s in my mind. (I say it anyway.) “I want to fence,” I say, **insistent**. “I want to be the best.”

insistent = in an eager, sure way

Stop & Discuss

How are Donte and Coach alike?

Talk with a partner about how they each feel about fencing.

SPOTLIGHT BENCHMARK: ELA.4.R.1.2 Explain a stated or implied theme and how it develops, using details, in a literary text.

Explain a Theme

- The **theme** of a story is an important message or lesson about life that the author wants to share.
- As you read, notice how a theme develops. Pay attention to the **conflicts**, or problems the characters face. Think about how the characters respond to the problems and what they learn during the course of the story.

Reread/Think

Reread *Black Brother, Black Brother.* Think about what the characters do, say, think, and feel as they try to solve their problems. Complete the chart by answering the questions with details from the story.

Beginning	Middle	End
What is the conflict, or problem?	How do the characters respond to the conflict?	What do the characters learn from the experience?

Theme
What important message or lesson about life does the author want to share?

Talk

Share your chart with a partner. Discuss how Donte responds to the conflict and what he learns from the situation. Make changes to your chart if you need to.

Donte's conflict is ___. He responds by ___.

In the end, Donte learns that ___.

I think the theme is ___.

Write

What is the theme of *Black Brother, Black Brother*? What does Donte learn about winning and losing? Use details from the story to show how the theme develops.

WRITING CHECKLIST

- ☐ I stated the theme.
- ☐ I included details from the story to explain what Donte learns.
- ☐ I used complete sentences.
- ☐ I used correct spelling, punctuation, and capitalization.

from President of the Whole Fifth Grade

by Sherri Winston

Brianna Justice is running for fifth-grade class president. She is willing to do anything to win. Just the day before, she cheated in a very important election contest and lost. Now, Brianna is at Mrs. Wetzel's bakery, where she has been making cupcakes. Brianna's hero, Miss Delicious, is also there. Miss Delicious is a world-famous baker and millionaire.

1 "Miss Delicious, have you ever done something bad? Like really, really bad? And you wished you could take it back, but you can't? Something so bad that maybe you felt like you didn't deserve to wish for anything good ever again?"

2 She and Mrs. W. exchanged looks, then they doubled over with laughter. "If you're asking if we've made mistakes that either one of us wish we could take back, then, *baaaaybeee*, the answer's absolutely, positively, one hundred percent yes!"

3 Mrs. W. came around the kitchen work island, still laughing, then straightening and looking more serious. "But if you're asking us how to deal with a mistake, then let's talk it out. We all make mistakes in life, Brianna. How you handle your mistakes is what can **determine** who you really are."

determine = decide

Stop & Discuss

Why do you think Brianna asks Miss Delicious for advice?

Look for clues in the text and discuss your answer with a partner.

4 And that was what I really needed to know. How could I handle my mistakes, and who was I, really?

5 After we finished up in the kitchen, we drank coffee and talked.

6 Like any smart kid knows, even when you're feeling all close and connected to grown-ups you don't tell them all the dirty details. Hey, too much information would just confuse them.

7 But I did talk about my problem at school. My friends had warned me not to get carried away with the election. They had warned me about wanting to win more than I wanted to be a good president.

Stop & Discuss

What two pieces of advice did Brianna's school friends give her?

Underline the sentences that describe the advice.

passionate = having strong feelings and beliefs

motivated = hard working, excited to get things done

8 "Even if you did get carried away," said Miss Delicious, delicately holding the teacup as she sipped her cream-and-sugared coffee. "Even if that's true, you've learned from it. Making that mistake, getting carried away, heck, that just means you're **passionate**. So what? It doesn't mean you wouldn't make a great president. I think it's wonderful that you're so **motivated** and that you're a young lady with goals and dreams. But keep in mind, you're a kid. So be a kid. Take your time. Enjoy your life. Play basketball. Hang out with your friends. Don't be in a rush to grow up. Trust me, you'll have plenty of time to make your millions!"

9 If I was going to be president of the whole fifth grade, I needed to act like a leader now rather than later.

10 And with that, I let out a big breath and did my best to start fixing what I'd messed up!

Stop & Discuss

What advice does Miss Delicious give Brianna?

Miss Delicious shares with Brianna that ___.

Explain a Theme

- To find the theme of a story, think about how the characters respond to the conflicts. What do the characters learn?
- Then think about what readers can learn from the story. What message or lesson can readers apply to real life?

Reread/Think

Reread *President of the Whole Fifth Grade*. Complete the chart by answering the questions with details from the story. Notice how the theme develops.

Beginning	Middle	End
What is the conflict, or problem?	How do the characters respond to the conflict?	What do the characters learn from the experience?

Theme
What important message or lesson about life does the author want to share?

SESSION 4 PRACTICE

Talk

Share your chart with a partner. Explain how Brianna responds to the conflict and what she learns from her experience. Make changes to your chart if you need to.

Brianna's conflict is ___.

Brianna responds to the conflict by ___.

In the end, Brianna learns ___.

Write

What is the theme of *President of the Whole Fifth Grade*? How does the theme develop in the story? Use at least two details from the story to support your response.

WRITING CHECKLIST

- ☐ I stated the theme.
- ☐ I explained how the theme develops during the story.
- ☐ I used text details.
- ☐ I used complete sentences.
- ☐ I used correct spelling, punctuation, and capitalization.

The Trouble with Talent

by Lee Lewis

1 My heart pounds out a wild drum solo as I near the music teacher's door. What had made me think I could sing in the talent show?

2 I had signed up last Wednesday, after eating turkey loaf for lunch. Eating the gray lump was mistake #1. Signing up for the show may have been mistake #2.

3 I take a deep breath and open Mrs. Ramirez's door.

4 She looks up from her desk and smiles. "Hi, Riley."

5 "Can we, um, talk about the talent show?" I ask.

6 She pats the chair next to her desk, and I sit. I swallow nervously. Mrs. Ramirez helped me discover I love singing. But she has high **expectations** for her students—like, *really* high—and I don't want to disappoint her.

7 "What's on your mind?" she asks.

8 "Um, I like singing in your class," I begin, as I feel a river of sweat running down my neck. *Ew.*

9 Mrs. Ramirez tilts her head, waiting.

10 "But," I mumble, "I don't know if I can sing in front of the whole school." I look down at the floor.

11 Mrs. Ramirez is quiet for what seems like minutes. Then she picks up a photo on her desk and hands it to me.

expectations = a belief about how good someone can be at doing something

auditioned = did a short performance to show off a talent

12 The photo shows an all-girl band wearing leather jackets and spiky boots. The drummer looks like a younger Mrs. Ramirez. “Is that your daughter?” I ask.

13 “That’s *me*!” Mrs. Ramirez laughs.

14 My jaw drops to my feet. “*You* were in a *band?*”

15 Mrs. Ramirez’s eyes twinkle. “I still remember the day I **auditioned**. I was sixteen and absolutely terrified.” She pauses and says, “It’s not easy putting yourself out there.”

16 “No, but you did it,” I say.

17 “Yes, I did,” Mrs. Ramirez nods. “But guess what would’ve happened if I hadn’t taken that chance.”

18 “What?”

19 “Nothing. I’d still be the same old me,” she says.

20 “And you wouldn’t have been in the band.”

21 Mrs. Ramirez smiles. “Exactly.”

22 Mrs. Ramirez is right. If I drop out, nothing bad will happen, but nothing *amazing* will happen, either. I want to do something I love instead of making mistake #3—giving up.

23 “Thanks for the talk, Mrs. Ramirez.” I hand the photo back to her. “Maybe I’m ready to take my chance, too.”

Respond to Text

Reread/Think

Reread "The Trouble with Talent." Then choose the best response to each question.

1. What problem does Riley face in the story?

Ⓐ He is worried he is not a good singer.

Ⓑ He feels there is not enough time to practice.

Ⓒ He is scared to sing in front of the other students.

Ⓓ He needs to ask his teacher for help with a music lesson.

2. In paragraph 1, what does Riley mean when he says his "heart pounds out a wild drum solo"?

Ⓐ He feels nervous before talking with Mrs. Ramirez.

Ⓑ He wants to tell Mrs. Ramirez he feels ill.

Ⓒ He is eager to play a song for Mrs. Ramirez.

Ⓓ He is playing the drums outside Mrs. Ramirez's door.

3. PART A

What is the theme of the story?

Ⓐ Taking a risk can lead to success.

Ⓑ It can be hard to ask others for help.

Ⓒ To do something well, you have to practice it every day.

Ⓓ As you get older, it becomes easier to perform on stage.

PART B

Which detail from the text **best** supports the answer to Part A?

Ⓐ "I take a deep breath and open Mrs. Ramirez's door." (paragraph 3)

Ⓑ "The drummer looks like a younger Mrs. Ramirez." (paragraph 12)

Ⓒ "'I still remember the day I auditioned. I was sixteen and absolutely terrified.'" (paragraph 15)

Ⓓ "If I drop out, nothing bad will happen, but nothing *amazing* will happen, either." (paragraph 22)

SESSION 5 PRACTICE

Reread/Think

4. Why does Mrs. Ramirez show Riley an old photograph of herself?

Ⓐ to show that everyone has musical talent

Ⓑ to show the importance of trying something new

Ⓒ to show how clothing has changed over time

Ⓓ to show that practice is key to being a good drummer

Write

What is the theme of "The Trouble with Talent"? How does it develop throughout the story? Use details about Riley's experience in your response.

WRITING CHECKLIST

- ☐ I described the theme of the story.
- ☐ I explained how the theme develops.
- ☐ I used details from the story.
- ☐ I used complete sentences.
- ☐ I used correct spelling, punctuation, and capitalization.

Respond to the Focus Question

What life lessons can we learn from others?

Reread/Think

With your group, decide which story each of you will reread. Reread the story and answer the questions on the lines below.

TEXT: ______________________________

What lesson does a character learn in this story, and who do they learn it from? How can you use this lesson in your own life?

____

____

____

Talk

Talk with your group about the life lessons shared in each story. Take notes below.

In ___, the character ___ learned a life lesson. That lesson was ___.

Title	Lessons Learned

Write

Think about a time you lost a competition that was important to you, made a mistake, or were scared to try something. Who helped you deal with that situation, and how?

It's a Mystery

FOCUS QUESTION

What skills can people use to solve a mystery?

NOTICE AND WONDER

Look at the three texts you will read in this lesson. What do you notice? What do you wonder? Discuss your ideas with a partner.

WHAT MAKES A MYSTERY

A mystery is a type of story with a puzzling problem. The story ends when enough information has been gathered to solve the problem. Discuss the meaning of each word and why it might be important in telling about a mystery.

characters plot solution

setting problem clues

The word ___ means ___.

That word is related to mysteries because ___.

The Lost Medals
by Jo Pitkin

The Glitter Trap
by Brooks Benjamin

The Case of the Missing Plant
by Amira Shea

SESSION 1 READ

THE LOST MEDALS

by Jo Pitkin

1 Antonio and his older brother Javier sat on the front steps of their house, looking for something to do on a sunny Saturday afternoon. Antonio pointed to a sign across the street: *Community Yard Sale.*

2 "Let's go take a look, Javier," Antonio said. "Remember the comic books we bought there last year?"

3 "How could I forget?" Javier laughed as he stood up. "You read them out loud to me for weeks!"

4 As the brothers wandered down the block, they examined tables piled high with used books, fancy plates, tools, and toys. Antonio picked up a ***cazuela*** just like the one his grandmother had and shook it. *Thunk!*

cazuela = cooking pot

5 "There's something inside!" he exclaimed. Antonio turned to the seller. "How much for it?"

* * *

6 Antonio pried the pot's lid off and found a faded envelope. Inside the envelope were two tarnished medals and a folded piece of paper. The paper listed a recipe written in Spanish. Antonio put it aside. Then, the boys cleaned the darkened medals. Each had the outline of a baseball player and these words: *Garcia, Miami High School, 1964.* Who was Garcia? Was this person a famous player? Antonio and Javier wanted to find out.

Stop & Discuss

What mystery do Antonio and Javier want to solve?

Underline the question in the text that needs to be answered in order to solve the mystery.

7 After school on Monday, the boys went to Miami High School's Media Center to look through the 1964 yearbook. There, in the sports photos, was the baseball player's full name: *Rafael Garcia*. In 1964, Garcia had been the captain of the baseball team.

hijole = wow

mi abuela = my grandmother

8 "If I'd lost my medals," Javier said, "I'd definitely want them back."

9 Javier began searching online for information about where the medal winner could be today. He typed *Rafael Garcia*, *Miami*, and *baseball player* into the search engine. The headline of a recently published news article flashed on screen: "Moving with Miami's Champ." Rafael Garcia taught exercise classes at a nearby community center. The brothers smiled and bumped their fists.

10 The next weekend, the brothers visited the center. They walked by a room where an exercise class was in progress, and it looked like the teacher was the man in the news article! Once the class ended, the boys introduced themselves and explained why they had come.

11 "***Hijole!***" cried Mr. Garcia as he stared at his medals for the first time in years. "I lost them when my family moved."

12 "We also found this," Antonio said, giving him the recipe.

13 Mr. Garcia stared at the paper, his eyes shining with tears. "***Mi abuela*** sent me our family's *tres leches* recipe. Somehow, it got lost, too." He smiled at the boys. "Thank you for finding a way to bring back these priceless memories."

Stop & Discuss

How does Mr. Garcia feel about getting his medals and the recipe back?

Underline details in the text that are clues.

SESSION 2 PRACTICE

SPOTLIGHT BENCHMARK: ELA.4.R.3.2 Summarize a text to enhance comprehension. (a) Include plot and theme for a literary text.

Summarize a Story

- When you **summarize** a story, you retell the most important parts of the story in your own words.
- A summary includes only the most important details about the characters, setting, and **plot**, or what happens in the story. A summary may also include the theme of the story. A **theme** is the story's message or lesson about life.

Reread/Think

Reread "The Lost Medals." First, write the names of the characters and the settings of the story in the chart. Next, write important details about the plot, or what happens in each part of the story. Then write the theme of the story.

Characters	Settings

Beginning (Problem Introduced)	Middle (Actions to Solve Problem)	End (Problem Solved)

Theme

Talk

Tell your partner why you included each detail in the Beginning, Middle, and End boxes of your chart. Are there any details you want to add or remove? Then discuss what you think the theme of the story is, and why.

I included this detail because ___.

I did not include this detail because ___.

I think the theme is ___. I think this because ___.

Write

Use your chart to summarize "The Lost Medals." Include important details about the characters, settings, and plot. Also include the theme.

In the Beginning ______________________________

____

____

____

In the Middle ______________________________

____

____

____

In the End ______________________________

____

____

____

____

WRITING CHECKLIST

- ☐ I included the most important details about the characters, settings, and plot.
- ☐ I identified the theme.
- ☐ I used complete sentences.
- ☐ I used correct spelling, punctuation, and capitalization.

SESSION 3 READ

The Glitter Trap

by Brooks Benjamin

1 Sumiko rubbed away the sleep **blurring** her vision, but when she looked at her bookshelf again, it was the same. Books were shoved in upside-down and sideways, with some on the floor and others missing completely. It was the third time this week she'd found her perfectly organized bookshelf a total mess.

2 Sumiko stormed to her little brother's side of the room. Toshi often borrowed her stuffed animals—if borrowing meant hiding them under his bed. Sure enough, two stuffed animals were squished underneath.

3 "Toshi!" Sumiko yelled.

4 Toshi ran into the room. "Yeah?"

5 Just as Sumiko was about to accuse Toshi of stealing her books, it occurred to her that he was only four. He couldn't even read yet.

6 "Did you need something, Sis?"

7 Sumiko stared into Toshi's innocent eyes. "It's nothing. Forget it."

8 Sumiko knew it was time to rethink. Someone was taking her books, and she would need evidence in order to figure out who was doing it. Detectives in the books she read always used tape to pull fingerprints off stuff, so Sumiko grabbed the tape dispenser off her desk and pressed a strip of sticky tape along the edge of the bookshelf.

blurring = making unclear and difficult to see

Stop & Discuss

Why does Sumiko think someone is stealing her books?

Tell your partner what clues in the text support your response.

Sumiko thinks someone is stealing her books because ___.

9 "Whatcha doing?" Toshi asked.

10 "Finding evidence."

11 "Eddi-vets?"

12 Sumiko smiled. "Evidence. Like clues."

13 "Like cat hair?" Toshi pointed to a clump of orange fur on the tape Sumiko just pulled off the shelf.

14 "Bandit!" Sumiko yelled. Bandit was always knocking stuff down. Of course, he never put things back, but maybe he had an **accomplice**.

accomplice = someone who helps another do a crime

15 Sumiko stormed across the hall and into her older sister's room, where Bandit was stretched out next to Tomoko on the bed. Toshi followed Sumiko in.

16 "Um, why are you in my room?" Tomoko asked.

17 "Finding eddi-vets," Toshi replied.

18 Sumiko marched to Tomoko's bookshelf where she immediately found some of her own books mixed in with her sister's. "*You've* been taking my books!"

19 "No, I haven't," Tomoko said. "Now get out of my room!"

20 Sumiko left with her books, wondering how she could prove her sister was the thief. She decided to set a trap. She began by sprinkling green glitter over the tops of the books on her bookshelf.

21 The next morning, Sumiko found a trail of glitter leading from her bookshelf into Tomoko's room. She peeked at her sleeping sister's hands and feet. To her surprise, there was no trace of glitter.

Stop & Discuss

Why is Sumiko surprised to find no glitter near her sister?

Discuss your response with your partner.

22 Toshi walked in holding out a piece of banana. "Want some?"

23 Something sparkled on the banana. Sumiko's eye followed Toshi's hand, up his arm, and across his shirt. He was covered in glitter!

24 "Toshi, did you steal my books?"

25 "No," he said, finishing his banana. "I borrowed them."

26 "Why didn't you say anything the whole time I was looking for the thief?"

27 "Because I wasn't a thief," blinked Toshi.

28 "You can't borrow people's stuff without asking! And you put my books back in the wrong places and left some in Tomoko's room!"

29 "I just wanted to read like you," Toshi said softly.

30 "Toshi, you can't take my books, but maybe we can read them together," Sumiko said.

31 "Yay!" Toshi clapped, sending glitter everywhere.

32 Sumiko sighed. Although her trap had helped solve a mystery, she now had another problem to solve: how to clean up all this green glitter.

Stop & Discuss

Which sentence would Toshi agree with?

Check the answer that **best** explains his reasoning.

- ☐ Borrowing is what makes someone a thief.
- ☐ Borrowing is okay but only from your sister or brother.
- ☐ Borrowing and taking are two different things.

SPOTLIGHT BENCHMARK: ELA.4.R.3.2 Summarize a text to enhance comprehension. (a) Include plot and theme for a literary text.

Summarize a Story

- A summary of a story includes only the most important details and ideas from the story.
- A detail is important if someone who has not read the story would need to know it to understand the summary. A detail is less important if someone could still understand the summary without knowing that detail.

Reread/Think

Reread "The Glitter Trap." Write the characters and setting of the story in the chart. Next, write details from each part of the story. Then write the theme.

Characters	Setting

Beginning (Problem Introduced)	Middle (Actions to Solve Problem)	End (Problem Solved)

Theme

SESSION 4 PRACTICE

Talk

Use details from your chart to describe the plot of the story. Choose one detail and tell why it is important for understanding the plot. Then discuss what you think the theme of the story is.

One important detail is ___.

This detail helps readers understand that ___.

I think the theme is ___ because ___.

Write

Summarize "The Glitter Trap." Include important details about the characters, settings, and plot. Also include the theme.

WRITING CHECKLIST

- ☐ I included the most important details about the characters, settings, and plot.
- ☐ I identified the theme.
- ☐ I used complete sentences.
- ☐ I used correct spelling, punctuation, and capitalization.

The Case of the Missing Plant

by Amira Shea

abruptly = suddenly and without warning

1 Josephine and Thomasina strode through the thick grass of their grandmother's yard to her garden shed. Granny was hosting a yard sale, and the sisters could keep any money they made selling her old clay pots.

2 Thomasina stopped **abruptly** at the garden. "Oh no!" She pointed at a patch of bare earth among the scarlet tomatoes, green okra, and yellow squash. Granny's beloved pigeon pea plant was *gone*.

3 Everyone knew that their grandmother had a way with plants. Some people believed stems and leaves just sprung up around her wherever she walked. But it was love and attention that made Granny's garden grow. So, it was strange that anything would be missing—especially the prized plant of Granny's garden.

4 Josephine squatted to inspect the empty spot where the pigeon pea plant had once been.

5 "No animal prints or holes," Josephine stated, still looking at the ground. "This can only mean one thing."

6 "What?" Thomasina asked.

7 "Only a human could've taken the plant," Josephine concluded.

8 Thomasina nodded and stepped carefully in the garden, looking for clues. There, behind the okra, was a yellow garden glove with a palm tree on it. However, Granny wore dark blue gloves. So, there *was* a plant thief!

9 "We should tell Granny," Thomasina said.

10 "No," Josephine said. "Let's not worry her. We'll find the thief ourselves."

11 That afternoon, as people arrived, the girls **scanned** the crowd. Josephine suddenly grabbed her sister's elbow.

12 "Look at the apron Mrs. Mavis is wearing," Josephine whispered. "It has the same palm tree as the glove we found!" The sisters moved closer and overheard Mrs. Mavis chatting about a new pigeon pea plant. They raced inside to tell Granny, who listened patiently. The sisters were breathless by the time they were done.

13 Smiling, Granny said, "I grew that plant as a present for Mrs. Mavis. She just moved here from Barbados. When she looks in her yard, she'll be reminded of home."

14 "We're sorry, Granny," Thomasina said sheepishly. "We shouldn't have thought the worst."

15 "You may have reached the wrong conclusion, but you had the right reason—to look out for your granny." Granny reached out and brought both girls in for a hug.

scanned = looked around to find something

Respond to Text

Reread/Think

Reread "The Case of the Missing Plant." Choose the best response to each question.

1. Which detail is **most** important to the plot of the story?

Ⓐ the old clay pots that are stored in a shed

Ⓑ the things that are for sale at the yard sale

Ⓒ a yellow glove with a palm tree on it

Ⓓ a garden shed surrounded by thick grass

2. **PART A**

Which statement **best** summarizes paragraph 12 of the story?

Ⓐ Granny is patient when she listens to the sisters.

Ⓑ The sisters believe that Mrs. Mavis took the glove.

Ⓒ Mrs. Mavis chats about her new pigeon pea plant.

Ⓓ Josephine whispers as she looks at the crowd.

PART B

Fill in the bubbles **before two** sentences that support the answer to Part A.

Ⓐ "Look at the apron Mrs. Mavis is wearing," Josephine whispered. Ⓑ "It has the same palm tree as the glove we found!" Ⓒ The sisters moved closer and overheard Mrs. Mavis chatting about a new pigeon pea plant. Ⓓ They raced inside to tell Granny, who listened patiently. Ⓔ The sisters were breathless by the time they were done.

SESSION 5 PRACTICE

Reread/Think

3. In paragraph 14, what does the word sheepishly show about Thomasina?

Ⓐ She is excited.

Ⓑ She is sure of herself.

Ⓒ She is embarrassed.

Ⓓ She is angry.

4. Which sentence **best** states a theme of the story?

Ⓐ Be careful not to make up your mind too quickly.

Ⓑ Good neighbors watch out for one another.

Ⓒ Be patient with people who are getting used to a place.

Ⓓ It takes hard work and love to grow a garden.

Write

How do Josephine and Thomasina solve the mystery? What important lesson do they learn? Use details from the story and your own words to summarize the plot and theme.

WRITING CHECKLIST

- ☐ I answered the questions.
- ☐ I included important details about the plot.
- ☐ I used my own words to tell what happened.
- ☐ I included the theme.
- ☐ I used complete sentences.
- ☐ I used correct spelling, punctuation, and capitalization.

Respond to the Focus Question

What skills can people use to solve a mystery?

Reread/Think

Choose one text from the lesson to reread.

TEXT: ____

What did you learn from the text you chose about how people solve mysteries?

1. ____

2. ____

Talk

What is the most important thing you learned about solving problems from these stories? Take notes on what you learned from talking to the other students in your group.

I learned ___ from ___.

One skill a good problem solver has is ___.

Skills for Solving Mysteries

Write

What have you learned from these mysteries that could help you solve a problem or answer a question? Use details from all three stories in your response.

Future Worlds

FOCUS QUESTION

How do people feel when they face challenges?

NOTICE AND WONDER

Look at the science-fiction stories you will read in this lesson. What do you notice? What do you wonder? Discuss your ideas with a partner.

SHADES OF MEANING

Circle the word in each pair that shows the stronger feeling. Think of words that describe similar feelings that could be added to each row. Write the words.

startled / shocked ______________________

excited / pleased ______________________

terrified / nervous ______________________

surprised / amazed ______________________

I think ___ shows a stronger feeling than ___ because ___.

I added the word ___ because it means something like ___.

from *Cog*
by Greg van Eekhout

The Flying Test
by Sara Matson

Down to Earth
by Salima Alikhan

from COG

by Greg van Eekhout

Cog is a robot who looks like an ordinary boy. He stays with Gina, the scientist who built him.

1 I remain bad at sleeping. Gina said sleep is difficult for me because my brain is always working, thinking, and learning, and she didn't want to "go monkeying around" in my brain before she fully understood what was going on inside my head.

2 Gina is not very good at sleeping, either. Even though she is not a robot, we have some of the same **bugs**.

bugs = mistakes that cause unexpected results

3 On one such night, I prepared two mugs of hot cocoa in the microwave oven, which is a machine that is not capable of learning but is very good at making hot cocoa. Gina was in the laboratory, sitting at her computer. I put her mug on the desk.

4 Usually she would say "thank you," which is standard behavior. And then I would say "you're welcome" or "no problem" or "think nothing of it," all of which are standard responses. But this time she didn't say anything. She didn't even seem to notice I was there. She just stared at her computer screen with abnormally **hydrated** eyes. A drop of fluid fell down her cheek.

hydrated = containing water

Stop & Discuss

What is Cog doing? What is Gina doing?

Use details from the text to explain your ideas.

5 A face stared out from the screen. Eyes, brown like mine. Skin the same shade of brown as my syntha-derm sheath. Hair like mine, only longer, tied into a ponytail that hugged the left side of the neck.

6 At the bottom of the picture were three letters: ADA.

7 "Who is that?"

8 "Oh!" Gina said, startled. She looked at me, then at the mug on her desk. She took a sip. "Thank you, Cog."

9 "Think nothing of it."

10 I was pleased that we had returned to standard behavior.

11 I waited a moment, and when Gina did not answer my question, I again asked whose face was on the computer screen.

12 Gina wiped the fluid from her face. "That's ADA," she said. "Your sister."

13 I blinked, **processing**.

14 "That's how I think of you two. Brother and sister. Because I designed and built you both."

15 I continued to blink.

16 Gina's eyes continued to hydrate. She sniffed.

17 "Where is ADA now?" I asked.

18 Gina clicked her mouse, and the face disappeared. Her screen went into sleep mode. "I lost her."

Soon, Cog would find out where ADA had gone.

processing = figuring out the meaning

Stop & Discuss

What does Cog learn about ADA?

Place a star next to paragraphs that explain who ADA is and where she is.

SPOTLIGHT BENCHMARK: ELA.4.R.1.1 Explain how setting, events, conflict, and character development contribute to the plot in a literary text.

Analyze Story Elements

- Story elements, also called literary elements, are the parts that make up a story.
  - — The **setting** is where and when a story takes place.
  - — A **character** is a person, animal, or creature in a story.
  - — A **conflict** is the challenge or problem that characters face in a story.
  - — The **plot** is the series of events that happen in a story. All the story elements contribute to the plot.

Reread/Think

Reread the excerpt from *Cog*. Complete the chart by describing the setting, characters, and conflict. Support your descriptions with details from the text. Then describe the plot.

Story Element	Description	Details from the Text
Setting	some time in the future in an unnamed place	Cog is a robot; the illustrations look like the future
Character: Cog		
Character: Gina		
Conflict (What confuses Cog?)		

Plot (What happens?) ____

____

Talk

Use the details in your chart to discuss the story elements of *Cog* with a partner. Consider these questions as you discuss:

- How would you describe the characters of Cog and Gina?
- How would you describe the setting and events?

Cog is ___. Gina is ___.

The setting is ___.

Cog tries to figure out ___.

Write

What conflict does Cog experience in this story? Include details about the setting, characters, and events in your response.

WRITING CHECKLIST

- ☐ I explained what I learned about Cog's conflict.
- ☐ I included details about the setting, characters, and events.
- ☐ I used complete sentences.
- ☐ I used correct spelling, punctuation, and capitalization.

The Flying Test

by Sara Matson

It's September 3012, and Captain Amara Rivera is coming home after leading a journey to Jupiter's moon Europa. Everyone's excited about the astronaut's return—except her daughter, Luna, who's thinking about passing her flying test before she turns thirteen.

examiner = person who gives and grades a test

navigating = following a route or path

1 Luna rode into the test pod, sat down, wiped her sweaty hands on her jacket, and took a few deep breaths. Finally, the **examiner's** voice filled the pod: *Luna Rivera, your flying test will now begin.*

2 An hour later, Luna exited the testing area feeling totally drained. Hovering had been easy, but parking hadn't gone so well. She hadn't dented anything, but she had scratched the test pod while **navigating** into a narrow slot between an aerovan and a rover hybrid. She hoped that what she'd done correctly was enough to earn her a passing grade.

3 She had just reached the aerobus station when her communication watch beeped with a message.

4 TEST RESULT: FAIL. LICENSE DENIED.

Stop & Discuss

What happens during and after Luna's test?

Use details from the text to explain your ideas.

During the test, ___.

After the test, ___.

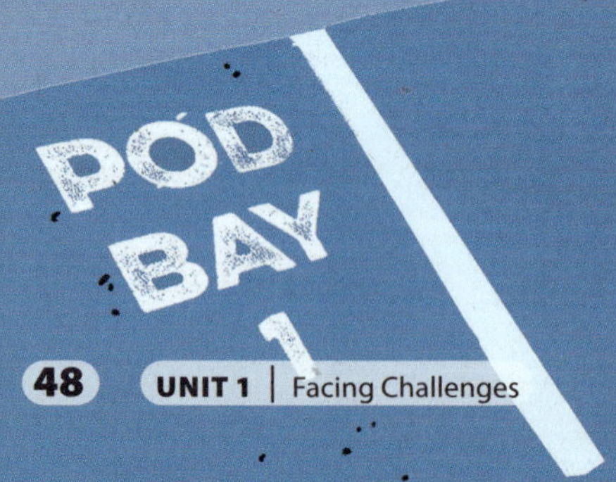

5 No! Luna got on the bus and slumped into a seat.

6 Another beep. This message was from Dad.

7 *MOM HOME. CAN'T WAIT TO SEE YOU. HURRY!*

8 Mom. Luna felt like she'd eaten a pound of moon dust. It was the worst thing that had ever happened to her! She pictured the headlines: *Famous Flier Amara Arrives Home to Husband and Daughter, the Flying Failure.*

9 After the bus let her off, Luna walked home as slowly as possible, and once she was outside the apartment, she hesitated. What if she just didn't go in?

10 Another beep. *WHERE ARE YOU?*

11 There was no avoiding it. She slid her watch under the scanner and unlocked the door.

Stop & Discuss

What does Luna do after she gets her dad's message? Why?

Underline details in paragraphs 8 and 9 that show what she does.

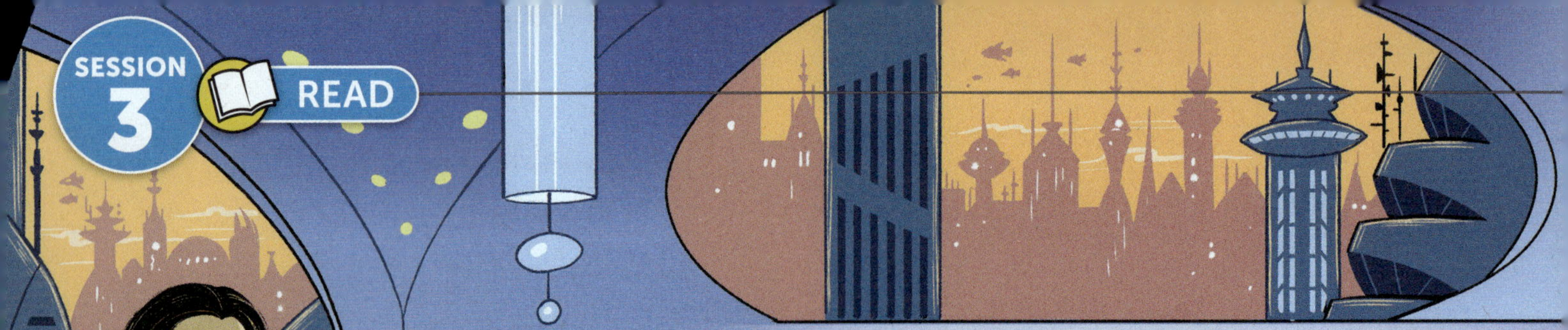

12 "Luna?" Dad called as she stepped inside the entryway.

13 She sighed. "Yep."

14 She heard footsteps and then both her parents were there, and Mom was hugging her. In spite of how awful she felt—or maybe because of it—the hug was pretty good. You couldn't get hugs like that over cosmovision.

15 "You're late," Dad said. "How did the test go?"

16 Luna looked down. "I failed. I messed up on parking."

17 Surprisingly, Mom laughed. "That pesky parking is the curse of the Riveras. Haven't you heard about the person who crashed her test pod and—"

18 "Made the examiner spill raspberry smoothie all over himself? That was *you*?" Luna said. "I thought it was just a story."

19 Mom grinned. "That was me, famous astronaut Amara Rivera, at twelve years old."

20 "No way," Luna said, suddenly feeling as weightless as if she were in an antigravity chamber.

21 "It's true," Mom said, sliding her arm around Luna's shoulder. "I'll tell you about it."

Stop & Discuss

What does Luna learn about her mom?

Use details from the text to explain your ideas.

SPOTLIGHT BENCHMARK: ELA.4.R.1.1 Explain how setting, events, conflict, and character development contribute to the plot in a literary text.

Analyze Story Elements

- The **plot** describes the events that happen in the beginning, middle, and end of a story. All story elements contribute to the plot.
  - **Conflict** is the challenge or problem that a character faces in a story. How the character responds to the conflict affects the plot.
  - **Character development** shows the way a character changes from the beginning to the end of a story.

Reread/Think

Reread "The Flying Test." Complete the chart by describing the setting, characters, and conflict at the beginning, middle, and end of the story.

Literary Elements	Beginning (paragraphs 1–4)	Middle (paragraphs 5–11)	End (paragraphs 12–21)
Setting	Earth in the year 3012, flying test		
Characters: Who are they? What are they doing, feeling, and thinking?	• Luna, 12 years old, failed her flying test		
Conflict	What is the conflict? Luna takes her flying test and fails.	How does the main character respond to the conflict?	How is the conflict resolved? How has the main character changed?

Talk

Discuss the plot of the story with your group.

- What is Luna's conflict? How does she respond to the conflict?
- What happens in the end? How does Luna change?

In the beginning, Luna's conflict is ___.

In the middle, Luna feels ___ because ___.

In the end Luna feels ___ because ___.

Write

Think about the plot of "The Flying Test." What is Luna's conflict in the story? How does she change as she works to resolve the conflict? Include details about the setting, characters, and events in your response.

WRITING CHECKLIST

- ☐ I explained Luna's conflict.
- ☐ I described how Luna changes in the story.
- ☐ I included details about the setting, characters, and events to support my response.
- ☐ I used complete sentences.
- ☐ I used correct spelling, punctuation, and capitalization.

Down to Earth

by Salima Alikhan

1 "I don't want to move to Earth," Raina told Kestra, her best friend at the space station. "I'll miss you *terribly*," she said, sniffling.

2 Kestra floated down on her hoverboard next to Raina and hugged her. "I'll miss you, too," Kestra said, her green antennae shaking, "but think of all the cool stuff there, like swimming and *pizza*." Kestra's antennae now waved with excitement. "All those Earth movies we've watched make pizza look *so* yummy—molten cheese on hot bread!"

3 Raina's family was originally from Earth, but she'd grown up on the space station. Because of her mom's new job, the family was relocating to a place Raina barely knew. "Mom scheduled a video call with my cousin Parker on Earth. What am I supposed to say to someone I've never met? What if he thinks I'm strange?"

4 "Keep an open mind and wait to see what happens," Kestra suggested. "Your cousin might surprise you."

5 Later that afternoon, Raina chewed on her nails as she waited for the call to start. Outside her window, Earth appeared so cold and distant.

6 The call connected, and a grinning boy with curly brown hair just like hers appeared on the screen. “Raina?”

7 “Hi.” She looked down and shifted in her seat.

8 “It’s exciting to finally meet you!” exclaimed Parker. “Are you nervous at all about moving?”

9 She took a breath. “Maybe a little . . .”

10 “I’ve moved before, too,” Parker said, “so I know how hard it is.” He paused. “So, um, we live near the mountains, and I thought we could go camping once you’re here.”

11 “I’ve never *really* been camping before,” Raina said. “But I *have* hiked **virtual reality** forests in the Holospace. They say it’s supposed to be realistic.”

virtual reality = a realistic but imaginary place created using technology

12 “Whoa, really? I want to know ALL about it!”

13 She nodded. “Yeah, it’s pretty cool.” Then her eyes lit up. “But I want to know ALL about pizza. Like, what does it taste like?”

14 “You’ve never had pizza? We can *definitely* grab some slices with my friends. They can’t wait to meet you!”

15 Raina glanced out at Earth again. It was a peaceful-looking blue-green globe wrapped in swirling clouds. A warm smile spread over Raina’s face.

SPOTLIGHT BENCHMARK: ELA.4.R.1.1 Explain how setting, events, conflict, and character development contribute to the plot in a literary text.

Respond to Text

Reread/Think

Reread "Down to Earth." Choose the best response to each question.

1. PART A

Based on paragraph 2, which sentence **best** describes Kestra?

Ⓐ She misses eating food on Earth.

Ⓑ She often travels to Earth.

Ⓒ She wants to move with Raina.

Ⓓ She cares a lot about Raina.

PART B

Which detail from paragraph 2 **best** supports the answer to Part A?

Ⓐ "Kestra floated down on her hoverboard next to Raina and hugged her."

Ⓑ "'think of all the cool stuff there, like swimming and *pizza*'"

Ⓒ "Kestra's antennae now waved with excitement."

Ⓓ "'those Earth movies we've watched make pizza look *so* yummy'"

2. Read this sentence from paragraph 5.

> Outside her window, Earth appeared so <u>cold and distant</u>.

What does the phrase <u>cold and distant</u> tell the reader about how Raina feels about Earth?

Ⓐ She thinks it will take a long time to get there.

Ⓑ She is afraid the people there will be unfriendly.

Ⓒ She worries that she will not like the weather there.

Ⓓ She is hopeful her cousin will show her where to camp.

Reread/Think

3. Which detail from the text **best** shows that Raina is nervous about talking to her cousin?

Ⓐ "Raina chewed on her nails as she waited for the call to start." (paragraph 5)

Ⓑ "boy with curly brown hair just like hers appeared on the screen." (paragraph 6)

Ⓒ "'It's exciting to finally meet you!'" (paragraph 8)

Ⓓ "A warm smile spread over Raina's face." (paragraph 15)

Write

How do Raina's feelings change from the beginning to the end of the story? What happens that makes her feelings change? Use two pieces of text evidence to support your response.

WRITING CHECKLIST

- ☐ I described how Raina's feelings changed.
- ☐ I explained why her feelings changed.
- ☐ I included two pieces of text evidence.
- ☐ I used complete sentences.
- ☐ I used correct spelling, punctuation, and capitalization.

Respond to the Focus Question

How do people feel when they face challenges?

Reread/Think

Choose one story to reread.

TEXT: ______________________________

1. In the story you chose, what challenge does a character face? How do they feel?

____

____

____

2. Do their feelings change? If so, how and why do they change?

____

____

____

Talk

In your group, discuss the following questions.

Which character do you relate to the most?

I relate to ___ because ___.

How does that character feel? Why? What helps them feel better?

First, ___ feels ___ because ___.
Then, ___ helps them feel better.

If you were the character's friend, how would you try to help them feel better?

I would try to help them feel better by ___.

Write

How do people feel when they face challenges? What helps them feel better? Use examples from the stories to support your ideas.

Imagining Possibilities

FOCUS QUESTION

How can imagination help people deal with challenges?

NOTICE AND WONDER

Look at the three parts of the story you will read in this lesson. What do you notice? What do you wonder? Discuss your ideas with a partner.

WHAT IS IMAGINATION?

Choose one of the words below. How is the word connected to imagination? Explain your ideas to a partner.

possible	mind	create
idea	picture	dream
exists	reality	

The word __ means __.

I think __ is related to imagination because __.

from *Zoe in Wonderland*, Parts 1–3

by Brenda Woods

from
Zoe in Wonderland

by Brenda Woods

Part 1

Eleven year-old Zoe Reindeer lives with her parents, sister, and brother in Pasadena, California. She helps out at her family's business, Doc Reindeer's Exotic Plant Wonderland, where they grow and sell plants.

1 Sort of like a seed, there's this thing inside of me that's nothing like my outside, and it's alive.

2 Some days it comes alive a lot, and other days it happens maybe only once or twice, kind of like a sneeze or hiccup.

3 I really never know when it's going to come alive, but once it gets going, it's kind of like a bowling ball that's rolling faster than fast down the lane toward the pins—impossible to stop.

4 Like yesterday, for example.

5 After school, I was walking home past the park where a girls' soccer game was being played. I was on a soccer team once, but I quickly found out that I stink at sports. But sometimes it's fun to watch, so I stopped and stared through the chain-link fence.

6 And suddenly, it—the thing that's inside of me, which I guess you could call my wild imagination—came alive and she—*Imaginary Zoe*—appeared.

Stop & Discuss

What does Zoe think is like a seed? How is it like a seed?

Underline a sentence that supports your answer. Then explain your answer to a partner.

7 *Zoe G. Reindeer, super forward, was on the field with the ball, in a perfect position. She aimed and kicked with all of her might. Their tall goalkeeper stretched sideways like she was made of rubber, trying desperately to guard the net, but she failed, and the ball crossed the goal line. Zoe's teammates* ***hoisted*** *her in the air!*

8 When the buzzer signaling the end of the game sounded, I blinked, and just like that, the real Zoe was back.

9 The real me never stands out, not at school, not at home, not at anywhere. Mostly, the real me likes the quiet of the Wonderland's pond and greenhouse and of half-empty movie theaters. If they gave awards for being boring, I'd get a gold medal.

10 But *Imaginary Zoe* is everything the real me isn't. Instead of being eleven years old, she's alrcady a teenager and even has her driver's license. Plus she doesn't stink at sports.

11 Sometimes I try very hard to keep *Imaginary Zoe* from disappearing, but because my real world keeps interrupting with all of its stuff like chores and homework and getting annoyed and having to brush my teeth and sometimes being forced to eat pickled beets, *Imaginary Zoe* vanishes.

12 Now that I've explained how I'm sort of like a seed and also about *Imaginary Zoe*, I can tell you about the real seeds.

hoisted = lifted

Stop & Discuss

How is real Zoe different from *Imaginary Zoe*?

Support your answer with details from the text.

Real Zoe ___, but *Imaginary Zoe* ___.

Unlike real Zoe, *Imaginary Zoe* ___.

SPOTLIGHT BENCHMARK: ELA.K12.EE.3.1 Make inferences to support comprehension.

Make Inferences

- Authors do not explain everything that happens in a story. If something is unclear in the story, you can make an inference to help you better understand the characters and events.
- An **inference** is an idea you form when you combine details in the text with information you already know.

Reread/Think

Reread Part 1 of *Zoe in Wonderland*. Complete the chart by using text details and what you already know to make inferences about *Imaginary Zoe*.

What the Text Says +	What I Know =	Inference
What I want to know: What is *Imaginary Zoe* like?		
Paragraph 2 "Some days it comes alive a lot, and other days it happens maybe only once or twice, kind of like a sneeze or hiccup."	You can't control sneezes or hiccups.	
Paragraph 8 "When the buzzer signaling the end of the game sounded, I blinked, and just like that, the real Zoe was back."		
What I want to know: How does real Zoe feel about *Imaginary Zoe*?		
Paragraphs 9 and 10 • "The real me never stands out" • "But *Imaginary Zoe* is everything the real me isn't."		

Talk

Share one inference from your chart with a partner. Then discuss the questions below. Support your ideas with details from the text and what you already know.

- When does *Imaginary Zoe* appear?
- When does *Imaginary Zoe* disappear?

The text says ___. I already know ___. So, I can infer ___.

Imaginary Zoe appears/ disappears when ___.

Write

What inference can you make about what causes *Imaginary Zoe* to appear? What inference can you make about what causes her to disappear? Support each inference with at least one detail from the text.

WRITING CHECKLIST

- ☐ I made inferences about what causes *Imaginary Zoe* to appear and disappear.
- ☐ I supported my inferences with details from the text.
- ☐ I used complete sentences.
- ☐ I used correct spelling, punctuation, and capitalization.

from Zoe in Wonderland

by Brenda Woods

Part 2

A tall man from Madagascar comes to Wonderland, Zoe's family business, looking for a baobab tree, but Zoe tells him the shop doesn't have any. He invites her to an open house at the lab where he works as an astronomer. When he leaves, Zoe and her friend Quincy research baobab trees.

1 With Quincy sitting beside me, I looked up *baobab tree* on the computer. Unexpectedly, there were a bunch of sites. I popped on one that called it "the tree of life" and a photo came up of about thirty baobab trees growing in a grassy Madagascar plain. The clear blue sky behind the trees made them look strangely beautiful. "Wow!"

2 I studied the tall, fat trunks and leafy branches closely.

3 Quickly I began to read. "Says they can live for thousands of years and that there are nine species."

4 "And it's one of the top **endangered** trees in the world," he read.

5 Abruptly, I stopped reading. "Endangered?" I repeated.

6 *Zoe was standing at the podium. The auditorium was packed and reporters pointed video cameras at the guest of honor:* ***environmentalist*** *Zoe G. Reindeer. At the end of Zoe's inspiring speech, people clapped and began popping up around the room like popcorn until finally everyone was standing. Single-handedly, Zoe had saved the baobabs from certain extinction.*

endangered = at risk of dying out because there are so few left

environmentalist = a person who works to protect nature

Stop & Discuss

What does Zoe imagine in this part of the story? Why?

Underline a sentence that shows what *Imaginary Zoe* accomplishes. Then describe the scene in your own words.

Inspired by her research, Zoe orders and plants baobab seeds in coffee cans. When she is working at Wonderland, the tall man returns.

7 The tall man smiled, showing both his top and bottom teeth. "Hello again, young lady."

8 Young lady is not a name, I thought. "Zoe," I informed him.

9 "Hello, Zoe. I'm Ben . . . Ben Rakotomalala."

10 I'd never heard a last name like that before.

11 "Actually one of the shorter names in Madagascar and quite common. Most people call me Ben."

12 Seeing him again made me instantly un-forget about the baobabs. Since the day I'd planted the seeds, I'd completely ignored them. As soon as the man leaves, I promised myself, I'll head to the greenhouse.

13 "We still don't have any baobab trees," I told him. "And I asked my daddy, but he didn't want to buy any, so my friend and I bought some seeds and I planted them, so we should have some pretty soon, maybe."

14 "So Zoe is an **entrepreneur**?"

15 I didn't know what an entrepreneur was, but I felt ashamed to ask, so I just shrugged. "Spoze so?"

16 "Didn't see you at the open house we had at JPL last week."

17 "Oh. I forgot all about it, plus I'm not really into science. My brother, Harper, he's the scientist. He knows a whole bunch of stuff."

18 "But you're the imaginer?"

19 Because he was right, I nodded.

entrepreneur = someone who starts or organizes a business

Stop & Discuss

How does Ben describe Zoe? How does this compare to the way she describes herself?

Support your answer with details from the text.

20 “Imagination is sometimes more valuable than having a head full of facts. Without imaginers, it’s likely we’d still be living in caves. Imaginers and adventurers can change the world.”

21 “But I’m not an adventurer,” I told him.

22 “I’ll be right back. I have something for you!” he exclaimed as he dashed outside.

23 Seconds later, he slammed the trunk closed, and quickly, his long-as-stilts legs brought him back to where I was standing. He was holding a book. He handed it to me. “A small gift for you.”

24 I took it from his hand and read the title. *Adventurers, Explorers, Inventors, Dreamers, and Imaginers: People Who Changed Our World.*

25 “I hope this will open your mind, Zoe,” he said. “And that your life will be a marvelous adventure,” he added.

26 “Thank you.”

27 “You are very welcome, Zoe. Time for me to go.” Before he ducked outside, he told me, “Promise you’ll save one for me.”

28 “One what?”

29 “Baobab.”

30 “I promise.”

31 I stared at the picture of the telescope on the back of his T-shirt as he walked away and wondered exactly how far away you can see with one. I studied the cover of the book again, then gazed up at the sky.

Stop & Discuss

What characteristics do adventurers, explorers, inventors, dreamers, and imaginers have in common? Does Zoe share those qualities?

Explain your answer to a partner, using details from the text.

SPOTLIGHT BENCHMARK: ELA.K12.EE.3.1 Make inferences to support comprehension.

Make Inferences

- **Text evidence** can be a detail, an example, or a quote from the text.
- Use text evidence, along with your own knowledge and experience, to support each inference you make when you read.

Reread/Think

Reread Part 2 of *Zoe in Wonderland*. Use text details and what you already know to make inferences about *Imaginary Zoe*. Complete the chart with your inferences.

What the Text Says +	What I Know =	Inference
What I want to know: Why does *Imaginary Zoe* appear in paragraph 6?		
Paragraphs 1–6 • "Wow!" • "'one of the top endangered trees in the world'"	If something is endangered, it might disappear forever.	
What I want to know: Why does Ben think Zoe is an "imaginer"?		
Paragraphs 12–18 "'my friend and I bought some seeds and I planted them, so we should have some pretty soon, maybe.' 'So Zoe is an entrepreneur?'"		
What I want to know: Why does Ben give Zoe the book?		
Paragraphs 20–31		

Talk

With a partner, take turns sharing an inference from your chart. Then discuss the questions below.

- What does *Imaginary Zoe* do with baobab trees?
- What does real Zoe actually do with baobab trees?
- How are *Imaginary Zoe* and real Zoe similar?

In the story, *Imaginary Zoe* ___ the baobab trees, but real Zoe ___.

Both real Zoe and *Imaginary Zoe* ___.

Write

Make an inference about how the real Zoe is similar to *Imaginary Zoe* in this part of the story. Use details from the text to support your response.

WRITING CHECKLIST

- ☐ I made an inference about how real Zoe and *Imaginary Zoe* are similar.
- ☐ I supported my inference with at least two details from the text.
- ☐ I used complete sentences.
- ☐ I used correct spelling, punctuation, and capitalization.

from Zoe in Wonderland

by Brenda Woods

Part 3

Ben stops by the store to give Zoe another book. Shortly after that, a fire at Wonderland destroys everything except one baobab sprout. Zoe's family decides to sell the land and move. Ben visits the apartment where Zoe's family is staying until they move.

1 "How did you find us?" I asked.

2 "The man who bought the Wonderland told me," he replied. "I came to express my sorrow and to replace these." He handed me copies of the two books he'd given me. "I assumed they were lost in the fire."

3 I took them from his hand. "They were . . . Thank you."

4 Daddy got tears in his eyes. "You're a kind man, Ben."

5 "We're moving to Kauai in Hawaii. Our plane leaves tomorrow. We bought a flower farm," I blurted.

6 "The Garden Isle, they call that one. I was there years ago when I worked on the Big Island at the University of Hawaii Institute for Astronomy. If you ever get to the Big Island, you'll have to make sure you visit the Mauna Kea Observatories. By 2022, the island will be home to the world's biggest telescope, allowing scientists to see thirteen billion light-years away. Well, it's time for me to say my good-byes," the tall man said. His words had a little sadness sprinkled on them.

7 "Bye, and thank you for the books," I told him.

8 He said good-bye one last time and turned to leave, heading toward the elevator.

9 Suddenly, I glanced at the baobab seedling in the Kona coffee can that was sitting on the table.

10 "Daddy?" I picked up the baobab. "Can I give this one to Ben? Please? I promised him."

11 "Ben!" Daddy called out. "Hold up! My Zoe has a gift for you."

12 I flew down the hallway to Ben Rakotomalala. "It's a baobab. For you."

13 He took the can from my hand. "Thank you, Zoe!"

14 "Don't water it too much or it might die," I warned him.

15 The elevator door was closing when he stopped it with his hand and it reopened. Ben stared into my eyes. "One more thing, Zoe. Promise you'll put that wonderful imagination of yours to good use."

16 "I promise."

17 Back inside the apartment, I plopped on the sofa beside Harper and together we flipped open the book by Carl Sagan, *Cosmos*.

18 Just like before, Ben had written on the first page:

19 *To my friend Zoe Reindeer—May your life be an amazing adventure.*

Respond to Text

Reread/Think

Reread Part 3 of *Zoe in Wonderland*. Choose the best response to each question.

1. PART A

Which inference about Zoe is **best** supported by paragraphs 1–3?

Ⓐ She is worried about seeing Ben.

Ⓑ She does not want to talk to Ben.

Ⓒ She is surprised to see Ben.

Ⓓ She feels sad when she sees Ben.

PART B

Which sentence from the story **best** supports the answer to Part A?

Ⓐ "'How did you find us?' I asked." (paragraph 1)

Ⓑ "'The man who bought the Wonderland told me,' he replied." (paragraph 2)

Ⓒ "'I came to express my sorrow and to replace these.'" (paragraph 2)

Ⓓ "I took them from his hand." (paragraph 3)

2. Which sentence **best** explains why Daddy has tears in his eyes in paragraph 4?

Ⓐ He is sad to sell the family business.

Ⓑ He is grateful for Ben's kindness.

Ⓒ He is sorry that the books were lost.

Ⓓ He is proud of Zoe for thanking Ben.

3. Why does Zoe give the baobab seedling to Ben?

Ⓐ Zoe thinks Ben will take good care of the tree.

Ⓑ Ben asked Zoe to promise to save one for him.

Ⓒ Zoe is using the tree to pay Ben for the books.

Ⓓ Ben asks Zoe's father again for a baobab tree.

Reread/Think

4. Read this sentence from paragraph 2.

"'I assumed they were lost in the fire.'"

What does assumed mean?

Ⓐ discovered

Ⓑ told someone

Ⓒ believed to be true

Ⓓ heard from someone

Write

Why does Ben make Zoe promise that she will put her imagination "to good use"? Use details from the text to support your inference.

WRITING CHECKLIST

- ☐ I made an inference about Ben.
- ☐ I supported my inference with at least two details from the text.
- ☐ I used complete sentences.
- ☐ I used correct spelling, punctuation, and capitalization.

Respond to the Focus Question

How can imagination help people deal with challenges?

Reread/Think

Revisit Parts 1–3 from *Zoe in Wonderland*. How does Zoe use her imagination in the story? How does it help her? Complete the chart with details from each part.

How Zoe Uses Her Imagination	How Zoe's Imagination Helps Her
Part 1	
Part 2	
Part 3	

Talk

With a small group, discuss how Zoe's imagination helps her throughout the story.

In the beginning/middle/end, Zoe imagines ___.

Zoe's imagination helps her ___.

Write

How have you used your imagination to face a challenge or solve a problem?

Dealing with Your Fears

TALK ABOUT WHAT YOU KNOW

Talk with a partner about different ways people can face challenges, based on the texts you have read in this unit. Use the images and the sentence frames to help you.

> People can figure out something tricky in their lives by ___.

> People can learn life lessons from others by ___.

> People can help others get through new experiences by ___.

LESSON 1

Learning from Others

LESSON 2

It's a Mystery

LESSON 3
Future Worlds

LESSON 4
Imagining Possibilities

CHALLENGES I HAVE FACED

Use some of the words below to write about a challenge you faced in your life and how you were able to face it.

prepare | scared | excited | questions

new | trouble | help | difficult

different | solve

SESSION 2 READ

Satchmo's Master Plan

from *Look Both Ways*

by Jason Reynolds

Satchmo Jenkins has a terrible fear of large dogs.

1 Today, after school, Satchmo Jenkins worked out a **master plan** to save his life.

master plan = perfect plan

2 A plan he wished he'd come up with a long time ago.

3 Small dogs didn't bother him. As long as they were no bigger than a football, he could deal. Anything bigger caused his back to tighten. Made his heart bark. Thankfully, since living in Marlow Hill, his walks home had been dogless.

4 Until yesterday.

peripheral = at the outer edge of an object

5 Yesterday, he was walking down Nestle Street when he passed Mr. Jerry's house and saw something out of the corner of his eye. Something big. And furry. It darted across the patch of grass Mr. Jerry had along the side of his house, blocked off by a chain-link fence.

6 Satchmo's stomach dropped to his feet, his throat twisted like twines making rope. He turned his head to see what he knew he'd already seen. To make sure that his first thought—and **peripheral** vision—hadn't lied. Mr. Jerry had gotten a dog.

Stop & Discuss

Why does Satchmo feel the need to make a master plan to save his life?

Underline details that help you explain to a partner why he feels this way.

7 Mr. Jerry's wife had passed away a few months ago. A week later, Satchmo stood with his mother at Mr. Jerry's front door, a house plant in his hand. His mother was holding a pound cake she'd made him as a way to say *Sorry for your loss.* And Satchmo wished the pound cake was enough and that his mother didn't have to keep talking and suggest Mr. Jerry get a dog. Adopt one from a shelter.

8 *Pound cake. Not a dog from the pound,* Satchmo thought.

9 "Lose a life, save another," his mother said to Mr. Jerry sweetly.

10 *To take mine,* Satchmo had thought.

11 Mr. Jerry said *no, no, no.* Said he wasn't ready. Guess he was ready now.

12 That was all he needed to see to start **devising** plans. Escape routes.

devising = thinking of

Stop & Discuss

How does Satchmo feel when his mother suggests that Mr. Jerry get a dog?

Underline the thoughts Satchmo has that help you understand his feelings.

haze = confusion

mission = special purpose

13 Today, after school, Satchmo Jenkins left his last class of the day, math, and headed to his locker in a **haze**. He opened it, swapped out books and stuck his head in his locker for a moment to take a few deep breaths to get himself together. This walk home was going to be a big one.

14 After he got outside, he started running down his game plan, amping himself up for the **mission**. That's what this was for him—a mission.

15 *Okay, Satch. You're prepared.*

16 *You've thought it all through.*

17 *You will not get bit. You will not get eaten.*

18 *Breathe, Satch. Breathe* *and work it*

19 *all out.*

20 *If the dog jumps the fence,*

21 when *the dog jumps the fence* *don't panic.*

22 *Just do what you've planned.*

23 *Break to the right.* *If Mr. Jerry's pickup truck is*

24 *parked on the street, jump into*

25 *the* *back of it and*

26 scream *for help.*

27 *That's the first base. That's your go-to. But*

28 *if for some reason Mr. Jerry's truck isn't there,*

29 *if for some reason he's out, I don't know,*

30 *saving* *other dogs while his neighbors run for their lives,*

31 *then keep going right onto the Carters' property.*

Stop & Discuss

Why does Satchmo say this walk home is going to be "a big one"?

Discuss your response with a partner.

When Satchmo walks home today, he ___.

32 This is what Satchmo told himself, what he was ready to **execute**—the master plan to save his life—as he approached Mr. Jerry's house. Satchmo had purposely walked on the other side of the street to give himself a little bit of an advantage. No need to bait the beast. As he slinked past Mr. Jerry's front door, coming up on his side yard, Satchmo's backbone became rawhide, his stomach a squishy chew toy, his palms wet but his fingers dry like dog treats, when he heard the bark. Well, not really a bark, but the **gruff** voice of an old man.

execute = complete, do

gruff = sounding rough and unfriendly

33 "Satch! Satch!"

34 Mr. Jerry was calling out for him. He was kneeling behind the fence, rubbing the dog's head, its tongue slapping the old man's cheeks. No bite-bite.

35 Love-love.

36 "Satch, come here," Mr. Jerry said, his face a touchdown dance all its own. "I want to introduce you to my friend."

Stop & Discuss

What does Satchmo notice about Mr. Jerry and his dog?

Discuss details from the text with a partner.

Respond to Text

Reread/Think

Reread "Satchmo's Master Plan." Choose the best response to each question.

1. PART A

What inference can be made about Satchmo based on evidence in the story?

Ⓐ He wants his mom to bake more pound cake.

Ⓑ He used to live in a neighborhood with only small dogs.

Ⓒ He enjoys math more than other school subjects.

Ⓓ He makes jokes to himself when he is nervous.

PART B

Which quotation from the story **best** supports the answer to Part A?

Ⓐ "As long as they were no bigger than a football, he could deal." (paragraph 3)

Ⓑ "His mother was holding a pound cake she'd made him as a way to say *Sorry for your loss.*" (paragraph 7)

Ⓒ "*Pound cake. Not a dog from the pound*, Satchmo thought." (paragraph 8)

Ⓓ "Today, after school, Satchmo Jenkins left his last class of the day, math, and headed to his locker in a haze." (paragraph 13)

2. How do Satchmo's thoughts in paragraphs 15–31 affect the plot of the story?

Ⓐ They introduce the other people in the neighborhood.

Ⓑ They develop the conflict that he faces.

Ⓒ They give details about the setting of the story.

Ⓓ They show how his feelings have changed.

3. Based on the story, what is the **main** reason Mr. Jerry gets a dog?

Ⓐ He hopes to train dogs not to bite.

Ⓑ He wants to keep people away from his property.

Ⓒ He thinks that a dog will be a good companion.

Ⓓ He wants to help people who are afraid of dogs.

4. What is a theme of the story?

Ⓐ Finishing a task can take careful planning.

Ⓑ Facing your fears can lead to unexpected results.

Ⓒ It is best to trust your feelings when making a decision.

Ⓓ Asking for help can be the best way to solve a problem.

5. Which **two** details should be included in a summary of the story?

Ⓐ Satchmo's mother suggests to Mr. Jerry that he get a dog.

Ⓑ Satchmo and his mother recently moved to Marlow Hill.

Ⓒ Satchmo decides he will run into the Carters' property.

Ⓓ Satchmo brings Mr. Jerry a houseplant as a gift.

Ⓔ Satchmo thinks that large dogs will attack him.

6. Fill in **one** bubble in each row to show when each event happens in the story.

	Beginning	Middle	End
Mr. Jerry invites Satchmo to meet his dog.	Ⓐ	Ⓑ	Ⓒ
Satchmo plans what to do if the dog attacks.	Ⓓ	Ⓔ	Ⓕ
Satchmo sees Mr. Jerry's dog behind a fence.	Ⓖ	Ⓗ	Ⓘ

Write

Think about the plot of "Satchmo's Master Plan." How is Satchmo's conflict important to the plot? How does his character change in the story? Use evidence from the text to support your response.

WRITING CHECKLIST

- ☐ I explained how Satchmo's conflict is important to the plot.
- ☐ I explained how Satchmo changes in the story.
- ☐ I used evidence from the text to support my response.
- ☐ I used complete sentences.
- ☐ I used correct spelling, punctuation, and capitalization.

Make Connections

Reread/Think

In this unit, you have read about how people solve mysteries and face challenges or new situations. Review the stories you have read in this unit. Which story character do you feel responds to a challenge in the best way? Why? Use details from one or more texts in your response.

My opinion: ____________________

____

____

____

Text evidence that supports my thinking:

1. ____________________

____

____

2. ____________________

____

____

Talk

Meet with a small group to discuss the character you wrote about and why you chose them. Use the sentence frames to get started.

The character __ responds to the challenge __ by __.

I think this is the best response because __.

Technology

LESSON 5
World-Changing Inventions
86

LESSON 6
Problem Solvers
102

LESSON 7
Young Inventors
118

UNIT 2

Perry's Pizza Palace
Welcome to our new and improved website

World-Changing Inventions

FOCUS QUESTION

How have inventions changed our world?

NOTICE AND WONDER

Look at the three texts you will read in this lesson. What do you notice? What do you wonder? Discuss your ideas with a partner.

TALK ABOUT INVENTIONS

Brainstorm words for the following categories:

- Examples of inventions
- Words that describe inventions
- Synonyms for the word *invention*

An example of an invention is ___.

___ said ___ is a synonym of ___. I agree/disagree because ___.

Capturing Moments

by Stephen Krensky

Speak Up!

by Scott Logan

So Cool

by Paul Davis

Capturing Moments

by Stephen Krensky

1 *Boom!* That's the sound a camera once made when taking a picture. It needed flash powder, like the kind used in firecrackers, to work. When the powder exploded, it produced sound and a flash of light. The camera had caught a single moment in time.

2 Capturing visual images made photographs seem incredible when they first appeared. For hundreds of years, artists had created realistic scenes and people. Artists needed a lot of talent and skill to make images look so real. Cameras, though, could capture a real scene using just light and flat metal plates coated in chemicals.

3 Early cameras were big and heavy, and only professional photographers operated them. Sometimes, people posing didn't smile because the camera took 15 to 30 seconds to take the picture—too long to hold a smile. People also had to stand or sit perfectly still or else the finished picture would be blurry. Moreover, cameras could take only one photo at a time. Afterward, the photographer had to **develop** the plate into a single photograph. The whole process could take months.

develop = to turn an image on film into a printed picture

4 By the 1880s, cameras were lighter and smaller. They were portable, which allowed more people to use them. The newer cameras could record many pictures on a small roll of film. Once people had taken all their photos, they could mail their cameras to a facility where the film was developed. Weeks later, the photographs were ready.

Stop & Discuss

How did the first cameras change the way people made images?

Support your response with details from paragraphs 2 and 3.

1839

The daguerreotype camera captured an image on a copper plate.

1900

The Brownie camera, which used film, was the first widely popular camera.

1948

The instant camera produced an image that came directly out of the camera.

5 Over the years that followed, cameras continued to be improved. They became smaller, using film that rolled up into a metal **canister** that could be removed from the camera for developing. The developing process improved too. Film was developed in a local shop, and finished photos were available in days instead of weeks. Eventually, one-hour processing became common.

canister = a container that stores something

6 Then, in the 1990s, digital photography arrived. Digital cameras created images electronically rather than using film. Digital photography allowed people to see their photos on a screen as soon as they were taken. This feature was a game-changer. Instead of waiting for film to be developed by someone else, people could take, review, and delete their photos with the simple touch of a button.

7 These days, photography doesn't seem so amazing. People take photos of anything and anyone whenever they want. But we do still take photographs of the people and events that matter to us. People can capture special moments with devices such as smartphones and then use the internet to share their photos in seconds with close friends and family around the world.

Stop & Discuss

How did digital cameras change the experience of taking and looking at pictures?

Support your response with details from paragraphs 6 and 7.

Digital cameras allowed people to ___.

SESSION 2 PRACTICE

SPOTLIGHT BENCHMARK: ELA.4.V.1.2 Identify and apply knowledge of common Greek and Latin roots . . . and affixes to determine the meaning of unfamiliar words in grade-level content.

Use Word Parts

- Many words are made up of parts. Knowing the meaning of the parts can help you figure out the meaning of the whole word.
- A **root** is a word part that gives a word its basic meaning. It usually cannot stand alone. Many roots come from Greek or Latin.
- A **prefix** is a word part added to the beginning of a word or root. A **suffix** is a word part added to the end of a word or root. A prefix or suffix changes the meaning of a word.

Roots
- *cred* = believe
- *fac* = do, make
- *graph* = write
- *port* = carry
- *photo* = light

Prefixes
- *in-* = not
- *re-* = again
- *un-* = not, opposite of
- *inter-* = between, among

Suffixes
- *-er/-or* = person who or thing that does an action
- *-ible/-able* = is, able to be
- *-ing* = action of
- *-ity* = state of

Reread/Think

Reread "Capturing Moments." Complete the chart by using the meanings of roots, prefixes, and suffixes to explain the meaning of each word.

Word	Word Parts	Meaning
photographer (paragraph 3)	• photo = light • graph = write • -er = person who	person who "writes with light" by making pictures with a camera and film
incredible (paragraph 2)		
portable (paragraph 4)		
facility (paragraph 4)		

Talk

Choose one of the words from your chart to discuss with your group. Explain how the meaning of the word parts helps you understand the meaning of the whole word. Then discuss how the word helps you understand the text.

The word part ___ means ___. This helps me know that the word ___ means ___.

The word ___ helps me understand the text because ___.

Write

How has photography changed over time? What has improved about cameras and the way people use them? Use at least two words from your chart in your response.

WRITING CHECKLIST

- ☐ I described how photography has changed over time.
- ☐ I explained how cameras and the way people use them have changed.
- ☐ I included at least two words from my chart.
- ☐ I used correct spelling, punctuation, and capitalization.

Carrier pigeons were an early method of long-distance communication.

Speak UP!

by Scott Logan

1 You hear a buzz and a few seconds of your favorite song. Your phone is ringing. It's your cousin, and even though you live hundreds of miles away from each other, you're connected in seconds.

2 Thousands of years ago, it was almost impossible to communicate with someone who was far away. The Romans, French, and Germans used carrier pigeons, birds that could carry and deliver messages from one place to another. One problem with this method, however, was that pigeons can fly only so far.

3 A huge improvement in long-distance communication came in the 1830s, when the telegraph was invented. Messages called telegrams traveled over electric wires for hundreds of miles in an instant.

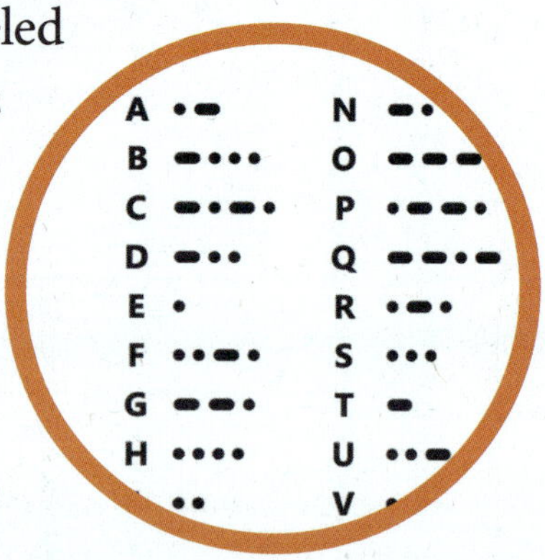

4 Communicating this way was complicated, because in order to send a telegram, a telegraph operator had to translate all the letters into Morse code. This "language" used dots and dashes instead of letters. Once the telegram was received, another operator had to translate the dots and dashes back into words.

Stop & Discuss

How did the telegraph change the speed at which people communicated?

Underline a sentence in paragraph 3 that supports your response.

Telephone operators used switchboards to connect callers.

Can you figure out how to use this early telephone?

5 Then, in 1876, a **device** was invented that could actually send a person's voice from one room to another. It was called the *telephone*, a word with Greek roots that means "far sound."

device = a mechanical or electronic object that has a special purpose

6 At first, making a telephone call involved many steps. A telephone user had to call an operator first. The operator managed a switchboard, a machine that used electrical cords, or "switches," to connect callers. Next, the operator would ask the caller for the number of the person to receive the call. Then, the operator moved cords on the switchboard to connect the two callers.

7 These calls may not have been easy to make, but at least there were no dots or dashes! People just talked. They could share news and stories with someone across town or across the country. Firefighters and police officers could be quickly alerted when needed.

Stop & Discuss

What made the telephone unlike earlier forms of communication?

Discuss your response with a partner.

The telephone allowed people to ___.

SESSION 3 READ

Callers using a wall telephone talked through a handset connected to the phone by a cord.

8 The telephone system transformed over the years. By the 1920s, telephones that could be dialed allowed people to make local calls without the help of an operator. Telephones themselves became smaller and easier to use. Up until 1970, all telephones plugged into the wall, and people talked through a handset attached to the phone by a cord. Later, the invention of the cordless telephone allowed people to walk freely as they chatted, but the phone still relied on wires to send the sound.

introduced = used for the first time

9 Then, in the 1980s, cell phones were **introduced**. Cell phones had no cords or wires at all—voices were sent by electrical signals through the air. People were free to talk inside or outside. But the world was changing fast, with computers popping up in offices and homes everywhere. Inventors wondered why phones couldn't do more than just send voices back and forth.

10 The first smartphone was invented in 1992. This multimedia device became more affordable in the 2000s. Now people could do much more than talk. They could also look up information, listen to music, send messages, take photos, and play games.

11 Our methods of telecommunication have changed immeasurably over hundreds of years. Who knows what the next century might bring! Will people be signing up for a planet-to-planet phone plan?

Stop & Discuss

What did smartphones allow people to do that they could not do before?

Underline details in paragraph 10 that support your response.

SPOTLIGHT BENCHMARK: ELA.4.V.1.2 Identify and apply knowledge of common Greek and Latin roots . . . and affixes to determine the meaning of unfamiliar words in grade-level content.

Use Word Parts

- Sometimes, you can figure out the meaning of an unfamiliar word by breaking the word into smaller parts.
- Look inside the word for parts you know. Put together the meaning of the parts to figure out the meaning of the whole word.

Roots	Prefixes	Suffixes
• *cir/circum* = around	• *de-* = opposite of	• *-ment* = state of being, act of
• *form* = shape	• *im-* = not	• *-ion/-tion/-sion* = act or process of
• *multi* = many	• *dis-* = not, opposite of	• *-ness* = state or condition of
• *phone* = sound	• *trans-* = across	• *-ly* = how something is done
• *tele* = far		• *-ate* = make, have, become
		• *-less* = without
		• *-able/-ible* = able to be done

Reread/Think

Reread "Speak Up!" Choose words from the text that have word parts you know and write them in the chart. Complete the chart by using the meanings of roots, prefixes, and suffixes to figure out the meaning of each word.

Word	Word Parts	Meaning
impossible (paragraph 2)	• im- = not • poss + -ible = able to be done	

SESSION 4 PRACTICE

Talk

Choose one of the words from your chart. Share with your group how you figured out the word's meaning and how this helps you understand the text.

> The word parts ___ and ___ are in the word ___. I can figure out that this word means ___.

> The word ___ helps me understand the text because ___.

Write

What does the word immeasurably mean in paragraph 11? Identify the word parts and explain how they helped you figure out the word's meaning.

WRITING CHECKLIST

- ☐ I broke the word into its parts.
- ☐ I found the root, prefix, and suffixes.
- ☐ I explained how the parts of the word helped me find the word's meaning.
- ☐ I used correct spelling, punctuation, and capitalization.

SO COOL

by Paul Davis

1 When you think of important inventions in the world, what comes to mind? Maybe the automobile, the camera, or the telephone? How about air conditioning? Even if we live in a cool climate, it's still a major invention that has changed our way of life.

2 Before air conditioning was invented, some people relied on handheld fans made of silk or lace to keep themselves cool on hot, sticky days. In the late 1800s, the electric fan was invented, which could circulate air automatically. But these fans could not make the air any colder, and they could **relieve** only a few people at a time.

relieve = to remove an unpleasant feeling

3 That's where air conditioning comes in.

4 In 1902, the first advanced air-cooling system was created. However, the purpose of this invention was not to cool people off. Instead, it was built to help a printing plant do business. Cooling and dehumidifying the air during hot, damp days helped the ink in the printing machines stick better to the paper running through them.

The first air-cooling systems were used in 1902 in printing plants like this one.

5 Then, in the 1920s, movie-theater owners had a great idea. Their theaters were very hot in the summer. Could a cooling system like the one used at printing plants benefit their business, too? In other words, would a colder theater bring in more customers?

6 The answer was yes. Definitely, yes.

7 After that, air conditioning quickly became important for homes, offices, libraries, and laboratories. Sometimes air conditioning was more than just a luxury. In hospitals, patients had a better chance to recover if their bodies didn't have to fight the heat.

architects = people who design buildings

8 By the 1950s, more buildings were designed with air conditioning in mind. **Architects** no longer worried about the sunlight making rooms too warm. They put in large windows and sliding glass doors. Skyscrapers, which were usually made with stone, now glittered in the sun with floor-to-ceiling glass.

9 When the first air-conditioned mall opened in Houston, Texas, in 1956, shoppers had a new reason to visit their favorite stores. They could shop in air-conditioned spaces in perfect comfort.

10 Once soaring temperatures no longer mattered, moving to the South became much more appealing. The population of Florida, for example, grew from 5 million in 1960 to more than 21 million today.

11 So, when you think about it, air conditioning really is a "cool" invention.

Movie theaters proudly advertised their air conditioning to bring in more customers.

SPOTLIGHT BENCHMARK: ELA.4.V.1.2 Identify and apply knowledge of common Greek and Latin roots . . . and affixes to determine the meaning of unfamiliar words in grade-level content.

Respond to Text

Reread/Think

Reread "So Cool." Choose the best response to each question.

1. Read the sentence from paragraph 4 of the passage.

   Cooling and dehumidifying the air during hot, damp days helped the ink in the printing machines stick better to the paper running through them.

   What does the prefix *de-* tell you about the meaning of dehumidifying?

   Ⓐ It means the opposite of humidifying.

   Ⓑ It means that something is humidifying again.

   Ⓒ It means that something is not able to humidify.

   Ⓓ It means the act or process of humidifying.

2. Using knowledge of word parts, what is the meaning of the word circulate in paragraph 2?

   Ⓐ to be moving across a circle

   Ⓑ to cause to move in a circle

   Ⓒ away from a circle

   Ⓓ without a circle

3. Read the sentence from paragraph 5, which describes the use of air conditioning in movie theaters.

   Could a cooling system like that used at printing plants benefit their business, too?

   Benefit has two word parts, *bene* and *fit*. *Bene* means "well." *Fit* means "to make or do something." What does benefit **most likely** mean?

   Ⓐ to make money

   Ⓑ to make cold

   Ⓒ to do something again

   Ⓓ to do something good

Reread/Think

4. Why did air conditioning let architects use more glass in skyscraper windows?

Ⓐ Air conditioning caused glass to shine in the sun.

Ⓑ Air conditioning made windows more affordable.

Ⓒ Air conditioning kept buildings cool on sunny days.

Ⓓ Air conditioning worked best in buildings made of glass.

Write

Read the following sentence from paragraph 2.

> In the late 1800s, the electric fan was invented, which could circulate air automatically.

Auto means "self," and *matic* means "doing something." The suffix *-al* means "related to," and the suffix *-ly* means "how something is." Explain the meaning of automatically in the sentence and tell how its word parts help to show that meaning.

WRITING CHECKLIST

- ☐ I explained the meaning of the word.
- ☐ I described how the word parts show the meaning of the whole word.
- ☐ I used complete sentences.
- ☐ I used correct spelling, punctuation, and capitalization.

Respond to the Focus Question

How have inventions changed our world?

Reread/Think

Choose one text from this lesson to reread. From that text, choose the invention or improvement that you find most interesting.

TEXT and INVENTION: ______________________________

What did you learn from your text about the invention and how it affected people's lives?

____

____

____

____

____

Talk

In a small group, share your responses from Reread/Think. Take notes about what your group members share.

Next, as a group, discuss how you would respond to this question:

How have the inventions described in this lesson changed the world?

The camera has changed the world because ___.

The telephone has changed how people ___.

Air conditioning has affected people because ___.

Write

Which of the inventions in this lesson do you think is the most important? Use information from at least one of the texts to support your response.

Problem Solvers

FOCUS QUESTION

How can people use technology to solve problems?

NOTICE AND WONDER

Look at the titles and images of the texts you will read in this lesson. What do you notice? What do you wonder? Discuss your ideas with a partner.

WORD SORT

How are the words below connected to the process of invention? Sort the words into the categories in the chart.

problem scientist experiment
design idea solve
invention test engineer

Who Invents	Why They Do It	How They Do It	What They Create

Googly-Eyed and Gobbling Garbage

by Helen Walz

The Strongest Thread

by Tracy Vonder Brink

Meet Stevie

by Corinne Purtill

SESSION 1 READ

Googly-Eyed and Gobbling Garbage

by Helen Walz

1 A floating monster guards Baltimore's Inner Harbor. Bigger than a school bus, the monster has a snail-like shell and huge googly eyes. The flowing water powers the monster's yawning mouth so it can eat. *Chomp.* It munches a soda can. *Slurp.* It snacks on some plastic bags. *Gulp.* It swallows a tire.

2 That's right. It's eating garbage! This monster is actually a machine named Mr. Trash Wheel. John Kellett designed this unusual machine to deal with a big problem: trash in the river.

3 Back in 2006, there was nothing to stop garbage as it made its way from the Jones Falls River, through the harbor, and out into the open ocean. Most of the trash was plastic. Plastic in the ocean is a big problem because it harms sea life and destroys their habitats.

disgusted = upset, angered

4 People who saw all the trash in the river and in the harbor felt **disgusted**. Kellett saw the trash every day on his walk to work at the Baltimore Maritime Museum. When it rained, he says, "you [would] see the flow of trash just dumping into the harbor, making it look terrible. I thought about it every day."

Stop & Discuss

What problem did Kellett think about every day?

Talk with a partner about details in paragraph 4 that tell about what he observed.

HOW MR. TRASH WHEEL WORKS

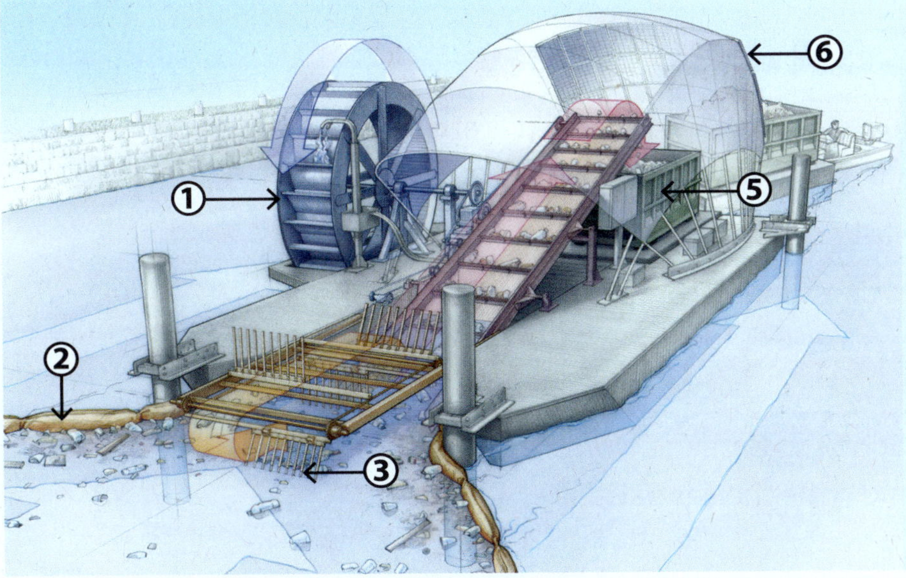

1. A waterwheel is one source of power for the machine.
2. Floats capture trash, moving it toward Mr. Trash Wheel's mouth.
3. Rakes pick up the trash and drop it on the conveyor belt.
4. The conveyor belt moves the trash into a dumpster.
5. When the dumpster is full, workers take it away.
6. Large solar panels are another source of power for Mr. Trash Wheel.

5 But Kellett didn't just think about the problem. He also invented a way to solve it. He imagined a waterwheel that could pick up trash. He talked to other people about his idea and got funding to build a prototype, or a rough model of an invention.

6 The original prototype needed work. It looked like a floating garden shed, and it wasn't strong enough to handle the large amount of trash in the river. So Kellett got back to work, improving his design with strong steel parts, extra solar panels for more power, and a new look.

7 The new garbage gobbler got to work in 2014. So far, Mr. Trash Wheel has **guzzled** more than one million water bottles, 4,600 sports balls, a guitar, and many other things. Mr. Trash Wheel also has a family of monster friends: Professor Trash Wheel and Captain Trash Wheel, which work on nearby rivers.

8 Kellett is surprised and delighted by how famous his invention has become. Mr. Trash Wheel encourages people to think about where litter and non-recycled plastic could end up. Kellett says that the trash wheel is "an **inspiration** to people to become part of the solution to the problem."

guzzled = eaten in a messy, hurried way

inspiration = something that excites and brings change

Stop & Discuss

What problems did the prototype have? How did Kellett improve his invention?

Reread paragraph 6 and discuss it with a partner.

SESSION 2 PRACTICE

SPOTLIGHT BENCHMARK: ELA.4.R.2.2 Explain how relevant details support the central idea, implied or explicit.

Explain a Central Idea

- The **topic** is a word or phrase that tells what the text is about.
- The **central idea** of a text is the most important idea the author wants you to know about the topic. You state it in a complete sentence.
- **Relevant details** are facts that support, or tell about, the central idea.

Reread/Think

Reread "Googly-Eyed and Gobbling Garbage." Write the topic of the text. Then identify important details and write the central idea.

Topic ______________________________

Central Idea		

Relevant Details (paragraphs 1 and 2)	Relevant Details (paragraphs 3–5)	Relevant Details (paragraphs 6–8)

Talk

Use the details in your chart to discuss the central idea with a partner. How do the relevant details support the central idea? Should any details be added or removed from your chart?

> The central idea the author wants the reader to know about the topic is ___.

> The relevant detail ___ supports the central idea by showing/explaining ___.

Write

What is the central idea of "Googly-Eyed and Gobbling Garbage"? Choose two relevant details and explain how they support the central idea.

WRITING CHECKLIST

- ☐ I described the central idea of the text.
- ☐ I included relevant details that support the central idea.
- ☐ I used information from the chart in my response.
- ☐ I used correct spelling, punctuation, and capitalization.

THE STRONGEST THREAD

by Tracy Vonder Brink

1 Stephanie Kwolek peered at the chemical mixture on the table. All her other test batches had been thick and clear, but this one was thin and cloudy. She frowned. Had something gone wrong with the experiment?

2 Kwolek was a chemist, a scientist who studies materials in the world around us. She was trying to find new ways of making threads and fabric out of chemicals. Ten years before, in 1955, her company had given her a huge challenge: create the strongest **fibers** ever made, fibers even stronger than steel!

fibers = thin threads

3 Over time, Kwolek and her team had mixed batch after batch of chemicals. They were looking for chemicals that would stick together to form strong fibers. To test their mixtures, the team sent them to the spinning room.

4 Spinning chemicals into thread is complicated. First, the liquid chemicals are poured into a machine that pushes them through tiny holes in a steel plate. This step creates solid fibers from the liquid. The fibers are then wound around a spool, creating a kind of thread.

Stop & Discuss

Why was Kwolek doing experiments?

Discuss paragraph 2 to identify at least two goals behind Kwolek's work.

Kwolek proudly displays her invention.

5 Kwolek and her team had tested more than 100,000 mixtures in the ten years since the challenge was given. None of them had worked. Now she was staring at this strange new cloudy, watery batch. It wasn't like any other she had seen before. Was it just another failure? Should she throw it out?

6 No! Just because this mixture was puzzling didn't mean it was bad. Maybe she should take it to the next step. The scientist who **operated** the spinning machine didn't want to test Kwolek's mixture, however. He was afraid it would **clog** and break the machine, so he told her no.

7 But Kwolek wasn't ready to give up. She checked the mixture again and told the scientist she didn't think it would break anything. Finally, he agreed to test it.

8 Kwolek waited. Would her mixture be a success? Or would it wreck the machine? Then she heard from the spinning room—her mixture had been turned into thread! That was a relief. Now the thread needed to be tested.

operated = managed, controlled

clog = block up

Stop & Discuss

Why did Kwolek think of throwing out her new batch?

Talk with a partner about the details in paragraph 5.

She thought it was ___.

penetrate = make a hole in

9 When the results came back, Kwolek was amazed. Her thread was five times stronger than steel! In fact, a sewing needle couldn't **penetrate** fabric woven from the thread. The needle bent instead of poking through.

10 It took the company five more years to figure out how to turn her super-strong invention into a fabric that could be made in large amounts. When they did, in 1970, it was named Kevlar®.

determination = strength to move forward with a goal even when it's difficult

11 Today, Kevlar strengthens helmets, skis, skateboards, and other sports equipment. It's used in tires and in the outer shells of space rockets. Kevlar's super-strong thread is even used to create bulletproof vests for police officers and soldiers.

12 Stephanie Kwolek could have thrown out the strange mixture or given up when she was told she shouldn't test it. But because of Kwolek's **determination** and her willingness to experiment, the world now has this incredible thread.

Stop & Discuss

What did Kwolek discover about the new mixture?

Reread paragraph 9 and underline what was extraordinary about the strength of this new material.

Kevlar is also used in parachutes and protective suits.

Explain a Central Idea

- Think about the important details in each part of the text.
- Put the details together to figure out the central idea of the whole text.

Reread/Think

Reread "The Strongest Thread." Write the topic of the text. Then identify important details and write the central idea.

Topic ______________________________

Central Idea		
Relevant Details (paragraphs 1–4)	**Relevant Details** (paragraphs 5–8)	**Relevant Details** (paragraphs 9–12)

SESSION 4 PRACTICE

Talk

Use the details in your chart to discuss the central idea with a partner. How do the relevant details support the central idea? Should any details be added or removed?

> The central idea the author wants the reader to understand about the topic is ___.

> The relevant detail ___ supports the central idea by showing/explaining ___.

Write

What is the central idea of "The Strongest Thread"? Use relevant details from the text to explain your thinking.

WRITING CHECKLIST

- ☐ I explained the central idea of the text.
- ☐ I included details that support the central idea.
- ☐ I used correct spelling, punctuation, and capitalization.

Meet Stevie

by Corinne Purtill

1 Phil Soriano, age 86, hosts fun sing-alongs at his retirement community. Today, Soriano wants to sing while a special guest, Stevie, leads the crowd through the song's dance moves. This dance party will be special, though. Why? Because Stevie is a robot.

2 While Soriano sets up the music, Niamh Donnelly, an engineer who helped create the robot, works with Stevie. "We could try to make him dance," says Donnelly. She types commands on a laptop, and the robot stretches its peg-like arms while a grin flashes on its digital face.

3 Researchers are working hard to learn what staff and **residents** might want from a robot. In fact, there are a lot of ways Stevie can add to the retirement community.

4 Stevie is a social robot. It's designed to **interact** with people. People talk to Stevie, and the robot responds with speech and movements. For example, tell Stevie you're sick, and it frowns and says, "I'm sorry to hear that." Compliment Stevie, and its screen changes to a smile. At other times, its digital eyes blink, waiting for a command.

residents = people who live in a certain place

interact = talk to or communicate with

5 Stevie can answer about 100 common questions, such as "How are you?" A person has to type the words for Stevie to say in other kinds of conversations. The team even had Stevie tell a joke: "What did the left eye say to the right?" Answer: "Between you and me, something smells!"

session = meeting; gathering

6 Researchers thought people would want Stevie to do chores. But surprisingly, residents didn't want to give Stevie an order and have the robot roll away. They wanted Stevie to stay and keep them company. When the team asked residents what they liked most about the robot, they said, "It made me laugh."

7 When Stevie showed up at a recent bingo **session**, staff member Menbere Gebral wasn't sure what to expect. But then Stevie began to call out the numbers, and it all made sense. This meant Gebral could keep doing the part of her job that she likes best—interacting with and helping residents.

8 What about the sing-along? It was a success! Phil led the singing while Stevie's arms circled around, doing its best to copy the dance moves. Stevie's dancing wasn't perfect, but it didn't matter. The audience was happy. Stevie was a fun, helpful addition to the community.

SPOTLIGHT BENCHMARK: ELA.4.R.2.2 Explain how relevant details support the central idea, implied or explicit.

Respond to Text

Reread/Think

Reread "Meet Stevie." Then choose the best response to each question.

1. PART A

What is the central idea of the text?

Ⓐ Stevie is one of the only robots that has the same feelings that humans have.

Ⓑ Researchers built Stevie so it could teach people how to dance at sing-alongs.

Ⓒ Stevie is helping researchers understand how robots can be useful for retirement communities.

Ⓓ Researchers created Stevie to answer questions from people who live in retirement communities.

PART B

Which detail from the text **best** supports the answer to Part A?

Ⓐ "Researchers are working hard to learn what staff and residents might want from a robot." (paragraph 3)

Ⓑ "For example, tell Stevie you're sick, and it frowns and says, 'I'm sorry to hear that.'" (paragraph 4)

Ⓒ "Stevie can answer about 100 common questions, such as 'How are you?'" (paragraph 5)

Ⓓ "Phil led the singing while Stevie's arms circled around, doing its best to copy the dance moves." (paragraph 8)

2. Read this sentence from paragraph 1.

> Phil Soriano, age 86, **hosts** fun sing-alongs at his retirement community.

What is the meaning of the word *hosts*?

Ⓐ plays with

Ⓑ entertains guests

Ⓒ listens to musicians

Ⓓ watches closely

SESSION 5 PRACTICE

Reread/Think

3. What did researchers discover residents wanted Stevie to do?

Ⓐ to roll away from them

Ⓑ to take orders from them

Ⓒ to help them with chores

Ⓓ to keep them company

4. What did Stevie do at the bingo game?

Ⓐ Stevie helped the residents.

Ⓑ Stevie answered questions.

Ⓒ Stevie called out numbers.

Ⓓ Stevie danced and sang.

Write

Describe what makes Stevie a special robot. Explain how Stevie affects the people around it. Use at least three relevant details from the text.

WRITING CHECKLIST

- ☐ I explained what makes Stevie a special robot.
- ☐ I used at least three relevant details from the text.
- ☐ I used complete sentences.
- ☐ I used correct spelling, punctuation, and capitalization.

Respond to the Focus Question

How can people use technology to solve problems?

Reread/Think

Choose one text from this lesson to reread.

TEXT: ______________________________

What interesting thing did you learn about how or why the technology was created?

____

____

Talk

Share with your group how the technology you read about is useful to others.

The ___ is useful to others because it ___.

As a group, discuss these questions. Take notes in the chart.

How do people use technology to solve problems? List some examples of technologies that you use in your own life and explain how they help solve problems.

What is the technology?	How is this technology helpful?

Write

Tell about an example of technology that has improved your life. How has it helped you? How does it work?

Young Inventors

FOCUS QUESTION

How can a young person become an inventor?

NOTICE AND WONDER

Look at the titles and images of the texts you will read in this lesson. What do you notice? What do you wonder? Discuss your ideas with a partner.

WHAT TRAITS DOES AN INVENTOR NEED?

How could the traits below help someone become an inventor? Discuss your ideas with a partner. Then add two more traits that inventors need.

creativity

persistence

____

____

Inventors need to have ___ because ___.

___ helps inventors ___.

Gitanjali Rao: Steps Toward Success

by Amanda Baker

Anything Is Paws-ible

by Mary Lindeen

Toying with a Challenge

by Lynda Jones

Gitanjali Rao: Steps Toward Success

by Amanda Baker

1 Gitanjali Rao saw a problem, and she wanted to solve it so she could help people. But solving it wasn't easy.

2 In 2016, the news was full of stories about unsafe drinking water in Flint, Michigan. The water had too much lead in it. Lead is a metal, and in water it is invisible and tasteless. When people drink water that contains lead, they can become very sick. Gitanjali was 11 years old at the time. She thought about how scary it must be to have polluted water coming out of your home faucet.

3 Test kits could detect lead in water. But they took too long to give results, and often those results were wrong. Gitanjali wondered if she could make a better test kit.

4 One day, Gitanjali read a news story about how tiny tubes were being used to test for poison in the air. Scientists would cover these tubes with a chemical that **attracted** a poison. When poison stuck to the chemical, it changed the way electricity flowed through the tubes. Scientists checking the electric flow could then see how much poison was in the air. Gitanjali wondered if she could detect lead in water this way, too.

attracted = pulled to itself

Stop & Discuss

What was the problem with the water? How did Gitanjali think she could help?

Explain the problem. Then underline a sentence that describes how she thought she could help.

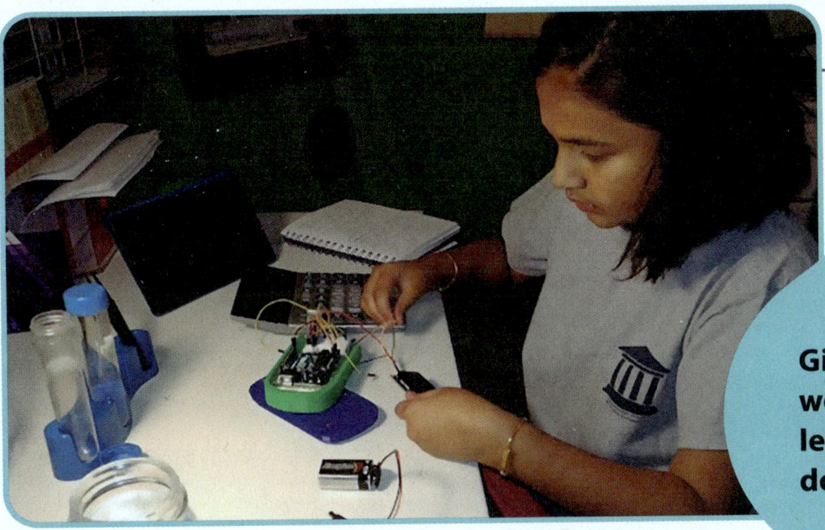

Gitanjali Rao working on her lead test kit design

5 Gitanjali found a chemical that could attract lead. She got some tubes. But she couldn't test her idea at home. She needed a lab with the right equipment. She wrote to large labs about her idea, but they didn't write back.

6 Finally, Gitanjali realized she did not need help from a fancy lab. She emailed a chemistry teacher at her local high school. The school didn't have a big lab, but its lab had everything she needed.

7 The chemistry teacher agreed to help. They started by testing clean water. Next, they added tiny scoops of lead. They weren't successful right away, but after many, many **attempts**, they finally got Gitanjali's lead detector to work.

8 Gitanjali wasn't finished yet. Next, she made a phone app so anyone using her kit could see the results instantly on their phones. She entered her idea in a big national competition. And she won, becoming the youngest-ever winner of the Discovery 3M Young Scientist Challenge.

9 Gitanjali has continued to explore new ideas. "Don't be afraid to fail," she has said, "because that's just another step toward success."

An early version of Gitanjali's invention

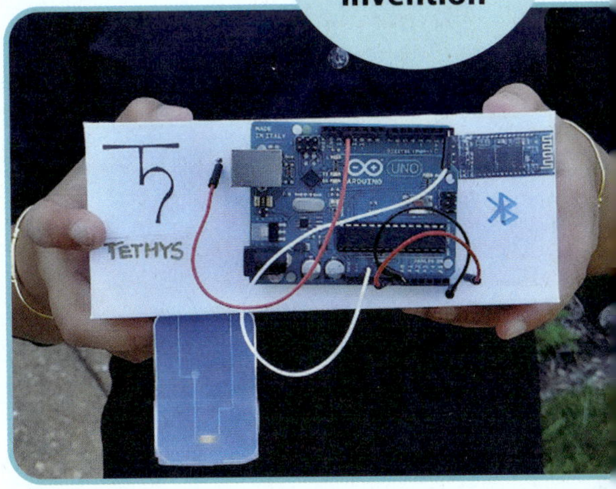

attempts = efforts to try to do something

Stop & Discuss

What does Gitanjali mean when she says failure is a "step toward success"?

Explain what she means using evidence from the text.

SPOTLIGHT BENCHMARK: ELA.4.R.3.2 Summarize a text to enhance comprehension. (b) Include the central idea and relevant details for an informational text.

Summarize a Text

- To **summarize** a text means to retell the most important ideas in the text.
- A **summary** includes the central idea and relevant details from the text.
- The **central idea** is the most important idea the author wants you to know about a topic. **Relevant details** are the most important details that support the central idea.

Reread/Think

Reread "Gitanjali Rao: Steps Toward Success." Think about the topic of the text. Then complete the chart with the central idea and relevant details that support it.

Topic Gitanjali Rao

Central Idea		

Relevant Details (paragraphs 1–4)	Relevant Details (paragraphs 5–7)	Relevant Details (paragraphs 8 and 9)

Talk

Use the details in your graphic organizer to tell a summary of the text to a partner. Make sure to include at least one detail from each section of the text.

The main thing to know about Gitanjali Rao is ___.

The problem she saw was ___. She thought she could help by ___.

She tried ___. Finally, she ___.

Write

Write a summary of "Gitanjali Rao: Steps Toward Success." Include the central idea and relevant details you listed to describe the problem Gitanjali heard about and what she did to help.

WRITING CHECKLIST

- ☐ I included the central idea of the text.
- ☐ I included relevant details.
- ☐ I explained who Gitanjali Rao is and what she did.
- ☐ I used correct spelling, punctuation, and capitalization.

Anything Is

by Mary Lindeen

1 Brooke Martin loved her dogs, Kayla and Zoey. And Kayla and Zoey loved Brooke. In fact, Brooke and her dogs really missed each other whenever they were apart. Brooke thought about how sometimes she and her friends and family would check in with each other using video chats. Brooke wondered if she could check in with her dogs that way, too. And that's what started 12-year-old Brooke on her path to becoming an inventor. She thought of a clever way for pet owners and their pets to stay connected using technology.

2 Working in a garage with her dad, Brooke built a new device. A small stand held a phone or tablet that automatically turned on whenever the owner called home. The device let owners and their pets see and hear each other so pet owners could "chat" with their pets.

dispense = give out in small amounts

3 To make the connection between pets and people even better, the machine also held treats. Owners could push a button on their phones to **dispense** a snack to their pet at home no matter where they were calling from. Brooke's machine made sure pets were safe from eating too many treats and getting sick. It was also designed to stop pets from getting into the snacks on their own.

Stop & Discuss

How did Brooke's love for her dogs lead to her first invention?

Use evidence from the text to explain your ideas.

Brooke Martin and her dog Kayla

Paws-ible

4 At first, Brooke shared her invention with family and friends. But then she started entering contests and going to meetings where inventors shared their ideas. People were interested in this young inventor who loved her dogs. Reporters wrote articles about Brooke. She was even invited to appear on a TV show where judges decide whether to give money to inventors to help them make and sell their product. Brooke didn't win any money, but that didn't stop her! She started her own company and sold her invention around the world.

Beorn the dog with Brooke Martin's invention that combines video chat with a dog treat dispenser

5 Then Brooke thought of a way to build on her idea to solve another problem. She thought about her grandmother, whose health problems made it difficult for her to use a phone or tablet. Brooke realized that with a few small changes, her original invention could help people!

6 Here's how Brooke's new invention worked. Caregivers would call a loved one who might need help with medications. The call would automatically connect them for a video chat to check in with each other. The dispenser would help people take medicine at the right time and in the right amount. Brooke, who was 15 years old by then, had come up with her second big invention.

Stop & Discuss

How did Brooke's first invention lead to her second invention?

Explain your ideas using evidence from the text.

Brooke Martin with her invention at the Global Pet Expo

7 Brooke went to college, where she studied engineering, which is the science of planning and building structures, machines, and systems. Engineers love to solve problems, so engineering was a good fit for an inventor. Brooke also learned how technology can help people better connect with each other.

8 Brooke Martin is proof that young people can be inventors. Maybe you'd like to be an inventor, too. Are you curious and willing to put in the effort? Great! All you need, then, is a problem to solve and a creative way to solve it.

Stop & Discuss

According to the text, what helps a person become an inventor?

Explain your ideas using evidence from the text.

___ can help a person become an inventor.

An inventor needs ___.

SPOTLIGHT BENCHMARK: ELA.4.R.3.2 Summarize a text to enhance comprehension. (b) Include the central idea and relevant details for an informational text.

Summarize a Text

- A summary should be brief. To help keep it short, include only relevant details. Do not include less important details.
- Not all details are relevant. A detail is not relevant if it is *not* necessary for understanding the central idea of the text.

Reread/Think

Reread "Anything Is Paws-ible." Write the topic of the text. Then identify the central idea and the relevant details that support it.

Topic ____

Central Idea		
Relevant Details (paragraphs 1–3)	Relevant Details (paragraphs 4–6)	Relevant Details (paragraphs 7 and 8)

SESSION 4 PRACTICE

Talk

Review the details in your graphic organizer and discuss them with your partner. Then tell a summary of the text to your partner that includes the central idea and relevant details. You can add or remove details from your chart as needed.

> The main thing to know about Brooke Martin is ___.

> A relevant detail about her first/second invention is ___.

> I think/do not think this is a relevant detail because ___.

Write

Write a summary of "Anything Is Paws-ible." Include the central idea and relevant details.

WRITING CHECKLIST

- ☐ I included the central idea of the text.
- ☐ I included relevant details and left out unimportant details.
- ☐ I explained who Brooke Martin is and what she did.
- ☐ I used correct spelling, punctuation, and capitalization.

Toying with a Challenge

by Lynda Jones

Shubham Banerjee, founder and chief executive officer of Braigo Labs, Inc., with his Braille printer made of LEGO® bricks

1 Twelve-year-old Shubham Banerjee loved a challenge, and he loved helping others. One day in 2014 he wondered, *How do people who are blind read?* After doing some research, Shubham learned that many people who are blind or have low vision read Braille, a system of raised dots that represent letters and symbols. To read Braille, people pass their fingers along each arrangement of dots, moving from left to right and **identifying** each letter as they go.

identifying = telling what something is

2 In his research, Shubham learned something else. Braille printers, which connect to a computer, are very expensive. They can cost from $2,000 to $5,000. If someone could build a less expensive Braille printer, he thought, people everywhere could more easily buy this assistive technology.

3 Shubham got to work. With the help of his family, he bought a high-tech set of LEGO® bricks. This kit included motors, **sensors**, and a computer. The kit cost less than $400, much less than the most affordable Braille printer!

sensors = pieces of equipment that detect changes in heat, light, sound, or motion

prototype = the first model of an invention that tests if it will work

4 Building the printer wasn't easy. Shubham spent many late nights at the kitchen table learning about robotics, writing computer code, and making the **prototype** work.

5 Shubham built and took apart seven prototypes until he built one that correctly printed the raised Braille dots. It also weighed only a few pounds. He called his invention "BRAIGO," a combination of *Braille* and *LEGO*®, and entered it into his seventh-grade science fair. BRAIGO was a hit at the fair. Later, Shubham's invention caught the attention of a major technology company, which helped fund his future work.

6 In 2014, Shubham started his own company, Braigo Labs, and began working with others to improve the printer. Henry Wedler, a chemist who was born blind, wanted to help. Wedler had read about Shubham's invention and contacted the teen to find out how the amazing printer worked. Now, Wedler is an advisor at Braigo Labs.

7 Shubham and his team are still perfecting BRAIGO. He hopes to have an affordable product available soon for people all over the world who are blind and have low vision.

Shubham Banerjee working on his Braille printer at home

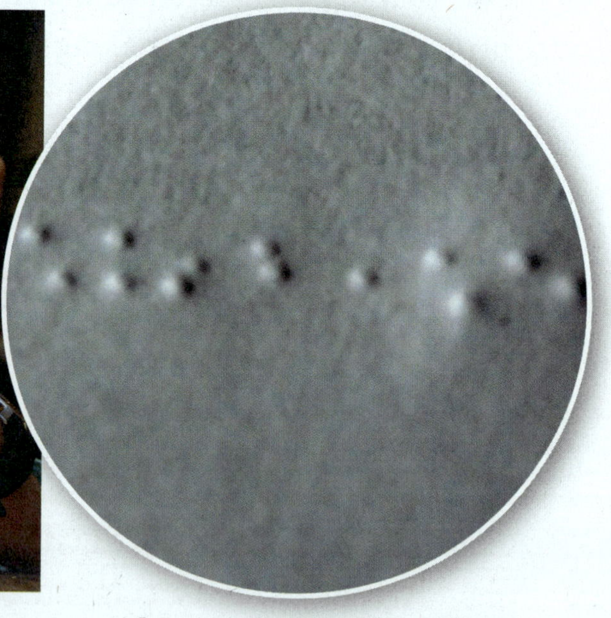

A test printout of Braille

LEGO® is a trademark of the LEGO Group of companies, which does not sponsor or endorse this content.

SPOTLIGHT BENCHMARK: ELA.4.R.3.2 Summarize a text to enhance comprehension. (b) Include the central idea and relevant details for an informational text.

Respond to Text

Reread/Think

Reread "Toying with a Challenge." Choose the best response to each question.

1. Which sentence **best** describes the central idea of the whole article?

Ⓐ Shubham Banerjee loved helping others and wanted to learn more about how people who are blind read.

Ⓑ Shubham Banerjee solved a problem by making an affordable Braille printer out of LEGO® bricks.

Ⓒ Shubham Banerjee bought a set of LEGO® bricks with motors and sensors that cost less than $400.

Ⓓ Shubham Banerjee built seven different prototypes before he made one that worked correctly.

2. Read the sentence from paragraph 6.

Now, Wedler is an <u>advisor</u> at Braigo Labs.

What is the meaning of the word <u>advisor</u>?

Ⓐ someone who advertises an invention

Ⓑ someone who funds scientific research

Ⓒ someone who knows how to read Braille

Ⓓ someone who offers helpful advice

3. Which details would be **most** important to include in a summary of the text? Select **two** details.

Ⓐ Shubham was in seventh grade when he learned about Braille.

Ⓑ Shubham started a company called Braigo Labs.

Ⓒ Shubham's family helped him buy the parts he needed.

Ⓓ Shubham's invention weighed only a few pounds.

Ⓔ Shubham wanted to invent something that would help people.

SESSION 5 PRACTICE

Reread/Think

4. How was Shubham's printer an improvement over other printers?

Ⓐ It was easier to use.

Ⓑ It was less expensive.

Ⓒ It printed more quickly.

Ⓓ It did not require a computer.

Write

Write a summary of "Toying with a Challenge." Include the central idea and relevant details.

WRITING CHECKLIST

- ☐ I included the central idea of the text.
- ☐ I included relevant details that support the central idea.
- ☐ I explained who Shubham Banerjee is and what he did.
- ☐ I used complete sentences.
- ☐ I used correct spelling, punctuation, and capitalization.

Respond to the Focus Question

How can a young person become an inventor?

Reread/Think

With your **team**, reread the beginning of "Toying with a Challenge." What problem did Shubham Banerjee want to solve? How did he solve it?

____

____

With a **partner**, reread the beginning of "Gitanjali Rao: Steps Toward Success." What problem did Gitanjali Rao want to solve? How did she solve it?

____

____

On your own, reread the beginning of "Anything Is Paws-ible." What problem did Brooke Martin want to solve? How did she solve it?

____

____

Talk

As a team, discuss the process each young inventor followed.

- What was similar about their creative ideas? What was different?
- What steps did they take to develop, test, and build their inventions?

All three of them ___.

___ was the only one who ___.

Write

Imagine your own idea for an invention that will solve a problem. Describe the steps you could take to develop, test, and build the invention.

From Idea to Invention

FOCUS QUESTION

How and why do people design and build new technologies?

NOTICE AND WONDER

Look at the three texts you will read in this lesson. What do you notice? What do you wonder? Discuss your ideas with a partner.

THE DESIGN PROCESS

People develop new inventions by following certain steps. Read the words below. Then put them in the order you think they happen. Explain your reasoning.

test	research	idea
prototype	redesign	brainstorm

☐ → ☐ → ☐ → ☐ → ☐ → ☐

After you come up with an idea, it is important to ___.

Before you test your idea, you must ___ and ___.

The Roots of Inspiration

by Morgan Parsons

Behind the Design Process

with DIY Girls InvenTeam

by Johanna Arnone

Built to Go Against the Flow

by Vila McHenry

SESSION 1 READ

The Roots of Inspiration

by Morgan Parsons

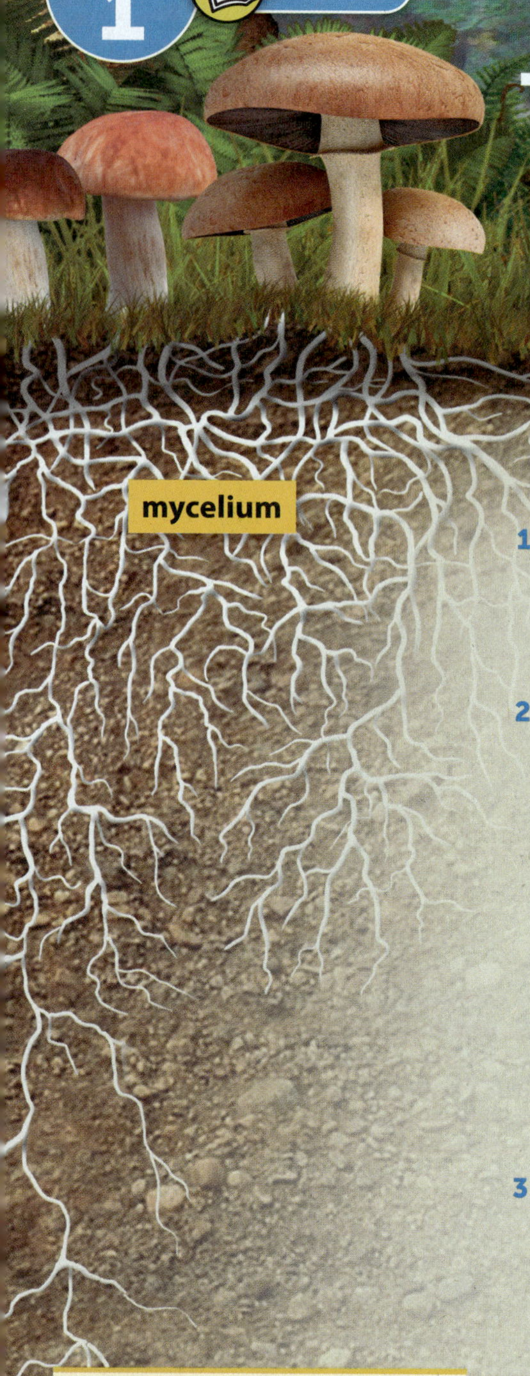

1 Inspiration can come from almost anywhere. Believe it or not, fungi—yes, fungi—are inspiring many new inventions.

2 What are fungi, you ask? Well, they are neither plant nor animal. But they are living things that interact with other organisms. Perhaps the most familiar part of a fungus is the mushroom. You might see the colorful caps dotting a forest floor. But hiding below the ground is their tangle of tiny, root-like threads called mycelium. These threads have two important characteristics. They grow quickly, spreading out into huge networks. And, when they tangle together, they're unusually strong.

3 Inventors have looked at the strength of mycelium and gotten big ideas. For example, Eben Bayer was first inspired by mycelium as a child in Vermont. One day, he noticed something strange about a pile of wood chips. Threads of mycelium had grown through the pile and, like glue, they held the chips together. As an adult, Bayer wanted to create a material to replace plastic, which harms the environment. And he remembered mycelium. His company invented a process that turns living mycelium into different products. These include an alternative to Styrofoam packaging and a material that **mimics** hard plastic. But unlike plastic, mycelium is biodegradable. It can break down in a landfill.

mimics = looks or acts like

Stop & Discuss

Why was Eben Bayer inspired by mycelium?

Underline details about mycelium and what Bayer noticed about it.

4 Mycelium is not only strong but lightweight. Both of these features have inspired **architects** to create new materials. For instance, some have turned it into building materials that are lighter than bricks and stronger than concrete. The architects hope to use these materials instead of concrete, which has negative effects on the environment. For example, concrete production releases carbon dioxide into the air and uses water we need for drinking. So, "growing" building material from mycelium would be much less harmful to the environment.

architects = people who design buildings

Vera Myer is a mycologist, or a person who studies fungi. She is holding a block of building material grown from mycelium.

5 If building with mycelium-based materials works on Earth, how about on Mars? This might be the most exciting example of its possible uses. If humans ever inhabit other planets, they'll need structures to live in. Sending heavy building materials to Mars would be too expensive. Lynn Rothschild, an astrobiologist at NASA, thinks mycelium-based housing is the answer. "How cool would that be . . . to grow your own habitats off-planet?" she wonders. To test the idea, her team created a "soil" mixture that mimics the dirt on Mars. With a little water and food, they were able to grow mycelium in it! Now her team is working on how to grow an entire structure.

6 What's next for this fascinating fungus feature? Mushroom motels? Mycelium malls? The possibilities are limitless. But one thing is certain: Nature is infinitely inspiring.

Stop & Discuss

What makes mycelium a good building material?

Talk with your partner about ways mycelium is a better building material than concrete.

SESSION 2 PRACTICE

SPOTLIGHT BENCHMARK: ELA.4.R.2.1 . . . identify the text structures of . . . sequence and description in texts.

Identify Text Structure

- Authors organize information in a text in different ways. The way they organize information about a topic or idea is called the **text structure**.
- Authors use a **descriptive text structure** to give information about a topic or idea. A text with this structure is organized into sections. Each section describes characteristics, features, or examples of a main topic.
- Descriptive text structures often include phrases such as *for example, for instance, characteristics of, features*, and *includes.*

Reread/Think

Reread "The Roots of Inspiration." Identify the text structure. Then complete the chart with information that shows the text structure.

Type of Text Structure: ______________________________

What Is the Section About?	Details or Examples	Signal Words
Paragraph 2 describes fungi and the characteristics of mycelium	quick growing, strong	two important characteristics
Paragraph 3		
Paragraph 4		
Paragraph 5		

Talk

Talk with a partner about the descriptions in paragraphs 3–5. What do these sections of the text help you understand about the features of mycelium? Include details from your chart.

> This section helps me understand that one characteristic of fungi/mycelium is ___.

> An example of how this characteristic has inspired inventors is ___.

Write

How does the text structure of "The Roots of Inspiration" help you understand how fungi are inspiring people? Use details from the text to support your response.

WRITING CHECKLIST

- ☐ I identified the text structure and explained how it helped me understand the topic.
- ☐ I used details from the text to support my response.
- ☐ I used complete sentences.
- ☐ I used correct spelling, punctuation, and capitalization.

Behind the DESIGN PROCESS with the DIY Girls InvenTeam

by Johanna Arnone

How do people design and build new inventions? Through several steps and a great team. Consider the DIY Girls InvenTeam: Twelve high schoolers, all from the San Fernando Valley region of Los Angeles. Here's a peek at the steps in their design process.

Stop & Discuss

What does the DIY Girls InvenTeam do at the beginning of the design process?

Summarize with your partner what the team wants to figure out.

The first step of the design process is ___.

The team's goal in the first step is to help ___.

Step ① Identify a Need

1 First, team members consider different ways to have an impact in their community. They spend weeks reflecting on what their city needs. With time, they narrow their focus to one issue. There is a growing number of people who are experiencing homelessness in L.A. The team blogs about how there are people "at church, on the streets, and in our family" who do not have housing. But can the team really make a difference? The DIY Girls InvenTeam digs in deeper.

DIY stands for "Do It Yourself"—and this team of young inventors is showing people how.

Brainstorming often involves drawing rough pictures of how something might look.

Step ② Brainstorm and Sketch

2 Next, it's time to brainstorm. What are the requirements for a practical invention that people could really use? L.A. bans temporary shelters from streets during the day, so the team plans a tent that collapses into a backpack. It must be easy to use. It must be safe. The team plans two unique features. It will self-clean, and it will include a **renewable energy** source. Solar power will run fans and lights and charge devices. The students break into three technical teams: structures, materials, and solar power. Each group weighs the pros and cons of different features. Finally, they sketch plans.

renewable energy = energy that comes from a natural resource that does not run out, such as solar or wind power

Step ③ Research

3 The students learn more about the problem. They read articles and listen to podcasts. Then they interview community members who provide services to people without housing. The team visits a studio at the University of Southern California (USC) where architecture students build homes from **discarded** supplies. USC builders discuss tools, materials, and structures. After gathering information, the DIY Girls InvenTeam decides to design a tent for a mother and two kids. They research similar shelters that other people have designed, and the team envisions a better version.

discarded = thrown away

Stop & Discuss

What does the team decide to make? How do they decide?

Underline details in both paragraphs that answer the questions.

Step ④ Build a Prototype

4 The structures, materials, and solar power groups have big jobs. They evaluate every detail. They learn new skills. During this process, they frequently change their minds. Over many hours, the groups assemble the first model, or prototype, of their invention.

Inventors build prototypes to test their ideas.

Step ⑤ Test and Improve

5 Testing comes next. The DIY Girls InvenTeam also presents the first tent to fellow students, engineers, teachers, family, and officials. They gather feedback. Then the team makes technical tweaks to their design. There's no end to an invention's possible improvements.

Step ⑥ Share the Results

6 Next, the DIY Girls InvenTeam travels to Cambridge, Massachusetts. There, they present a working prototype to fellow inventors at an event sponsored by the Massachusetts Institute of Technology. The prototype tent is made of insulating, breathable material. It has solar-powered lights, a phone charger, and sanitation features. This design meets technical goals. It also meets the team's larger goal: to create a convenient place for a family to rest. What are the next steps? Further testing. Filing for a **patent** to get the legal rights to their invention. And finally, distributing the invention to people who could use it. No doubt about it. These inventors put in the work!

patent = a legal document that gives inventors the right to make, use, or sell their invention

Stop & Discuss

Why do you think the team tests their ideas?

Discuss with your partner why testing might be important, based on details in the text.

Identify Text Structure

- Authors use different text structures to organize information.
- Texts organized by a **sequential text structure** show the **sequence**, or order of steps, in a process. Authors use this text structure to explain how to do or make something.
- Texts with a sequential text structure often include numbered steps and words that show order, such as *first, second, third, before, next, after,* and *finally.*

Reread/Think

Reread "Behind the Design Process." Identify the text structure. Then complete the chart with information that shows the text structure.

Type of Text Structure: ______________________________

What Is the Section About?	Signal Words
Paragraph 1 explains the first step in the design process: how the team thinks about what their community needs	• the number "1" • First • With time
Paragraph 2	
Paragraph 3	
Paragraph 4	

Talk

What does each section of the text explain? What signal words are used, and what do they help you understand about the text structure?

Each section of the text explains ___.

The signal words ___ show that the text structure is organized by ___.

Write

Identify the text structure of "Behind the Design Process." How does it help you understand the team's design process? Use details from the text to support your response.

WRITING CHECKLIST

- ☐ I identified the text structure.
- ☐ I explained how this text structure helped me understand the topic.
- ☐ I supported my response with details from the text.
- ☐ I used complete sentences.
- ☐ I used correct spelling, punctuation, and capitalization.

Built to GO Against the Flow

by Vila McHenry

1 At a water park, after people scream their way down the log flume and splash-land at the bottom, they might wonder: How did all that water get *up* the hill in the first place? How does it move against gravity? How is it carried?

2 One example of transporting water up a slope is based on a 2,500-year-old technology called the Archimedes screw, named after a Greek mathematician and inventor. But according to legend, it was likely invented even earlier, so the King of Babylon could water his high garden **terraces**.

3 The design includes just two simple parts: a tube and a screw. The screw spins inside the tube so that its threads scoop up water at the bottom. As the screw rotates, the threads carry the water higher, spiraling upwards inside the tube until it reaches the top.

4 Today, people are still inspired to find new uses for this design. For example, the Archimedes screw is used on farms to transfer animal feed up into a storage **silo**. A miniature version is used in artificial hearts to move blood from one part of the heart to another.

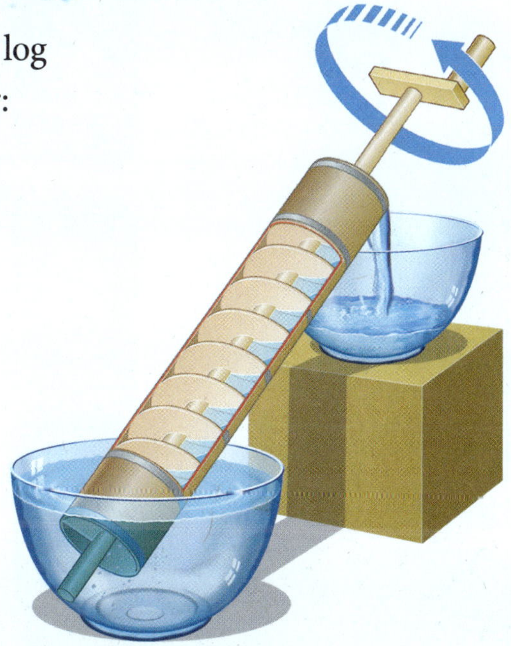

An Archimedes screw carries water from a lower area to a higher area.

terraces = raised flat areas next to a building

silo = a tall, round building that stores animal feed

5 Maybe you, too, will be inspired by this technology. Here are the steps to build your own model.

How to Build an Archimedes Screw

Materials

- 2-liter plastic bottle
- wooden spoon
- thin cardboard
- tape and scissors
- pencil
- large bowl of popped popcorn

1 Cut off the top and bottom of the bottle, turning it into a clear tube. Place one end of the tube on the cardboard. Trace a circle and cut it out.

2 Place the end of the spoon handle in the center of the cardboard circle. Trace a circle around the handle. Cut out the small circle by first making a slit from the outer edge to the inner circle. Using this shape as a pattern, make six more copies.

3 Tape the cut end of the first circle to the beginning of the second one. Continue connecting all the circles until you have a continuous spiral.

4 Slide the handle of the spoon through the center of the spiral, gently spreading out the spiral along the handle. Tape the top and bottom of the spiral to the spoon handle, with the spoon end sticking out of the top. Insert the screw into the tube.

6 Now test it with your bowl of popcorn! When you turn the top of the spoon, the screw should rotate inside the tube, carrying popcorn upward as it turns. Can you imagine any other uses for this design?

Respond to Text

Reread/Think

Reread "Built to Go Against the Flow." Choose the best response to each question.

1. How does the text structure of paragraph 2 contribute to the meaning of the text?

Ⓐ It gives information about a process.

Ⓑ It describes details about a topic.

Ⓒ It explains how to do something.

Ⓓ It shows how a problem was solved.

2. What is the meaning of continuous as it is used in Step 3 of "How to Build an Archimedes Screw"?

Ⓐ moving around in a circle

Ⓑ forming an unbroken whole

Ⓒ copied more than once

Ⓓ gathered into a solid bunch

3. Which quotation from paragraph 5 gives the **best** signal that the author is going to start using a different text structure in the passage?

Ⓐ "Maybe you, too, will be inspired"

Ⓑ "by this technology"

Ⓒ "Here are the steps"

Ⓓ "your own model"

Reread/Think

4. Fill in **one** bubble in each row to show the correct order of steps in building an Archimedes screw.

	First	Next	Then	Finally
Make six copies of a cardboard circle with a slit in one side and a hole in the middle.	Ⓐ	Ⓑ	Ⓒ	Ⓓ
Slide the handle of a spoon through the center, spreading out the spiral.	Ⓔ	Ⓕ	Ⓖ	Ⓗ
Tape the top and bottom of the spiral to the spoon handle.	Ⓘ	Ⓙ	Ⓚ	Ⓛ
Tape together the ends of the cardboard circles to form a spiral.	Ⓜ	Ⓝ	Ⓞ	Ⓟ

Write

Identify the text structure in each part of "Built to Go Against the Flow." How does each structure help you understand the topic? Use details from the text to support your response.

____

____

____

____

____

____

____

____

____

WRITING CHECKLIST

- ☐ I identified two text structures.
- ☐ I explained how these text structures helped me understand the topic.
- ☐ I used details from the text to support my response.
- ☐ I used complete sentences.
- ☐ I used correct spelling, punctuation, and capitalization.

Respond to the Focus Question

How and why do people design and build new technologies?

Reread/Think

Look back at the texts you read in this lesson. Then answer the questions below. Include an example from each text in your responses.

1. What did you learn about **why** people design new technologies?

____

____

____

2. What did you learn about **how** people design new technologies?

____

____

____

Talk

As a team, share the ideas you wrote about and discuss these questions:

Why do people design new technologies?

What steps do people take to make their ideas a reality?

People design new technologies because ___.

The first steps in the design process are ___, ___, and ___.

After people ___, they ___.

Write

Imagine a technology you would like to design. Explain why you would like to design it. Then describe the steps you would follow to create it.

How to Make a Prototype

TALK ABOUT WHAT YOU KNOW

Turn and talk with a partner about what you know about inventions, technology, and the design process. Use the pictures and the sentence frames to help you.

People have invented new technologies because ___.

Technology has helped people solve problems such as ___.

The design process helps inventors ___.

LESSON 5 World-Changing Inventions

LESSON 6 Problem Solvers

LESSON 7
Young Inventors

LESSON 8
From Idea to Invention

WRITE ABOUT INVENTIONS

Write a sentence about inventions, using some of the words displayed below. Challenge yourself to use several words.

create | process | design | invent | imagine

problem | idea | test | experiment | solve

What Is Prototyping?

by Eric Cook

1 Do you have an idea for an invention? If you do, you might ask yourself, *How do I turn my idea into something I can make?* Well, first, you need to write down your idea. Then, you need to think about the details: what your invention will look like, the materials it uses, and how it works. Next, you build a prototype, or a rough model of your idea, before you create the final thing. This step even has a special name—*prototyping.*

2 Prototyping lets inventors test their ideas before they decide on a final design. Artists often draw sketches before they start working on a painting. If artists sketch something and they decide that they don't like the design, they can improve the sketch or make another one. Similarly, inventors create early models of a project to uncover problems before it's too late to make changes. Like sketches, prototypes are quick, cheap, and easy to revise if the model doesn't turn out right.

Stop & Discuss

Why do inventors use prototyping?

Discuss your response with a partner.

Inventors use prototyping to explore ___

3 Let's meet one young inventor, named Leo, who learned the value of prototyping. Leo loved pizza, which he usually ordered online. The website of his favorite pizza shop, however, was old and **inefficient**. One day, Leo complained to his sister Sylvie about how hard it was to order different toppings.

inefficient = not making the best use of time and energy

4 "If it bothers you so much," she said, "why don't you design something better?"

5 And that's what Leo set out to do.

6 Leo imagined an online ordering system that would allow customers to drag pictures of toppings they wanted onto an image of a pizza. First, Leo used simple materials to create the a version of his invention. He sketched what the website might look like on paper. He drew pictures of toppings on sticky notes so they could be easily moved around.

7 Next, Leo showed Sylvie his paper prototype. But she paid more attention to details such as color than to how the website would work. Leo wanted feedback on his general idea, not on his drawings. So, he went back and drew a simpler set of black-and-white sketches.

Stop & Discuss

How did Leo think his invention would be better than the pizza shop's website?

Underline the sentence that describes Leo's idea.

8 After Leo revised his prototype, he began to test it out on his friends. They approved of his design. As they moved different ingredients onto and off of the paper prototype, they laughed and said things like, "This is so much fun!"

9 At the same time, testing showed that there were several **potential** areas for mix-ups. For instance, if someone put pepperoni on just half of the pizza, did that really mean the person only wanted pepperoni on half? Or was the person just being sloppy as they dragged the ingredients over? And what was the best way to show double orders of toppings? On paper, a single layer of mushrooms didn't really look that different from a double layer of mushrooms. And if someone wanted to order a pizza with nine different toppings, how could the designer be sure that all of the toppings were visible?

potential = possible

Stop & Discuss

What worked about Leo's prototype? What needed improvement?

Discuss your response with a partner.

10 By raising questions and identifying problems that needed to be solved, testing helped Leo figure out how to improve his design. He made changes again and again to his prototype. And then one day he couldn't think of any more changes to make. So, it was time to stop prototyping. He was ready to move on to building the real thing.

11 But Leo didn't take the next step alone. He collaborated with his sister. Sylvie had learned a lot about making websites in computer class at school, so she helped him create a final design that actually worked. Leo's success was possible only because he had started with prototypes.

12 Take a look around your world. What needs improvement, and how can you make it better? With ideas, creativity, and some prototyping, you could be on your way to the next greatest invention!

Stop & Discuss

How did Leo know when to stop prototyping?

Underline details in the text that support your response.

SESSION 3 PRACTICE

Respond to Text

Reread/Think

Reread “What Is Prototyping?” Choose the best response to each question.

1. According to the text, what is the first step you should take after coming up with an idea for an invention?

Ⓐ decide how the invention will look

Ⓑ ask others what they think of the idea

Ⓒ find the materials for the prototype

Ⓓ write down the idea for the invention

2. Which sentence **best** states the central idea of “What Is Prototyping?”

Ⓐ “Well, first, you need to write down your idea.” (paragraph 1)

Ⓑ “Prototyping lets inventors test their ideas before they decide on a final design.” (paragraph 2)

Ⓒ “Leo used simple materials to create the first version of his invention.” (paragraph 6)

Ⓓ “Once Leo revised his prototype, he began to test it out on his friends.” (paragraph 8)

3. Why did Leo test out his idea on his friends?

Ⓐ to show off his idea

Ⓑ to see how well his design would work

Ⓒ to make them laugh

Ⓓ to learn what they like on their pizza

4. The word revise contains the root *vis*, meaning “see.” What is the meaning of revise in paragraph 2, based on the meaning of the prefix *re-* and the root *vis*?

Ⓐ to look at something again to make changes

Ⓑ to look across something to see it clearly

Ⓒ to look at opposite things

Ⓓ to look among several things

5. Which detail would be **most** important to include in a summary of paragraphs 6–9?

Ⓐ Leo used sticky notes to help organize his ideas.

Ⓑ Leo found the design of the toppings difficult to create.

Ⓒ Leo drew his second sketches in black and white.

Ⓓ Leo improved his design after showing Sylvie his ideas.

6. Read this sentence from paragraph 11.

He collaborated with his sister.

The word "labor" in collaborated means "to work." What does the word collaborated mean?

Ⓐ worked carefully

Ⓑ worked for a long time

Ⓒ worked together

Ⓓ worked for a family member

7. Reread paragraph 11. Fill in the bubble **before** the sentence that **best** supports the central idea of the text.

Ⓐ But Leo didn't take the next step alone. Ⓑ He collaborated with his sister. Ⓒ Sylvie had learned a lot about making websites in computer class at school, so she helped him create a final design that actually worked. Ⓓ Leo's success was possible only because he started with a prototype.

SESSION 3 PRACTICE

Write

Identify the text structure that the author uses to organize information in paragraphs 6–11 of "What Is Prototyping?" How does this text structure help you understand what Leo did? Use details and signal words from the text in your response.

WRITING CHECKLIST

- ☐ I identified the text structure.
- ☐ I explained what the text structure helps me understand.
- ☐ I used details and signal words from the text.
- ☐ I used complete sentences.
- ☐ I used correct spelling, punctuation, and capitalization.

Make Connections

Reread/Think

Think back to the texts you have read in this unit. Which invention or inventing process that you read about is the most interesting to you? Why do you think it is important? Reread the text. Then explain your opinion about the invention or process.

The text I reread: ______________________________

My opinion: ______________________________

____

____

____

Text evidence that supports my thinking:

1. ______________________________

____

____

2. ______________________________

____

____

Talk

Meet with a partner to discuss your responses above. Use the sentence frames to get started.

I think the most interesting invention/process is ___ because ___.

I agree/disagree that ___ because ___.

Another reason that supports my thinking is ___.

Exploring

LESSON 9

Uncovering the Past

162

LESSON 10

Mapping the Unknown

178

UNIT 3

SESSION 1 TALK ABOUT THE TOPIC

Uncovering the Past

FOCUS QUESTION

What can we discover by exploring the world around us?

NOTICE AND WONDER

Look at the story you will read in this lesson. What do you notice? What do you wonder? Discuss your ideas with a partner.

EXPLORATION WORD PAIRS

Match each word on the left with a word on the right. Tell your partner why you connected these words.

rock	paleontologist
dig	fossil
scientist	chisel

___ means ___, which is similar to ___.

___ is related to ___ because ___.

Digging In,
Parts 1–3

by Brooks Benjamin

Digging In PART 1

by Brooks Benjamin

Dear Journal, June 25

1 I've been robbed. By my DAD. I was supposed to be spending my first week of summer break on a boogie board, being chased by monster waves.

2 But my dad just came in to tell me he canceled our trip to the beach because he has an even better surprise.

3 Spoiler alert: IT'S NOT BETTER.

4 We're staying home, in New Mexico, so he can camp out to study rocks for three days, and I have to go with him. Why do I have to go? I'm basically a teenager! (in 2 years, 4 months, and 13 days) I know how to take care of myself. I've made mac and cheese a million times! They put the directions ON THE BOX.

5 I don't understand him. I wish they put directions on parents sometimes, especially paleontologist ones because I really don't get the whole digging in the dirt thing.

—Maddox

Stop & Discuss

How does Maddox feel about the trip with his dad?

Underline at least one detail that shows how he feels.

Dear Journal,

June 26

6 Dad woke me up at five this morning. Getting up that early during summer has to be breaking some sort of law.

7 When we finally got to the excavation site and I stepped out of Dad's truck, I nearly passed out. It was like walking into an oven cranked up to 450 degrees.

8 Even in my lightest T-shirt, I was a melting stick of butter. If you find a Maddox-shaped puddle out in the desert, just stick me back in a refrigerator when you get a chance.

9 Also, I'm the only kid here. There are a few college students and another professor who works at the same college where my dad teaches. Her name's Aisha. She seems nice, but she's way too excited about hammering rocks. I mean, she even brought her toolkit to dinner like she thought I wanted to see it.

10 Not like the tools were special. Just regular tools, but smaller. A mini pickax, mini shovels, tiny little brushes, scrapers like they use at the dentist . . . whatever.

11 She showed me a picture of something she found that could be a dinosaur fossil and said I could help her excavate it tomorrow if I wanted to.

12 I don't know. Maybe I'll check it out. It will probably be less boring than spending all day in the tent.

—Maddox

Stop & Discuss

What does Maddox think about the site so far? Predict what he will do next.

Use details from the text to explain your ideas.

SPOTLIGHT BENCHMARK: ELA.4.R.3.1 Explain how figurative language contributes to meaning in text(s).

Explain Figurative Language

- Authors use **figurative language** to help readers imagine vivid images. Figurative language is made of words and phrases whose meanings go beyond their literal, or exact, meaning.
  - — A **simile** compares two things using *like* or *as*. For example, *He is as quiet as a mouse* is a simile.
  - — A **metaphor** compares two things without using *like* or *as*. For example, *You're a gem* is a metaphor.
  - — **Hyperbole** is the use of exaggerated statements. For example, *This weighs a ton!* is hyperbole.

Reread/Think

Reread Part 1 of "Digging In." Complete the chart by identifying the type of figurative language used in the example. Then explain its meaning.

Example	Type of Figurative Language	What It Means
"I've been robbed." (paragraph 1)	hyperbole	Maddox feels that not being able to go to the beach is as unfair as having something stolen from him.
"I've made mac and cheese a million times!" (paragraph 4)		
"It was like walking into an oven cranked up to 450 degrees." (paragraph 7)		
"I was a melting stick of butter." (paragraph 8)		

Talk

Choose an example of figurative language from your chart. Explain how the language helps you understand Maddox's experiences and emotions.

Maddox describes ___ as ___.

The figurative language ___ helps me understand ___.

Write

How does Maddox feel about going to the excavation site in Part 1 of "Digging In"? Identify an example of figurative language in the text and explain how it helps you understand Maddox's feelings. Use details from the text to support your response.

WRITING CHECKLIST

- ☐ I identified an example of figurative language in the text.
- ☐ I explained how figurative language helps me understand Maddox's feelings.
- ☐ I used details from the text to support my response.
- ☐ I used complete sentences.
- ☐ I used correct spelling, punctuation, and capitalization.

Digging In PART 2

by Brooks Benjamin

Dear Journal, June 27

1 The sun is definitely closer here, and it's got a serious attitude problem. Our tents are all at the base of the mountains, so at least we're in the shade in the evening. But in the morning? Forget about it.

2 I decided to go with Dad to see if Aisha had pulled out a T-Rex skull or anything, but I had no idea I had to hike halfway to the sun to see it. Two whole bottles of water later, I finally made it.

3 Thankfully, there were tents where I could rest in the shade. My dad stayed with me while I gulped down like five gallons of glorious water. No matter how fast I drank, though, I don't think my mouth felt it. The heat **evaporated** every drop before it ever had a chance to touch my tongue.

evaporated = changed from a liquid to a vapor by heat

4 Aisha walked over to talk to my dad, and when she was finished, do you know what she did? She looked right at me and said, "Ready to get your feet wet?"

5 As if the desert would even let a human enjoy something other than sand and sunburns. I told Aisha I just came to see the dinosaur bone, and she told me I'd come at the perfect time because she was about to uncover it.

6 I asked her if I could rest a little longer first. I wasn't really tired anymore, but I wanted to make sure I wrote all this down before I stepped out into the sun and melted.

—Maddox

Stop & Discuss

How does Maddox feel about working with Aisha?

Underline details that support your response.

Dear Journal, June 27

7 Okay, you know me. I never exaggerate, so when I say this next part, you know it's true. Seeing my dad and Aisha working with all those tools was actually kind of cool. They'd chisel away at some of the rock, scrape a section here, brush a section there.

8 My dad pointed to a part that was a different color and told me this was the fossil.

9 I asked him why they couldn't just **pluck** the thing out like a loose tooth, and they laughed.

pluck = pull out

10 "It's all about patience," Dad said.

11 Maybe that's why I'm not a paleontologist.

12 Except he handed me one of the tools and asked if I wanted to give it a shot.

13 My throat was sandpaper, my sunscreen was melting, and my clothes were sweat-glued to my skin.

14 But I took the brush. I had to see what it felt like to be that close to a real fossil. Just for a second.

Stop & Discuss

How does Maddox's attitude change? Why does it change?

Underline the sentence that *first* tells you Maddox's attitude has changed.

15 Aisha began trimming pieces of rock away with a tiny knife and hammer while I was in charge of sweeping away the dust. We settled into a rhythm where she'd trim and I'd sweep over and over again.

16 Before I knew it, we had nearly the whole thing uncovered. It was a piece of cake!

17 My dad and Aisha took some measurements and wrote some stuff down. And that's when he looked at me and told me we may have just found a tooth fossil!

18 From an actual dinosaur!

19 AND I ACTUALLY GOT TO HELP UNCOVER IT!

—Maddox

Stop & Discuss

What does Maddox think and feel about the trip to the desert now?

Support your response with details from the text.

I can tell Maddox ___ because ___.

Explain Figurative Language

- Authors use different types of figurative language to create vivid images.
  - **Personification** gives human characteristics to non-human things. For example, *The wind whispered through the trees* is an example of personification.
  - An **idiom** is a phrase that has a very different meaning from the literal meaning of its words. For example, *You're off the hook* is an idiom.

Reread/Think

Reread Part 2 of "Digging In." Complete the chart by identifying the type of figurative language in each example. Then explain the meaning.

Example	Type of Figurative Language	What It Means
"The sun is definitely closer here, and it's got a serious attitude problem." (paragraph 1)	personification	Maddox thinks the hot sun at the site is difficult to deal with.
"'Ready to get your feet wet?'" (paragraph 4)		
"As if the desert would even let a human enjoy something other than sand and sunburns." (paragraph 5)		
". . . asked if I wanted to give it a shot." (paragraph 12)		

Talk

Choose an example of figurative language from your chart. Talk with your partner about what the language means and how it helps you understand Maddox's experiences.

> Maddox describes ___ as ___.

> This example of figurative language helps me understand Maddox because ___.

Write

Choose an example of personification from Part 2 of "Digging In." What non-human thing is given human characteristics? How does the language help you understand what it's like for Maddox to be in the desert? Use details from the text to support your response.

WRITING CHECKLIST

- ☐ I identified an example of personification in the text.
- ☐ I explained how figurative language helps me understand Maddox's experience in the desert.
- ☐ I used details from the text to support my response.
- ☐ I used complete sentences.
- ☐ I used correct spelling, punctuation, and capitalization.

Digging In PART 3

by Brooks Benjamin

Dear Journal, June 28

1 The night lasted forever. I barely slept at all. I was too excited! And this morning, I even got up before Dad. Right now we're eating breakfast and everyone's talking about some of the things they found, but my mind refuses to let go of that tooth.

2 It's weird because I've seen dinosaur fossils in movies or TV shows or at a museum, but it's totally different when you see one still in the ground.

3 At least it is for me. It's like something in my brain clicked and I realized that these creatures stomped around in the exact same places we do today. Some of them were as tiny as toy cars, while others were mountains on legs, their feet squishing prints into the ground for us to find millions of years later.

4 Anyway, we're about to head out. I'll check in later with an update.

—Maddox

Dear Journal,

June 28

5 Dad's pretty sure we're looking at a tooth fossil FROM THE BIGGEST DINOSAUR THAT EVER ROAMED NORTH AMERICA!

6 This dinosaur may have had a huge body, but its head was pretty small. Even weirder, it was an **herbivore**. In the DESERT, which means that millions of years ago, New Mexico was covered in plants and filled with water. Right now, I'm probably standing on what was an actual beach with warm sand and cool waves.

herbivore = an animal that eats only plants

7 This paleontology stuff is wild . . . but kind of cool.

8 I got to do more than brushing away dust this time. Dad let me plop this goopy stuff onto the fossil. He said it was glue that would keep any cracks from widening.

9 We chiseled a little ditch around the tooth to free it from the rock. Dad said it was important to keep the rock attached because, while the scientists poke and prod around in the rock, the minerals whisper little clues about what dinosaur it was and when it was alive. He said finding fossils isn't just about finding and unearthing fossils. It's about finding everything else AROUND the fossils, too.

10 Also, I found out that today's our last day here.

11 Dad promised me we'd go to an actual present-day beach after this. But you know what I told him?

12 A few more days on this one wouldn't be too bad.

—Maddox

Respond to Text

Reread/Think

Reread Part 3 of "Digging In." Choose the best response to each question.

1. PART A

Which detail from the story contains a simile?

Ⓐ "I've seen dinosaur fossils in movies or TV shows" (paragraph 2)

Ⓑ "it's totally different when you see one still in the ground" (paragraph 2)

Ⓒ "Some of them were as tiny as toy cars" (paragraph 3)

Ⓓ "others were mountains on legs" (paragraph 3)

PART B

How does the simile in Part A help the reader understand the text?

Ⓐ It compares imaginary fossils with real fossils.

Ⓑ It shows why dinosaurs lived in some places.

Ⓒ It describes how small some dinosaurs were.

Ⓓ It tells where dinosaur fossils can be found.

2. Fill in the bubble **before** one sentence in paragraph 1 that shows hyperbole.

Ⓐ The night lasted forever. Ⓑ I barely slept at all. Ⓒ I was too excited! Ⓓ And this morning, I even got up before Dad. Ⓔ Right now we're eating breakfast and everyone's talking about some of the things they found, but my mind refuses to let go of that tooth.

3. What is the meaning of <u>unearthing</u> as it is used in paragraph 9?

Ⓐ taking pictures of

Ⓑ putting glue on

Ⓒ talking about

Ⓓ digging up

SESSION 5 PRACTICE

Reread/Think

4. What lesson does Maddox learn in Part 3 of "Digging In"?

Ⓐ It is easier to see fossils in a movie than in the real world.

Ⓑ Looking for fossils is a fun way to learn about the past.

Ⓒ Most fossils are found in hot places like deserts.

Ⓓ Cleaning fossils should only be done by experts.

Write

In paragraph 9, Maddox's father explains that "minerals whisper little clues" about dinosaurs. What type of figurative language is this? What does it help you understand about the text? Use details from the text to support your response.

WRITING CHECKLIST

- ☐ I identified a type of figurative language.
- ☐ I described what the figurative language helps me understand.
- ☐ I used details from the text to support my response.
- ☐ I used complete sentences.
- ☐ I used correct spelling, punctuation, and capitalization.

Respond to the Focus Question

What can we discover by exploring the world around us?

Reread/Think

Think about what happens to Maddox in the three parts of "Digging In." Revisit parts of the story to help you remember. In the space below, describe what Maddox discovers by exploring.

Talk

Share ideas about what Maddox discovers by exploring. Where would you like to explore? What do you think you might learn from that experience?

Maddox learns ___.

I would like to explore ___.
I think I would learn ___.

Write

Work with your group to create a podcast script about Maddox's discoveries. One person will be Maddox. The other group members will be interviewers. Work together to write the interviewers' questions and Maddox's answers. Include one question that asks Maddox what advice he has about trying new experiences.

Mapping the Unknown

FOCUS QUESTION

How do people create maps of new places?

NOTICE AND WONDER

Look at the three texts you will read in this lesson. What do you notice? What do you wonder? Discuss your ideas with a partner.

CREATE A WORD WEB

What are some words that are related to maps? Add words to the word web below. Then, discuss your choices with a partner.

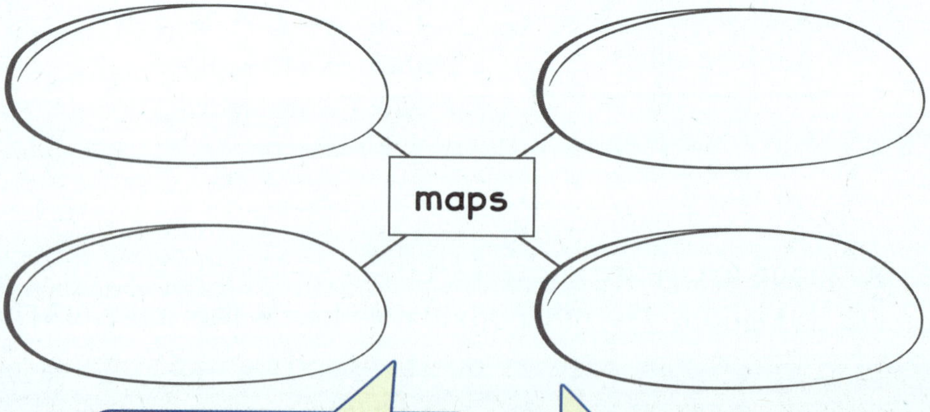

The word __ is related to maps because __.

When I think of maps, I think of __ because __.

Marie Maps the Sea

by Liz Huyck

Braving the Cave

by Lynda Jones

The Rainforest's Hidden Cities

by Kathryn Hulick

SESSION 1 READ

Marie Maps the Sea

by Liz Huyck

1 Young Marie Tharp thought her father had the best job ever. During the 1920s, he traveled around the Midwest, making maps. His maps were special—they revealed details about the soil that helped farmers know what to plant. He taught Marie to draw maps too.

2 In college, Marie took art, music, and math classes. She also took geology, the study of Earth's surface and how it has changed over time.

3 One day, Marie's geology teacher pointed to a big map of Earth. Almost three-quarters of it was plain blue ocean. What was under all that water? Was the sea floor flat, like a beach? Or were there mountains and valleys, as on land? No one knew. Marie Tharp was **intrigued**.

intrigued = curious about something

4 After college, in 1948, Tharp got a job in New York with a group of geologists who were studying the oceans. Women weren't allowed on research ships back then, so her job was to stay in the office and keep track of data that ships sent back. One number she often recorded was how deep the water was in different places.

5 Tharp noticed there were huge books in the office that listed how deep the ocean was along routes where ships had sailed in the past. The numbers gave her an idea. Could she use them to make a map of the whole sea floor?

6 Tharp recorded the numbers as dots on a graph. When she connected the dots, each line showed the changing depth of the water. She put the graphs together, like slices of bread, and created a 3-D view of the ocean floor.

Stop & Discuss

What was Tharp curious about in her college geology class?

Underline details in the text.

Tharp wanted to know more information about ___.

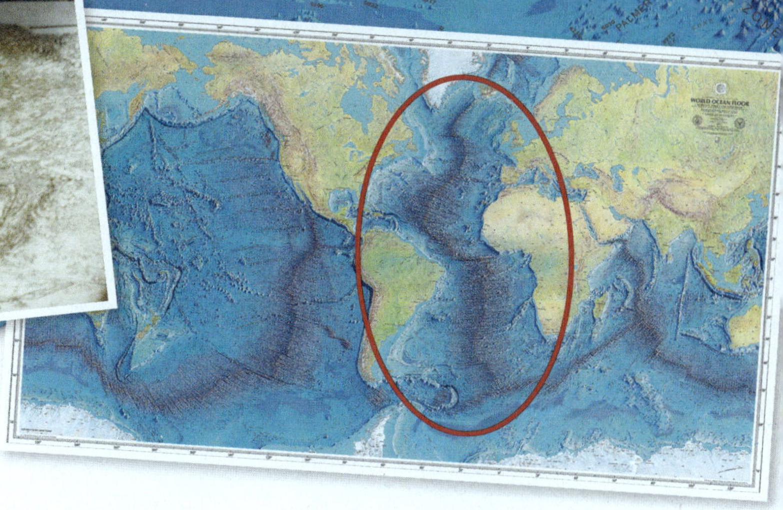

Marie Tharp (*left*) looks at the map of the sea floor that she created (*right*). The circled area shows a long rift through the Atlantic Ocean.

7 Another geologist, Bruce Heezen, collected more numbers to add to the map. Ocean scientists from other countries shared their measurements. Finally, in 1957, the first map of the ocean floor was complete.

8 This new map showed that the bottom of the ocean was full of mountains and valleys. A long mountain range went down the middle of the Atlantic Ocean. Running through the mountain range was another surprise—a crack, or rift, right down the center. That rift helped solve an old puzzle.

9 In 1912, a geologist named Alfred Wegener had suggested that the continents move. Most people laughed at or ignored his idea. But Tharp's map proved that Wegener was right. The Earth's crust is made of huge, rocky, slow-moving plates. Where the plates pull apart, **magma** bubbles up and hardens, forming new mountains. In other places, the plates move toward each other and crunch together.

10 Today, **satellites** can measure the continents moving—very slowly, a few centimeters a year. And Marie Tharp's map showed the way.

magma = liquid rock deep within Earth

satellites = objects in space that collect and send information

Stop & Discuss

What new information did Tharp's map provide?

Discuss details from the text with a partner.

SPOTLIGHT BENCHMARK: ELA.K12.EE.3.1 Make inferences to support comprehension.

Make Inferences

- An **inference** is an idea you form when you combine details in the text with what you already know.
- You can make inferences to help fill in details the author has not included.

Reread/Think

Reread "Marie Maps the Sea." Complete the chart by using text details and what you already know to make inferences about Marie Tharp's career.

What I Want To Know: How did Marie Tharp's experiences shape her career?

What the Text Says +	What I Know =	Inference
"Young Marie Tharp thought her father had the best job ever." "He taught Marie to draw maps too." (paragraph 1)	Children sometimes want to be like the adults they know.	
"What was under all that water? Was the sea floor flat, like a beach? Or were there mountains and valleys, as on land? No one knew. Marie Tharp was intrigued." (paragraph 3)		
"Women weren't allowed on research ships back then, so her job was to stay in the office and keep track of data that ships sent back." (paragraph 4)		

Talk

Share your chart with a partner. Discuss your inferences and the text details and background knowledge you used to support them.

The text says ___. I already know ___. So, I can infer ___.

I had a similar/different idea. I thought ___.

Write

How did Marie Tharp's experiences shape her career? Make at least one inference that answers this question. Be sure to include text evidence and your own knowledge to show how you made the inference.

WRITING CHECKLIST

- ☐ I made at least one inference in response to the question.
- ☐ I included text evidence and my own knowledge.
- ☐ I used complete sentences.
- ☐ I used correct spelling, punctuation, and capitalization.

SESSION 3 READ

Braving the Cave

by Lynda Jones

Stephen Bishop as a young man

1 One evening in the mid-1800s, enslaved 17-year-old Stephen Bishop entered the yawning entrance to Kentucky's Mammoth Cave to begin his night's work. He lit his kerosene lantern, raised it high, squeezed through a narrow passageway, and disappeared into darkness.

2 Bishop first entered Mammoth Cave in 1838 as an enslaved Black teenager. Frank Gorin, Bishop's enslaver, had purchased the cave to make it a tourist attraction. Gorin made Bishop work as a cave guide.

3 Bishop knew little about caves, but this changed as he began to explore them. It wasn't long before he knew the eight miles of the original cave routes. Soon, he began giving tours. Unlike White tour guides, however, Bishop wasn't paid for his work. Enslaved people were forced to do hard jobs every day without pay.

domes = rounded shapes

4 With only a lantern and a rope, Bishop spent many hours in Mammoth Cave. During his tours, he often spotted trails off the main routes. Later, he would explore beyond the known trails. He climbed up slick walls and high **domes** and down into deep pits. He saw rocks that looked like icicles growing down from the cave ceilings and up from the cave floor. He also discovered cave rooms filled with sparkling crystals shaped like roses.

Stop & Discuss

Why did Bishop first enter and then keep returning to Mammoth Cave?

Underline details in paragraphs 2 and 3 that support your response.

5 The Bottomless Pit, however, was one part of the cave that Bishop had not explored beyond. The pit was so wide and deep that no one had ever dared to cross it—until one day a visitor challenged Bishop to cross over the pit with him.

6 After placing a long, shaky ladder across the pit, Bishop carried a lantern between his teeth as he and the man made the journey to the other side. They entered a part of the cave that no one had ever seen.

7 Bishop returned again and again to this part of the cave. He discovered new creatures hiding in the walls and swimming in underground rivers. Bishop was becoming known for his explorations and findings. It was because of him that scientists traveled from all over the world to see animals they had never known existed. There, they saw eyeless cave fish and different kinds of bats.

8 Bishop discovered many miles of new passageways, domes, pits, and **caverns**. He gave his discoveries names like Snowball Room, Haunted Chamber, Giant's Coffin, and **Gothic** Avenue. These interesting names helped him remember details about each place.

caverns = large caves

Gothic = a style of building known for extremely high walls and pointed ceilings

Stop & Discuss

What happened as a result of Bishop crossing the Bottomless Pit?

Discuss with a partner what happened because Bishop crossed the pit.

When Bishop crossed the pit, ___.

9 After only a year of owning Mammoth Cave, Gorin sold the cave—and Bishop—to John Croghan. Because of Bishop's knowledge and the discoveries he had made, in 1842 Croghan told to him to **update** the map of the cave. He spent two weeks sketching the map without using any notes or drawings. Someone else wrote in the names of Bishop's findings. It was against the law for enslaved people to read and write.

update = add new information to

10 Copies of the map were made available at the cave, and the map was later published in a book. Bishop was given full credit for his **accomplishments**, which was unusual for an enslaved person to receive.

accomplishments = great actions

11 Stephen Bishop is known as Mammoth's greatest cave explorer of all time. While this is amazing, it is still important to remember that, as an enslaved person, Bishop had no choice but to work in that cave. Imagine the exciting things Bishop might have done if he was free to follow his own dreams.

Stop & Discuss

Why was it unusual for Bishop to get credit for mapping the cave?

Discuss with a partner what was unusual about Bishop receiving credit.

Stephen Bishop's map of Mammoth Cave, Kentucky, 1844

Make Inferences

When an idea in a text is unclear, make an inference to try to understand.

Reread/Think

Reread "Braving the Cave." Complete the chart by using text details and what you already know to make inferences about Stephen Bishop.

What I want to know: Why did Bishop bring a rope into the cave?		
What the Text Says +	**What I Know** =	**Inference**
"He climbed up slick walls and high domes and down into deep pits." (paragraph 4)	People attach themselves to ropes to stay safer while climbing.	
What I want to know: Why did Bishop return to the cave when he wasn't giving tours?		
• "Later, he would explore beyond the known trails." • "He discovered new creatures" (paragraphs 4 and 7)		
What I want to know: What skills helped Bishop create a map of the cave?		
• "These interesting names helped him remember details about each place." • "He spent two weeks sketching the map without using any notes or drawings." (paragraphs 8 and 9)		

SESSION 4 PRACTICE

Talk

Share your chart with a partner. Compare your responses and explain how the text details and your background knowledge support each inference.

> The text says ___. I already know ___. So, I can infer ___.

> I had a similar/different idea. I thought ___.

Write

What inferences can you make about Bishop's exploring and mapping skills? Support your response with text details and background knowledge.

WRITING CHECKLIST

- ☐ I answered the question.
- ☐ I included details from the text and my background knowledge.
- ☐ I used complete sentences.
- ☐ I used correct spelling, punctuation, and capitalization.

The Rainforest's Hidden Cities

by Kathryn Hulick

1 The rainforests of northern Guatemala hide a secret: **ruins** of ancient cities stretch across the forest floor. Pyramids, palaces, and roads built more than a thousand years ago tell the story of a large **empire** that once spread throughout Central America and Mexico. Some of the largest buildings rise above the trees. But thick forest has grown over other parts, covering up much of the past.

ruins = what remains after something has fallen apart

empire = kingdom

2 Today, about six million people trace their roots back to the Maya, the people who built these structures. Yet no one knows for sure why their empire didn't last. Was it disease? War? Archaeologists—scientists who study ancient buildings, tools, and other objects to understand past human life—have been trying for years to figure out what happened. The remains of these cities may give clues. But searching for ruins in a rainforest is slow, difficult work. Luckily, a special technology now allows scientists to take a closer look into areas with heavy vegetation, while also avoiding poisonous snakes, swarms of bees, and hot, moist air.

Some Mayan ruins are tall enough to rise above the rainforests of Central America and Mexico.

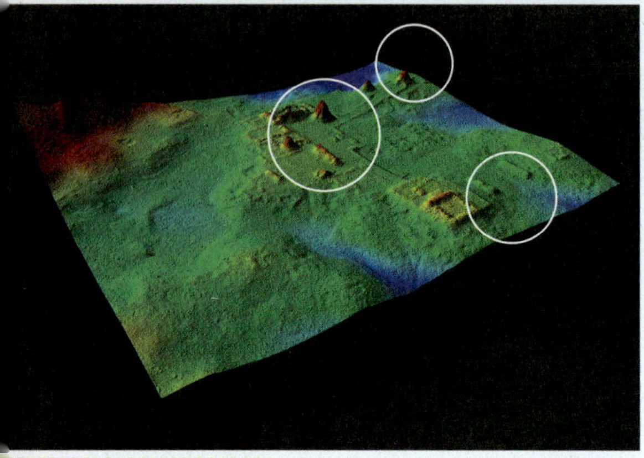

LiDAR technology sees through the thick rainforest (*above*) to create a map of the structures that stand within it (*below*).

3 The technology is called LiDAR. The letters stand for "**L**ight **D**etection **A**nd **R**anging." A helicopter flies over the forest while LiDAR equipment attached to the bottom of the helicopter shoots quick, powerful rays of light at the ground. These laser beams are narrow enough to pass through openings between branches and leaves. They hit the ground and then bounce back. The LiDAR equipment measures the distance the beams travel. When many measurements are put together, they show the shape of the ground and any buildings on it. The result is a 3-D map of the forest floor.

4 In 2015, the PACUNAM Foundation, a Guatemalan organization that **preserves** Mayan culture, teamed up with a group of archaeologists. They began using LiDAR to map the forest floor. By 2018, they had mapped more than 61,000 structures. "The **scale** of [the ruins] really blew our minds," said archaeologist Thomas Garrison.

5 Even when the forest isn't very thick, LiDAR maps make important details easier to see. In 2019, archaeologist Takeshi Inomata was studying a LiDAR map of part of Mexico. It showed 27 large shapes. From the ground, the shapes had seemed like part of the natural **landscape**. But the LiDAR map showed that they were flat, rectangular structures. They must have been built by humans. Researchers think the early Maya probably used these low platforms for special events and celebrations.

6 LiDAR has made mapping ancient ruins easier and faster than ever before. Each newly mapped site helps researchers learn more about the mystery of the Maya.

preserves = takes action to protect something

scale = size

landscape = everything that makes up an area of land, including buildings, hills, and forests

Respond to Text

Reread/Think

Reread "The Rainforest's Hidden Cities." Choose the best response to each question.

1. PART A

According to paragraph 2, why is searching for ruins in a rainforest "slow, difficult work"?

Ⓐ It takes years to collect the equipment needed for a search.

Ⓑ The region is difficult to explore.

Ⓒ Archaeologists must make a map of the area.

Ⓓ The Maya buried structures deep inside the thick forest.

PART B

Which key detail from the text **best** supports your answer in Part A?

Ⓐ ". . . the Maya, the people who built these structures."

Ⓑ "Yet no one knows for sure why their empire didn't last."

Ⓒ "The remains of these cities may give clues."

Ⓓ ". . . poisonous snakes, swarms of bees, and hot, moist air."

2. Which phrase helps you know what *laser beams* means in paragraph 3?

Ⓐ "attached to the bottom of the helicopter"

Ⓑ "quick, powerful rays of light"

Ⓒ "narrow enough to pass through openings"

Ⓓ "the shape of the ground"

SESSION 5 PRACTICE

Reread/Think

3. Why did the PACUNAM Foundation and a group of archaeologists work together to map the forest floor?

Ⓐ Locating Mayan ruins benefited both groups, helping one to preserve the ruins and the other to study it.

Ⓑ Both groups wanted to explore the natural landscape of the rainforest.

Ⓒ One team mapped half of the structures they found, while the other team mapped the other half.

Ⓓ Neither group wanted special events to celebrate the work they did.

4. Which statement describes an idea from paragraph 5?

Ⓐ An archaeologist studied a LiDAR map to prove that 27 shapes in the forest were natural parts of the landscape.

Ⓑ The 27 large structures discovered on a LiDAR map proved that the forest was easy to travel through.

Ⓒ A LiDAR map showed that 27 structures on the ground were probably platforms for Mayan events.

Ⓓ The forest was not very thick, so a LiDAR map was easily able to show 27 large shapes.

Write

Why were the LiDAR discoveries surprising? Use two details from the text in your response.

____

____

____

____

____

____

____

WRITING CHECKLIST

- ☐ I answered the question.
- ☐ I provided an introduction and a concluding sentence.
- ☐ I included details from the text.
- ☐ I used complete sentences.

Respond to the Focus Question

How do people create maps of new places?

Reread/Think

Choose one text from this lesson to reread.

TEXT: ______________________________

What did you learn from your text about how people create maps?

____

____

____

____

____

____

Talk

In a small group, first share your responses from Reread/Think. Then, discuss as a group how you would respond to this question:

How do people create maps of new places?

Marie Tharp measured ___.

Stephen Bishop explored ___.

People use LiDAR to ___.

Write

Think about how people create maps for new places. What would you do to create a map for your neighborhood or your school?

SESSION 1 TALK ABOUT THE TOPIC

Exploring Space

FOCUS QUESTION

What is an astronaut's job like?

NOTICE AND WONDER

Look at the four texts you will read in this lesson. What do you notice? What do you wonder? Discuss your ideas with a partner.

WORD SORT

Read the words about space exploration and sort them into the correct categories. Then add an example of your own in each column. Discuss your ideas with a partner.

astronaut
spacecraft
lunar module
Moon
International Space Station
NASA scientist
computer
rocket

Equipment	People	Locations in Space

The word ___ means ___.

I think ___ belongs in the category ___ because ___.

Stepping into History
by Shay Maunz

from *Reaching for the Moon*
by Buzz Aldrin

From the NFL to Space
by Wendell Riley

from *Chasing Space*
by Leland Melvin

Stepping into HISTORY

by Shay Maunz

NASA = National Aeronautics and Space Administration, the United States' space agency

1 On July 20, 1969, 500 million people watched a special event on live TV. They saw grainy black-and-white images beamed back from space. Then they heard the voice of American astronaut Neil Armstrong as he emerged from his spacecraft. He said, "That's one small step for [a] man, one giant leap for mankind."

2 Armstrong had just become the first person to walk on the Moon. His famous footsteps were the finale of a competition between the United States and the Soviet Union. Throughout the 1950s and 1960s, the two countries raced to achieve milestones in space exploration.

3 In 1961, U.S. president John F. Kennedy stood before Congress. He said, "This nation should commit itself to achieving the goal, before this decade is out, of landing a man on the Moon and returning him safely to the Earth." NASA accepted the challenge.

Stop & Discuss

What did Armstrong mean by "That's one small step for [a] man, one giant leap for mankind"?

Underline evidence showing that landing on the Moon was a "giant leap for mankind."

4 Neil Armstrong, Buzz Aldrin, and Michael Collins were launched into space 1969. They took off aboard *Apollo 11* on July 16, from the Kennedy Space Center in Florida. As they neared the Moon, their spacecraft split up into two sections. Collins was in *Columbia*, the command **module**. This is where the astronauts lived. Armstrong and Aldrin traveled in *Eagle*, the lunar module. It could travel from the command module to the surface of the Moon.

Buzz Aldrin setting up the Early Apollo Scientific Experiments Package, which included a seismometer, lunar dust detector, and solar panels

5 As Collins orbited, Armstrong steered *Eagle* to a flat surface area that astronomers called the Sea of **Tranquility**. After a few tense minutes, they touched down. "The *Eagle* has landed," Armstrong notified NASA's Mission Control, in Houston, Texas.

6 Armstrong and Aldrin spent 21 hours and 36 minutes on the Moon's surface. During that time, they set up science experiments and took rock and soil samples. They also planted an American flag in the powdery ground and left a plaque. It says, "We came in peace for all mankind."

module = a part of a space vehicle that can work alone

tranquility = calm and quiet

7 The crew returned to Earth on July 24, 1969, splashing down in the Pacific Ocean. They were picked up by a ship and taken to Hawaii. Like other travelers, they had to go through **U.S. Customs**. They declared their cargo as Moon rocks and dust.

U.S. Customs = an organization that controls what people bring into the United States.

8 The *Apollo 11* astronauts soon went on a tour to cities across the United States. They visited 24 countries. Around the world, they were celebrated as heroes.

Stop & Discuss

What did Armstrong and Aldrin do while they were on the Moon?

Discuss four details in paragraph 6 that show what the astronauts did.

SPOTLIGHT BENCHMARK: ELA.4.R.3.3 Compare and contrast accounts of the same event using primary and/or secondary sources.

Compare and Contrast Sources

- A **primary source** is an informational text about an event that was written by someone who was there when the event happened. Primary sources often include the author's thoughts and feelings.
- A **secondary source** is a text about an event that was written by someone who was not there when it happened. Secondary sources often include background information and factual details based on research.

Reread/Think

Reread "Stepping into History." Answer the questions below. Then complete the chart.

What event does the author describe? ______________________________

Is this a primary source or a secondary source? **primary source / secondary source**

Text Details	What the Details Help Me Learn
Paragraphs 1–3: • In 1969, 500 million people watched the Moon landing on TV. • Armstrong was the first person to walk on the Moon. • The United States and the Soviet Union competed to get to the Moon.	• People were interested in *Apollo 11* because no one had ever landed on the Moon before. • facts about when the first people landed on the Moon and who they were • information about the events leading to the first Moon landing
Paragraphs 4–6:	
Paragraphs 7 and 8:	

Talk

In a small group, discuss the details from one section of your chart.

- What do the details help you understand about the Moon landing?
- What are the details mostly about? Does the author tell more about facts and data or thoughts and feelings?

These details help me understand ___.

The details in this section are mostly about ___.

Write

Is "Stepping into History" a primary or secondary source? What does it help you understand about the *Apollo 11* Moon landing? Use details from the text to support your response.

WRITING CHECKLIST

- ☐ I described what type of source this is.
- ☐ I explained what the text helps me understand about *Apollo 11*.
- ☐ I supported my response with details from the text.
- ☐ I used complete sentences.
- ☐ I used correct spelling, punctuation, and capitalization.

SESSION 3 READ

Reaching FOR THE Moon

by Buzz Aldrin

Neil Armstrong, Michael Collins, and Buzz Aldrin

Buzz Aldrin describes his experience landing on the Moon in 1969. He was part of the Apollo 11 *mission along with fellow astronauts Neil Armstrong and Michael Collins.*

1 Four days after the launch, and after traveling 240,000 miles, we were in orbit around the Moon. *Apollo* separated into two parts: *Columbia*, where Mike would wait in orbit, and the *Eagle*, the lander. The *Eagle* was powerful enough to take Neil and me down to the Moon's surface and back up to *Columbia*. But its walls were so thin, I could have punched a pencil through them if I had tried.

2 The computer had chosen a spot for the *Eagle* to land. But through the window we could see that it was too rocky. We couldn't rely on the computer to land the *Eagle* safely. We would have to do it ourselves.

3 Neil took control. I called out to let him know how far we were from the ground. Two hundred feet. One hundred. Forty. By the time the *Eagle* landed, we had used up almost all our fuel with only twenty seconds left to spare.

4 But we had made it. We were safely on the surface of the Moon. I grinned at Neil. There was no need to say anything. We had work to do.

Stop & Discuss

What dangers did the astronauts face as they were landing on the Moon?

Work with your partner to find one danger in each of the first three paragraphs.

A view of the Earth from the Moon

Aldrin climbing down the ladder of the Eagle to the surface of the Moon

5 Flight and spaceflight had always meant motion to me. But now the *Eagle* stood perfectly still.

6 Neil and I put on our space suits. Neil climbed out first and descended *Eagle*'s ladder to the Moon's surface. Everyone listening back on Earth heard Neil's first words: "That's one small step for . . . man, one giant leap for mankind."

7 I climbed down the ladder and joined Neil. There was no color on the Moon. A flat landscape of rocks and craters stretched in all directions. Everything was gray or white. The shadows and the sky above were as black as the blackest velvet I had ever seen. I exclaimed: "Magnificent **desolation**."

desolation = land without plants or animals

8 I could see Earth, our home, in the sky overhead—blue water, white clouds, brown land. I could see the continents, and I knew that they were younger than the Moondust in which Neil and I were now leaving our footprints.

A footprint on the surface of the Moon

Stop & Discuss

What does Aldrin notice when he is on the Moon?

Discuss details that show what Aldrin sees, says, and thinks.

Buzz Aldrin with the American flag on the Moon

compartment = a separate part or area

9 I took out the American flag from the **compartment** where it was stored.

10 Neil and I could force the pole only a few inches into the Moon's soil. I knew that more than half a billion people back on Earth were watching on television, and I worried that the flag would sag or tip. But when we took our hands away, it stood straight. I snapped off a crisp salute, just as I was taught at West Point.

11 We moved quickly on to other tasks. I became a rock collector again, gathering samples for study back on Earth. Still, I remember that brief moment perfectly, so many years later. I remember the pride I felt and how I imagined the pride of every American on Earth.

Buzz Aldrin collecting a soil sample by hammering a tube into the surface of the Moon

12 Neil and I set up a plaque that would remain on the surface of the Moon with the simple words:

HERE MEN FROM THE PLANET EARTH
FIRST SET FOOT UPON THE MOON
JULY 1969, A.D.
WE CAME IN PEACE FOR ALL MANKIND

Aldrin feels ___ because ___.

Stop & Discuss

How does Aldrin feel when he is on the Moon?

Underline two feelings he has and discuss why he feels this way.

Compare and Contrast Sources

- Remember, a primary source is a text about an event written by someone who was there when the event happened. A secondary source is an account written by someone who was not there.
- A primary source often includes sensory details.
- Comparing primary and secondary sources can help you understand more about an event.

Reread/Think

Reread *Reaching for the Moon*. Answer the questions below. Then complete the chart with details from this source.

What event does the author describe? ______________________________

Is this a primary source or a secondary source? **primary source / secondary source**

Text Details	What the Details Help Me Learn
Paragraphs 1–4: • *Eagle* lander had very thin walls. • Astronauts had to land *Eagle* themselves. • They almost used up their fuel.	how dangerous it was for astronauts landing on the Moon
Paragraphs 5–8:	
Paragraphs 9–12:	

SESSION 4 PRACTICE

Talk

With your partner, compare and contrast "Stepping into History" and *Reaching for the Moon*. How are the primary and secondary sources alike? How are they different? Use the chart to record and organize your ideas.

"Stepping into History"	Both	*Reaching for the Moon*
	• tell about *Apollo 11* mission and Moon landing	• primary source

Write

Compare and contrast the two texts about the *Apollo 11* Moon landing. What did you learn from each source? Include details from the texts in your response.

____
____
____
____
____
____
____
____
____

WRITING CHECKLIST

- ☐ I compared and contrasted the texts.
- ☐ I explained what I learned from each text.
- ☐ I supported my response with details from each text.
- ☐ I used complete sentences.
- ☐ I used correct spelling, punctuation, and capitalization.

FROM THE NFL TO SPACE

by Wendell Riley

Leland Melvin as a college football player

1 Fresh out of college in 1986, Leland Melvin was living his dream. He had been a star football player in college, and the Detroit Lions had signed him to play in the National Football League. Then, something terrible happened. Melvin tore a muscle in the back of his leg. Unable to play, he was cut from the team. His football career was over. That kind of bad luck might have made anyone feel hopeless—but not Melvin.

2 Melvin had another great interest in his life: science. He had already earned a college degree in chemistry, and he was studying to become an engineer at the University of Virginia. While there, Melvin got a job at NASA (National Aeronautics and Space Administration). At first, he worked as a scientist. But after a few years, he decided to aim higher—he wanted to go into space.

3 As a boy in 1969, Melvin had watched with excitement as astronauts Neil Armstrong and Buzz Aldrin had taken the first walk on the Moon. Melvin never pictured himself as an astronaut, because all astronauts back then were White. But that changed in 1983, when Guion Bluford became the first African American astronaut in space.

Leland Melvin as a NASA astronaut

missions = trips to complete work in space

4 In 1998, Melvin was accepted into the astronaut program at NASA. Once again, Melvin was doing something most people only dream about. And once again, he suffered a serious setback.

5 Part of an astronaut's training is doing "spacewalks" deep underwater. One day, Melvin's helmet didn't work properly, and his ears were severely injured. He came out of the water with blood flowing from one ear and major hearing loss in both ears. Doctors told him he would never fly in space. They said he would only work for NASA here on Earth.

6 But Melvin proved the doctors wrong. Over the next five years, his hearing improved, and Melvin achieved his dream of becoming an astronaut. In 2008 and 2009, he flew two **missions** aboard the space shuttle *Atlantis*. The missions took him to the International Space Station, where astronauts from around the world live and work together high above Earth. Melvin would later say it was one of the most meaningful experiences of his life.

7 After leaving NASA in 2014, Melvin wrote a book about his life called *Chasing Space*. Now he travels around the country speaking about his experiences. Leland Melvin never gets tired of inspiring people of all ages to follow their dreams.

from CHASING SPACE

An Astronaut's Story of Grit, Grace, and Second Chances

by Leland Melvin

1 The countdown began.

2 Six seconds prior to liftoff, the main engines came to life. The **thrust** from them tilted the entire shuttle stack slowly forward and then back again. NASA folks call this the "twang" because, like a door spring used to stop a door from hitting the wall, it makes that sound as it bends back and forth.

3 Then there was the thunderous roar of the solid rocket boosters coming to life.

4 And we were off.

5 Imagine you're in a fast sports car going about 100 miles per hour. Our acceleration was 100,000 times more intense. We were pinned in our seats, feeling three times our weight on our chests. I remember laboring to breathe a bit for about two minutes until we used up the solid rocket boosters. The load got a little lighter and my breathing got easier.

6 *We were heading to space.*

7 From space, our views of Earth's bodies of water would challenge even a painter's vocabulary. There aren't enough words to describe all the shades of blue in the Caribbean Sea alone.

thrust = force made by an engine

After a three-day journey, Melvin reached the International Space Station where he worked with Commander Peggy Whitson and a team of astronauts from 16 countries.

aspects = parts

8 There are so many unforgettable **aspects** of life in space, including the experiments, the robotics, and the spacewalks, but I think my most memorable moment took place when Peggy and her crew invited us to have dinner over in the Russian service module.

9 "You guys bring the vegetables, we'll bring the meat," Peggy said. We gathered around a small table. Some of us were floating above it and others below. We were French, German, Russian, Asian-American, and African-American.

10 We were orbiting around the planet every 90 minutes at 17,500 mph. There were sunsets and sunrises every 45 minutes, and out the window we could see every place on the planet, from Afghanistan to Antarctica.

11 Two hundred and forty miles above the Earth, I sat in peace with people we had once counted among our nation's enemies. It was one of those amazing moments when you realize just how much we can accomplish when we all work together. It was one of the most inspiring moments of my life.

Respond to Text

Reread/Think

Reread "From the NFL to Space" and *Chasing Space: An Astronaut's Story of Grit, Grace, and Second Chances*. Choose the best response to each question.

1. Fill in **one** bubble in each row to choose whether each description is about "From the NFL to Space," *Chasing Space*, or both texts.

	From the NFL to Space	*Chasing Space*	Both
is a primary source	Ⓐ	Ⓑ	Ⓒ
is a secondary source	Ⓓ	Ⓔ	Ⓕ
describes Melvin's experience of the space shuttle taking off	Ⓖ	Ⓗ	Ⓘ
mentions Melvin's work with people from different countries	Ⓙ	Ⓚ	Ⓛ

2. Read the sentence from paragraph 3 of *Chasing Space*.

> Then there was the thunderous roar of the solid rocket boosters coming to life.

What does thunderous tell about the rocket boosters?

Ⓐ how loud they sounded

Ⓑ how powerful they were

Ⓒ how surprising they were

Ⓓ how large they appeared

SESSION 5 PRACTICE

Reread/Think

3. PART A

Which idea is **best** supported by paragraph 11 of *Chasing Space*?

Ⓐ Melvin had wanted to go to space since he was a boy.

Ⓑ Melvin was inspired by his time on the International Space Station.

Ⓒ Melvin felt hopeless after an injury ended his NFL career.

Ⓓ Melvin now travels around the country speaking to people about his life.

PART B

Which paragraph from "From the NFL to Space" expresses an idea similar to the answer in Part A?

Ⓐ paragraph 4

Ⓑ paragraph 5

Ⓒ paragraph 6

Ⓓ paragraph 7

Write

Explain how the primary and secondary sources describe different things about Leland Melvin's journey to space. Use details from both texts to support your response.

WRITING CHECKLIST

- ☐ I described what each source tells about Leland Melvin.
- ☐ I used examples from each text.
- ☐ I used complete sentences.
- ☐ I used correct spelling, punctuation, and capitalization.

Respond to the Focus Question

What is an astronaut's job like?

Reread/Think

Look back at the texts in this lesson. Then answer each question with an example from one of the texts.

What kinds of things do astronauts do in space?

____

____

What kinds of background and training do you think astronauts need?

____

____

Why do you think astronauts choose to explore the unknown?

____

____

Talk

Discuss with your group what it might be like to have an astronaut's job.

Which parts of an astronaut's job are the most interesting to you?

What do you think it would be like to travel in space?

One of the most interesting parts of an astronaut's job is __ because __.

I think traveling in space would be __ because __.

Write

Would you want to be an astronaut? Why or why not? Use details from the texts to support your response.

SESSION 1 MAKE CONNECTIONS

Under the Sea

TALK ABOUT WHAT YOU KNOW

In this unit, you read about explorers and exploration. Circle the pictures that show the type of exploration you find most interesting. Talk with a partner about why you think it is interesting.

I am interested in exploring __ because __.

I would like to read more about __ because __.

I would like to try __ because __.

LESSON 9

Uncovering the Past

LESSON 10

Mapping the Unknown

LESSON 11

Exploring Space

EXPLORING REWARDS AND CHALLENGES

Which words describe the rewards of exploring? Which words describe the challenges? Sort the words. Then add your own words. Explain your thinking to a partner, using examples from this unit.

fear	adventure	danger	discovery

Rewards	Challenges

Secrets of a Frigid World

by Morgan Parsons

Kirsten Carlson (right) before her last dive in Antarctica at Turtle Rock

insulated = has material to keep a person warm

1 The snowy, icy land of Antarctica might seem empty and bare. But beneath the ocean surface, a world full of life awaits.

2 This is the world artist Kirsten Carlson explored for seven weeks in 2017. She stayed at the McMurdo Station in Antarctica, where many scientists do research. Artists like Carlson are invited to the station so they can share the many wonders of Antarctica through their work.

3 Kirsten Carlson did her creative work underwater. Covered in **insulated** gear, she bravely dove beneath the ice 33 times. There, the water is around 28°F (–2°C), as cold as sea water can get without freezing solid. Because of the harsh environment, it is a place few people have studied. Carlson's drawings, photographs, and notes help reveal the secrets of this frigid and colorful world.

Stop & Discuss

What did Kirsten Carlson do in Antarctica? Why?

Underline details in the text that explain her work and what it has revealed.

McMurdo Station in Antarctica

Divers swimming up toward a hole in the ice

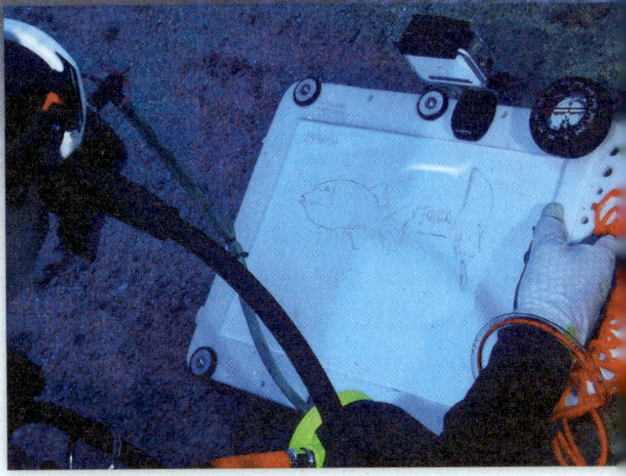

Kirsten Carlson's underwater drawing equipment

4 On her dives, Carlson heard the strange calls of Weddell seals. These animals spend much of their time hunting for food beneath the ice. She saw sea stars, sea slugs, jellyfish, and many other creatures. She sketched a naked dragonfish, a kind of fish without scales, hiding near its eggs. Two pointy teeth stuck up from its lower jaw, like a bulldog's. She also drew a giant sea sponge that was almost as big as she was.

5 Back at the surface, Carlson shared her discoveries with the world. She hopes that her team's work will encourage people to think about the connections between art, science, and the natural world in different ways.

Stop & Discuss

Why does Carlson think it is important to share what she has seen with the world?

Use evidence from the text to support your answer.

Carlson hopes that people will learn ___.

DRAWING UNDER ICE

by Kirsten Carlson

Kirsten Carlson is a scientific illustrator who traveled to Antarctica to explore an amazing undersea world.

1 Putting on all my warm, waterproof diving gear took longer than the dive itself. I prepared to enter the chilly water through a large round hole drilled through thick sea ice. These ocean temperatures are colder than a glass of ice water. But peeking through the hole was like looking at a starry nighttime sky. Through the crystal-clear water, sea stars on the ocean floor far below seemed to glow.

Stop & Discuss

How did Carlson prepare for her dive? Why did she need special equipment?

Use details from the text to support your answer.

Kirsten Carlson drawing underwater on an earlier dive

2 During my dive, I used a pencil and waterproof paper to sketch sea stars and a giant sponge, one that was shaped like a vase and almost as big as me. I drew a fish peeking out at me from the inside of the sponge. A white, ruffled sea slug hurried across the ocean floor. I used my camera to capture the colors I saw. Many of the creatures are white and pastel: pinks, pale yellows, and lavenders.

3 Thirty minutes into the dive, I felt my hands tingle and knew it was time to surface. Though Antarctica is an extreme environment, it is the best place for scientists to study the toughest animals on Earth.

Stop & Discuss

How did Carlson capture images of what she saw underwater?

Use details from the text to explain how she worked.

Carlson used ___ to sketch ___.

She also used ___ to ___.

Kirsten Carlson's sketches and paintings of sea creatures

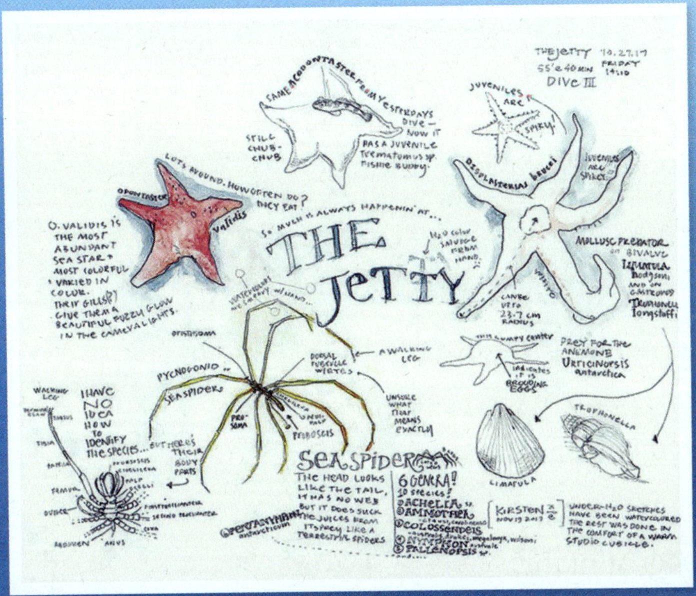

Respond to Text

Reread/Think

Reread "Secrets of a Frigid World" and "Drawing Under Ice." Choose the best response to each question.

1. Reread the underlined sentence in paragraph 3 of "Secrets of a Frigid World." Fill in the bubble **before** the sentence in the paragraph that provides the **best** clue to the meaning of the word harsh.

Ⓐ Kirsten Carlson did her creative work underwater. Ⓑ Covered in insulated gear, she bravely dove beneath the ice 33 times. Ⓒ There, the water is around 28°F (–2°C), as cold as sea water can get without freezing solid. Because of the harsh environment, it is a place few people have studied. Ⓓ Carlson's drawings, photographs, and notes help reveal the secrets of this frigid and colorful world.

2. Reread paragraph 1 of "Drawing Under Ice." Based on details in the text, why might getting ready to dive have taken Carlson longer than the dive itself?

Ⓐ She had to get dressed in the cold.

Ⓑ She had to put on a lot of special gear.

Ⓒ She had to stop and take pictures.

Ⓓ She had to drill a bigger hole in the ice.

3. Read the following sentence from paragraph 1 of "Drawing Under Ice."

But peeking through the hole was like looking at a starry nighttime sky.

How does the figurative language in the sentence contribute to the meaning of the text?

Ⓐ It compares the ocean animals to a sky full of stars.

Ⓑ It shows how the stars in the sky reflect in the water.

Ⓒ It explains that the ice is as dark as the sky at night.

Ⓓ It describes how far away the sky is from the ocean at night.

4. Which **two** details would be **most** important to include in a summary of "Secrets of a Frigid World"?

Ⓐ Carlson stayed at McMurdo Station with many other scientists.

Ⓑ Carlson heard the calls of Weddell seals hunting for food.

Ⓒ Carlson wanted to share her discoveries in Antarctica with the world.

Ⓓ Carlson sketched a dragonfish hiding in the water near its eggs.

Ⓔ Carlson made drawings, photos, and notes about the animals she saw.

5. Fill in **one** bubble in each row to show whether each description is about "Secrets of a Frigid World," "Drawing Under Ice," or both texts.

	Secrets of a Frigid World	Drawing Under Ice	Both Texts
is a primary source	Ⓐ	Ⓑ	Ⓒ
is a secondary source	Ⓓ	Ⓔ	Ⓕ
describes equipment needed to explore the ocean	Ⓖ	Ⓗ	Ⓘ
tells how many dives Carlson made	Ⓙ	Ⓚ	Ⓛ

6. What additional information does Carlson share in "Drawing Under Ice" that is not in "Secrets of a Frigid World"?

Ⓐ how her hands felt after 30 minutes in the water

Ⓑ how big a giant sea sponge looked next to her

Ⓒ the fact that she wore gear to keep her warm

Ⓓ the types of sea creatures she saw on her dives

Write

Compare the accounts "Secrets of a Frigid World" and "Drawing Under Ice." Describe how the two texts add to your understanding of Kirsten Carlson's work. Use at least one example from each text in your response.

WRITING CHECKLIST

- ☐ I compared the information in both texts.
- ☐ I used at least one example from each text.
- ☐ I used complete sentences.
- ☐ I used correct spelling, punctuation, and capitalization.

Make Connections

Reread/Think

In this unit, you have learned about exploration and discovery. Think about the texts you have read in this unit and the different reasons people explore and discover. Then answer the questions.

Why is exploration important? ______________________________

____

____

How does exploration help people? ______________________________

____

____

Text evidence that supports my thinking:

1. ____

____

____

2. ____

____

____

Talk

As a small group, discuss why exploration is important. Use the sentence frames to get started.

I think ___ because ___.

I agree/disagree with ___ because ___.

One detail that supports my thinking is ___.

Traditions

LESSON 12

Storytelling Through Art

224

LESSON 13

Generation to Generation

240

UNIT 4

Storytelling Through Art

FOCUS QUESTION

How do people tell stories through the arts?

NOTICE AND WONDER

Look at the three texts you will read in this lesson. What do you notice? What do you wonder? Discuss your ideas with a partner.

DISCUSS ART FORMS

What is one type of art, music, or dance that you know about? Talk with a partner about what you know about the art form.

I know about the art form ___. People use ___ to create ___.

This art is important because ___.

Hula: Keeping a Tradition Fresh

by the staff of the Smithsonian Museum

The Roots of Rap

by Alicia Williams

Cy Thao: Story Painter

by Missy McDonald

Hula
Keeping a Tradition Fresh

by the staff of the Smithsonian Museum

1 Aloha! Welcome to Hawaii (also spelled Hawai'i), the home of a special dance called the Hawaiian hula. Some might think it's just a dance for tourists—a performance with grass skirts and swaying hands. But the hula is actually a kind of storytelling that helps keep the original Hawaiian language alive.

2 Hula has been a part of Hawaiian culture since ancient times. The oldest form of hula involves chanting, drumming, and dance, including hand motions. The chants have been passed down for generations. Hula was a way for Hawaiians to share stories about their history and culture before they had written records. Each chant tells a story about the people's beliefs, values, and history.

missionaries = people who travel to spread a religion

3 When **missionaries** from New England arrived in Hawaii in the 1820s, the Hawaiian language existed only in spoken form. Throughout most of the 19th century, the missionaries made Hawaiians speak English in schools, and they banned hula. Over time, fewer and fewer native Hawaiian speakers remained.

Stop & Discuss

What is the purpose of the Hawaiian hula?

Underline two sentences that explain why Hawaiian people hula.

The Hawaiian people use hula to ___.

4 Thankfully, the Hawaiian language and hula did not disappear. In the 1960s, the Hawaiian culture preservation movement began with people like Edith Kanaka'ole who work to keep Hawaiian traditions alive. The hula school that Kanaka'ole's family opened is one example of this effort to save the culture. Students at the school spend years becoming skillful at hula in its many forms.

Learning hula is an important part of Hawaiian tradition.

5 Even though hula has very old roots, the dance is continually renewed with fresh ideas. For example, one newer style of hula uses stringed instruments. Some people believe that new music and new chants help keep the tradition alive.

6 George Na'ope, a well-known hula teacher, believed that learning hula was very important. He said, "I tell the young people to learn the culture and learn it well, preserve it, so their children and their children's children can continue . . . and that our culture will live forever."

Stop & Discuss

How does Edith Kanaka'ole's school help keep Hawaiian traditions alive?

Underline two sentences in the text that answer this question.

Hula Hand Motions and Meanings

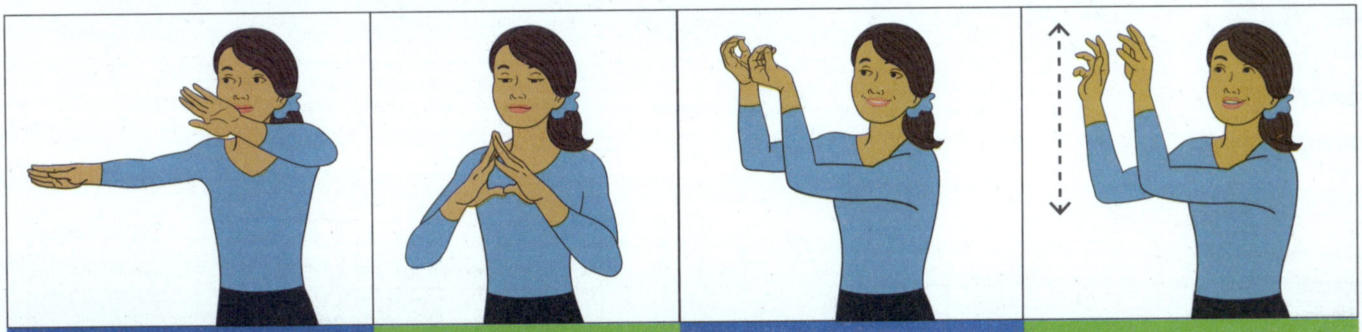

Nana: see, look—one hand by the side of your eyes and the other outstretched	**Hale:** house—two hands making the peak of a roof	**Pua:** flower—palm with hand cupped and fingers together	**Ua:** rain—both arms raised and then brought down with fingers fluttering

SPOTLIGHT BENCHMARK: ELA.4.V.1.2 Apply knowledge of . . . base words, and affixes to determine the meaning of unfamiliar words in grade-level content.

Use Word Parts

- Word parts can provide clues to the meaning of an unknown word.
- Many words are built from a base word. A **base word** is a word that has meaning. It can stand alone as a complete word, without a prefix or suffix. For example, the base word of *movement* is *move*.
- A **prefix** is a word part added to the beginning of a base word. A **suffix** is a word part added to the end of a base word. A prefix or suffix changes the meaning of a word.

Prefixes

- *im-*, *in-* = not, in
- *re-* = again
- *dis-* = not, opposite of
- *pre-* = before

Suffixes

- *-ful* = full of, having a lot of
- *-ion/-tion/-ation* = act or process of
- *-ed* = happened in the past, describes
- *-ment* = state or act of

Reread/Think

Reread "Hula: Keeping a Tradition Fresh." Complete the chart by using base words, prefixes, and suffixes to figure out the meaning of each word.

Word	Word Parts	Meaning
tourists (paragraph 1)	• tour = to travel and look around • -ist = person who does something	Someone who travel tour
disappear (paragraph 4)	dis= not appear= see	can not see it
skillful (paragraph 4)	S	

Talk

Choose one of the words from your chart to share with your group. Explain how the word parts help you understand the meaning of the word. Discuss how the word helps you understand the text.

> The word part ___ means ___. This helps me know that the word ___ means ___.

> The word ___ helps me understand the text because ___.

Write

Read this sentence from paragraph 5.

> Even though hula has very old roots, the dance is continually renewed with fresh ideas.

Using your knowledge of word parts, what does the word renewed mean? How does your understanding of the word add to your understanding of the sentence and to hula in general?

WRITING CHECKLIST

- ☐ I used word parts to explain the meaning of a word.
- ☐ I explained how the word renewed helps me understand more about hula.
- ☐ I used complete sentences.
- ☐ I used correct spelling, punctuation, and capitalization.

SESSION 3 READ

THE ROOTS

by Alicia Williams

1 You may have *heard* rap, but what *is* rap? It's like poetry, using rhythm and rhyme. But rap is performed over music.

2 Rap developed in the 1970s, but its roots are much older than that. In fact, rap can be traced back to the griots, or storytellers, of West Africa in the 13th century.

colonized = took control of a region

influenced = affected

3 How is rap related to griots of long ago? In the 1700s and 1800s, Europeans **colonized** West Africa. They enslaved millions of West Africans, including griots, and brought them to the Americas, including the United States. Griots took their storytelling tradition with them. This tradition later **influenced** Black musical styles, including rap.

Stop & Discuss

How is rap connected to griots?

Discuss your response with a partner.

Griots often used music to tell their stories.

OF RAP

A Storytelling Tradition

4 In West Africa, griots had an important place in their society. Their main job was to memorize stories and share them with the people of their villages. Griots shared stories with more than their words, though. They used songs, drums, stringed instruments, and dance to **enhance** their stories and entertain their audience. Like griots, the rappers of today tell stories through their words and music. However, most rappers don't play their own musical instruments. They need **DJs**, a band, or sound experts in a recording studio to provide the background of sounds for their rhythmic, rhyming, and repetitive lyrics.

enhance = improve

DJs = disc jockeys; people who introduce and play music on the radio or at dance clubs

5 Rhythm and repetition were also important parts of griot storytelling. Griots would repeat important words and sentences in their stories, and the audience would repeat them back. Why? Repetition helped both griots and villagers recall information more easily.

Stop & Discuss

In what ways are griots and rappers alike?

Discuss your response with a partner.

Rappers work with DJs and use technology to tell stories through words and music.

Modern-day griots continue to share current events as well as historical and political information.

politics = actions or beliefs related to government

Entertainment with a Purpose

6 Griots' stories were entertaining, but they often included a moral, or message, that showed a village's social beliefs. Griots also told the history of important people of the past, such as kings and queens. They memorized and kept track of villagers' birthdays, marriages, and other important family events. They informed people about **politics** and problems in their village.

7 Similarly, many rappers educate their listeners about social issues. Black and Latinx youth from New York City created rap as part of the art, music, and dance of hip-hop culture. Rap allowed them to communicate their stories in creative ways. Rappers have spoken about serious subjects such as love, injustice, and politics. They have expressed the importance of developing self-confidence and empowering people in the community. But rappers can be playful, too, and create songs that are simply entertaining.

More Alike Than Different?

8 There are important differences between griots and rappers. While griots shared their stories by traveling from village to village, rap artists perform both in their local communities and at concerts for larger crowds. Rappers also use radio, television, and social media to interact with audiences.

9 Still, griots and rappers have a lot in common. They are storytellers and artists who pass down stories, knowledge, and history from one generation to the next.

Stop & Discuss

What are rappers trying to do with their music?

Discuss with a partner the different purposes and goals behind rap performances.

Rappers use their music as a way to ___.

SPOTLIGHT BENCHMARK: ELA.4.V.1.2 Apply knowledge of . . . base words, and affixes to determine the meaning of unfamiliar words in grade-level content.

Use Word Parts

- To help figure out the meaning of an unfamiliar word, look for any word parts you know.
- Think about the meanings of each word part and how they fit together. The meanings of the word parts can often lead you to the meaning of the word.

Prefixes

- *en-/em-* = cause to
- *inter-* = between, among
- *non-* = not

Suffixes

- *-ize* = cause, make, become
- *-ate* = make, have, become
- *-ent/-ant* = an action or condition, person who
- *-ive/-ative/-itive* = described as

Reread/Think

Reread "The Roots of Rap." Complete the chart by using base words, prefixes, and suffixes to figure out the meaning of each word. Fill in the last two rows with words from the text that have familiar word parts.

Word	Word Parts	Meaning
enslaved (paragraph 3)	• en- = cause to • slave = person who is forced to work for someone else without freedom or pay • -ed = happened in the past	
empowering (paragraph 7)		

SESSION 4 PRACTICE

Talk

Choose one of the words from your chart. Share with your group how you figured out the word's meaning and how the word helps you understand the text.

The word __ has the word parts __.

The word means __ because I know __.

The word __ helps me understand the text because __.

Write

What does the word empowering mean in paragraph 7? How can rap be empowering? Use word parts and details from the text to support your response.

WRITING CHECKLIST

- ☐ I used word parts to explain the meaning of empowering.
- ☐ I used details from the text to explain how rap can be empowering.
- ☐ I used complete sentences.
- ☐ I used correct spelling, punctuation, and capitalization.

Cy Thao
Story Painter

by Missy McDonald

1 Cy Thao has a powerful story to tell. Like that of many immigrants coming to America, his experience was full of both hardship and hope.

2 Born in 1972, Thao was only two when his family had to leave their home in Laos, a country in Southeast Asia. A war had made the country unsafe, and many Hmong people were forced to escape. Thao's family traveled to Thailand, where they spent five difficult years in a Hmong refugee camp. Finally, in 1980, they were able to immigrate to the United States. St. Paul, Minnesota, became their new home.

3 At the age of eight, Thao had to adjust to a new life. Everything was different: sounds, smells, tall buildings, technology. Hardest of all, though, was having a new language to learn. Not knowing English made Thao feel invisible at school. But he was determined to communicate. So he drew pictures and gave them to his schoolmates. Slowly, he made friends.

4 Decades later, as an adult, Cy Thao decided to tell the story of his people's postwar experiences as immigrants in the U.S. But the Hmong people didn't have a written language. He asked himself, "How do you tell a story without words?" Then Thao remembered his childhood drawings. He remembered friendships made without words. And so Thao became a painter.

Thao's paintings tell stories about the Hmong community in the U.S.

5 Each of Thao's paintings resembles a quilt square, and each one tells a story about the Hmong experience. Many of the paintings describe a part of his own journey. Others show bigger ideas about change and hope: business opportunities, fun sports tournaments, and education.

6 Thao's paintings honor an ancient Hmong tradition called *paj ntaub*, or "flowering cloth." Long ago, Hmong women hand-stitched beautiful, colorful designs onto clothing. In the 1970s, Hmong women in refugee camps began to sew other kinds of images onto fabric. The women used needlework to tell stories of their experiences through their craft.

7 Thao uses his paintings in a similar way. Like the story cloths of the past, his artwork includes bright, detailed images that show important experiences. But his paintings focus on more recent Hmong experiences, and his stories are told with a paintbrush instead of a needle and thread.

8 Thao is helping his people by using an old tradition in a new way. As he points out, "To keep the culture alive, we have to **adapt**."

adapt = get used to a new situation

SPOTLIGHT BENCHMARK: ELA.4.V.1.2 Apply knowledge of . . . base words, and affixes to determine the meaning of unfamiliar words in grade-level content.

Respond to Text

Reread/Think

Reread "Cy Thao: Story Painter." Choose the best response to each question.

1. Read the sentence below from paragraph 2.

> Born in 1972, Thao was only two when his family had to leave their home in Laos, a country in Southeast Asia.

Which phrase helps you understand that Cy Thao's family did not want to leave Laos?

Ⓐ Born in

Ⓑ only two

Ⓒ had to

Ⓓ their home

2. Read the sentence below from paragraph 2.

> Thao's family traveled to Thailand, where they spent five difficult years in a Hmong refugee camp.

The base word refuge means "a place of safety from danger." The suffix *-ee* means "a person who receives an action." Based on these word parts, who lives in a refugee camp?

Ⓐ people who offer safety to other people in a place

Ⓑ people who work to create safety in a place

Ⓒ people who have left the safety of a new place

Ⓓ people who are given safety in a new place

3. Which word from paragraph 3 uses a prefix that means "not"?

Ⓐ adjust

Ⓑ different

Ⓒ invisible

Ⓓ determined

Reread/Think

4. In paragraph 4, the author says that Cy Thao wanted to tell about his people's postwar experiences. If the prefix *post-* means "after or later," what does postwar mean?

Ⓐ because of the war

Ⓑ when the war was over

Ⓒ affected by the war

Ⓓ as the war happened

Write

Read the following sentence from paragraph 1 of the passage.

> Like that of many immigrants coming to America, his experience was full of both hardship and hope.

The base word of immigrants is *migrate*, which means "to move from one place to another." What do you think the word immigrants means? What clues led you to this meaning?

WRITING CHECKLIST

- ☐ I explained the meaning of immigrants.
- ☐ I explained how I used word parts and clues from the text to figure out the meaning.
- ☐ I used complete sentences.
- ☐ I used correct spelling, punctuation, and capitalization.

Respond to the Focus Question

How do people tell stories through the arts?

Reread/Think

In this lesson, you have read three texts. Reread your favorite one. Then tell what you learned from that text about the different ways people tell stories through the arts.

TEXT: ______________________________

In this text, people tell stories through art by: ______________________________

____

____

____

____

____

____

Talk

As a small group, discuss the following questions.

What did you like about one of the ways to tell stories though art? Why?

What does this art form help people express?

I like the idea of sharing stories through ___ because ___.

The art form ___ helps people express ___.

Write

Which art would you use to tell a story? Why? Tell a story using that art form.

Generation to Generation

FOCUS QUESTION

What types of customs and ideas do people pass down from generation to generation?

NOTICE AND WONDER

Look at the story you will read in this lesson. What do you notice? What do you wonder? Discuss your ideas with a partner.

TALKING ABOUT CUSTOMS

A custom is an activity or celebration that happens in a similar way each time. Tell a partner about a custom in your family or community.

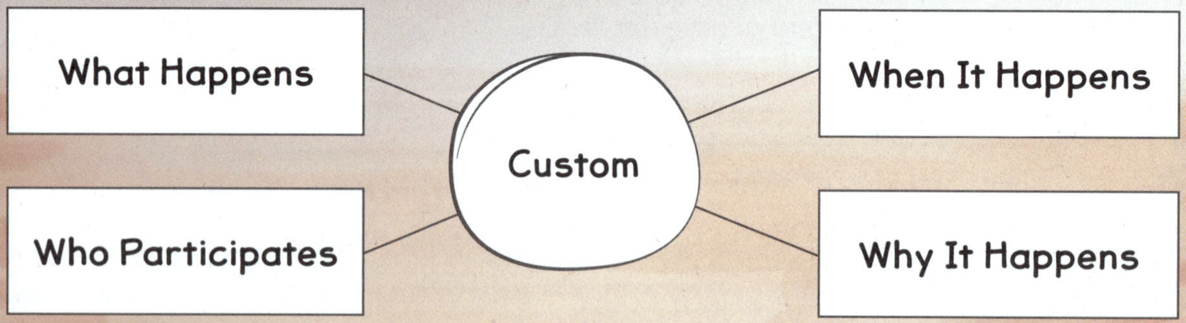

My custom is called ___.

What happens is ___. We do it because ___.

We do it every ___. The people who participate are ___.

from *Esperanza Rising*, Parts 1–3

by Pam Muñoz Ryan

SESSION 1 READ

from *Esperanza Rising*

by Pam Muñoz Ryan

Part 1

Esperanza, Mama, and Abuelita live in Mexico in 1930. Abuelita is teaching Esperanza how to crochet.

1 "Come, *mi nieta*, my granddaughter," said Abuelita, holding up yarn and crochet hooks. "I am starting a new blanket and will teach you the zigzag."

2 Esperanza's grandmother, whom everyone called Abuelita, lived with them and was a smaller, older, more wrinkled version of Mama. She looked very distinguished, wearing a respectable black dress, the same gold loops she wore in her ears every day, and her white hair pulled back into a bun at the nape of her neck. But Esperanza loved her more for her capricious ways than for her propriety. Abuelita might host a group of ladies for a formal tea in the afternoon, then after they had gone, be found wandering barefoot in the grapes, with a book in her hand, quoting poetry to the birds. Although some things were always the same with Abuelita—a lace-edged handkerchief peeking out from beneath the sleeve of her dress—others were surprising: a flower in her hair, a beautiful stone in her pocket, or a **philosophical** saying salted into her conversation.

philosophical = thoughtful ideas about life

Stop & Discuss

How would you describe the character of Abuelita?

Discuss details that show what Abuelita is like.

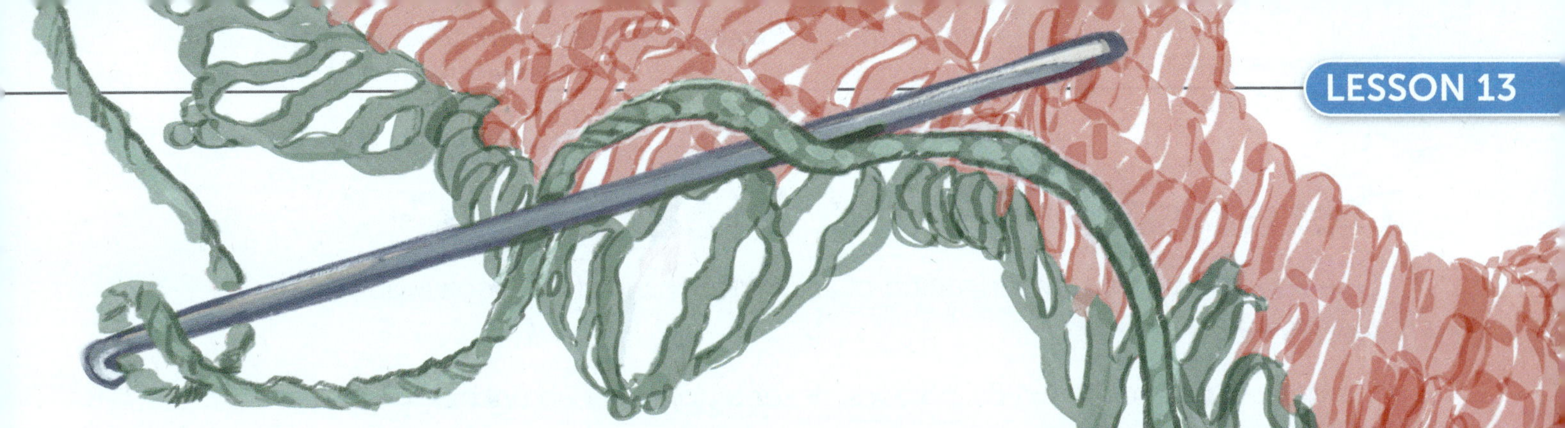

3 Esperanza complained, "Must we always crochet to take our minds off worry?" She sat next to her grandmother anyway, smelling her ever-present aroma of garlic, face powder, and peppermint.

4 "What happened to your finger?" asked Abuelita.

5 "A big thorn," said Esperanza.

6 Abuelita nodded and said thoughtfully, *"No hay rosa sin espinas.* There is no rose without thorns."

7 Esperanza smiled, knowing that Abuelita wasn't talking about flowers at all but that there was no life without difficulties. She watched the silver crochet needle dance back and forth in her grandmother's hand. When a strand of hair fell into her lap, Abuelita picked it up and held it against the yarn and stitched it into the blanket. "Esperanza, in this way my love and good wishes will be in the blanket forever. Now watch. Ten stitches up to the top of the mountain. Add one stitch. Nine stitches down to the bottom of the valley. Skip one."

8 Esperanza picked up her own crochet needle and copied Abuelita's movements and then looked at her own crocheting. The tops of her mountains were lopsided and the bottoms of her valleys were all bunched up.

9 Abuelita smiled, reached over, and pulled the yarn, unraveling all of Esperanza's rows. "Do not be afraid to start over," she said.

10 Esperanza sighed and began again with ten stitches.

Stop & Discuss

What does Abuelita teach Esperanza?

Underline details that explain Abuelita's instructions about crocheting and her advice about life.

SPOTLIGHT BENCHMARK: ELA.4.V.1.3 Use context clues, figurative language, word relationships, . . . and/or background knowledge to determine the meaning of multiple-meaning and unknown words and phrases, appropriate to grade level.

Determine Word Meanings

- One way to figure out the meaning of an unknown word is to look around the word for clues in the text.
- **Context clues** are the words, phrases, or sentences near an unknown word in a text that help you determine its meaning. There are different types of clues.
  - — **Synonyms** are words that have the same or similar meanings.
  - — **Antonyms** are words that have opposite meanings. When synonyms or antonyms are used together, you can use one word to figure out the other.
  - — An example shows what a group of things or a trait is like.

Reread/Think

Reread paragraphs 2 and 3 of *Esperanza Rising*, Part 1. Find each word from the chart below in the text. Identify the context clues that help you determine the meaning of each word. Write the clues, types of clues, and meanings in the chart.

Word	Context Clues	Types of Clues	Meaning
propriety (paragraph 2)	"respectable," hosting a formal tea	synonym, example	
distinguished (paragraph 2)	"looked very distinguished, wearing a respectable black dress"	example, synonym	
capricious (paragraph 2)			
aroma (paragraph 3)			

Talk

With a partner, discuss the context clues you used to figure out the meaning of one of the words in your chart.

> The context clue ___ helps me understand that the word ___ means ___.

> This context clue is a synonym/antonym/example that shows ___.

Write

In what ways does Abuelita show propriety? In what ways is Abuelita capricious? Use one other word from your chart and details from the text to support your response.

____

____

____

____

____

____

____

____

____

____

____

____

WRITING CHECKLIST

- ☐ I used details from the text to explain how Abuelita shows propriety and is capricious.
- ☐ I used one other word from my chart.
- ☐ I used complete sentences.
- ☐ I used correct spelling, punctuation, and capitalization.

from *Esperanza Rising*

by Pam Muñoz Ryan

Part 2

Tragedy strikes Esperanza's family. Her father dies, and their house burns down. She and Mama leave Mexico and move to the United States, and Abuelita stays behind. In this scene, Mama gets sick from a dust storm, and Esperanza takes care of her.

1 Esperanza almost never left Mama's side. She sponged her with cool water and fed her teaspoons of broth throughout the day.

2 The doctor came back a few weeks later with more medicine. "She is not getting worse," he said, shaking his head. "But she is not getting better, either."

3 Mama drifted in and out of fitful sleep and sometimes she called out for Abuelita. Esperanza could barely sit still and often paced around the small room.

4 One morning, Mama said weakly, "Esperanza . . ."

5 Esperanza ran to her and took her hand. "Abuelita's blanket . . ." she whispered.

Stop & Discuss

How does Mama feel?

Use details about what characters say and do to support your ideas.

I can tell Mama is feeling ___ because ___.

6 Esperanza pulled her valise from under the bed. She had not opened it since before the dust storm and saw that the fine brown powder had even found its way deep inside. As it had found its way into Mama's lungs.

7 She lifted out the crocheting that Abuelita had started the night Papa died. It seemed like a lifetime ago. Had it only been a few months?

8 She stretched out the zigzag rows. They reached from one side of Mama's bed to the other, but were only a few hands wide, looking more like a long scarf than the beginnings of a blanket. Esperanza could see Abuelita's hairs woven in so that all her love and good wishes would go with them forever. She held the crocheting to her face and could still smell the smoke from the fire. And the faintest scent of peppermint.

9 Esperanza looked at Mama, breathing uneasily, her eyes closed. It was clear she needed Abuelita. They both needed her. But what was Esperanza to do? She picked up Mama's limp hand and kissed it. Then she handed the strip of zigzag rows to Mama, who clutched it to her chest.

Stop & Discuss

Describe Abuelita's blanket.

Underline three details about what the blanket looks like and smells like. Discuss what these details show.

10 What had Abuelita told her when she'd given her the bundle of crocheting? And then she remembered. She had said, "Finish this for me, Esperanza . . . and promise me you'll take care of Mama."

11 After Mama fell asleep, Esperanza picked up the needlework and began where Abuelita had left off. Ten stitches up to the top of the mountain. Add one stitch. Nine stitches down to the bottom of the valley, skip one. Her fingers were more **nimble** now and her stitches were more even. The mountains and valleys in the blanket were easy. But as soon as she reached a mountain, she was headed back down into a valley again. Would she ever escape this valley she was living in? This valley of Mama being sick?

12 What else had Abuelita said? After she had lived many mountains and valleys they would be together again. She bent over her work, **intent**, and when her hair fell into her lap, she picked it up and wove it into the blanket. She cried when she thought of the wishes that would go into the blanket forever.

nimble = quick

intent = focused

Stop & Discuss

Why does Esperanza continue crocheting Abuelita's blanket?

Underline what Esperanza remembers Abuelita saying.

SPOTLIGHT BENCHMARK: ELA.4.V.1.3 Use context clues, figurative language, word relationships, . . . and/or background knowledge to determine the meaning of multiple-meaning and unknown words and phrases, appropriate to grade level.

Determine Word Meanings

- Different types of context clues can help you figure out the meaning of words.
  - — Look for nearby words that can help you make an inference about the meaning of a word or phrase.
  - — Look for comparisons and images in figurative language to help you understand the meaning of words or phrases as they are used in the text.
- You can also use context clues to understand words that have multiple meanings. Use context clues to figure out which meaning makes sense.

Reread/Think

Reread Part 2 of *Esperanza Rising*. Find each word from the chart below in the text. Identify the context clues that help you determine the meaning of each word. Write the clues, types of clues, and meaning in the chart.

Word or Phrase	Context Clues	Types of Clues	Meaning
fitful (paragraph 3)	"drifted in and out of sleep . . . called out"	inference	starting and stopping
mountain, valley (beginning of paragraph 11)	• "Ten stitches up to the top of the mountain." • "Nine stitches down to the bottom of the valley."	figurative language, inference	
valley (end of paragraph 11)	• "escape this valley she was living in?"		
many mountains and valleys (paragraph 12)			

SESSION 4 PRACTICE

Talk

Discuss the meanings of the words mountains and valleys as they are used in Part 2 of the story. Explain how context clues helped you figure out the meanings.

I know that the words *mountains* and *valleys* usually mean ___ and ___.

The context clue ___ shows Abuelita uses the words *mountain* and *valley* to explain ___.

Then Esperanza thinks about the word *valley* as a way of describing ___.

Write

Choose one meaning of the words mountains and valleys as they are used in Part 2 of *Esperanza Rising*. Explain the context clues you used to figure out their meanings. Use details from the text to support your response.

WRITING CHECKLIST

- ☐ I used context clues to figure out the meaning of words.
- ☐ I used complete sentences.
- ☐ I used correct spelling, punctuation, and capitalization.

from *Esperanza Rising* Part 3

by Pam Muñoz Ryan

Mama and Esperanza have lived in the United States for almost a year in a cabin with another family, including a child named Isabel. After Mama recovers from her illness, Abuelita visits them for the first time since they left Mexico.

1 Esperanza watched Abuelita walk to where Mama slept, resting on the **makeshift** lounge. She was framed by the vineyard, the grapes ripe and ready to drop.

2 Abuelita stopped a few feet from Mama and looked at her.

3 A stack of lace ***carpetas*** was at Mama's side as well as her crochet needle and thread. Abuelita reached out and stroked her hair, gently pulling the loose strands away from Mama's face and smoothing them against her head.

4 Softly, Abuelita said, "Ramona."

5 Mama did not open her eyes, but said as if she was dreaming, "Esperanza, is that you?"

6 "No, Ramona, it is me, Abuelita."

7 Mama slowly opened her eyes. She stared at Abuelita with no reaction, as if she was not really seeing her at all. Then she lifted her hand and reached out to touch her mother's face, making sure that the vision was true.

8 Abuelita nodded, "Yes, it is me. I have come."

makeshift = temporary substitute

carpetas = small, decorative mats

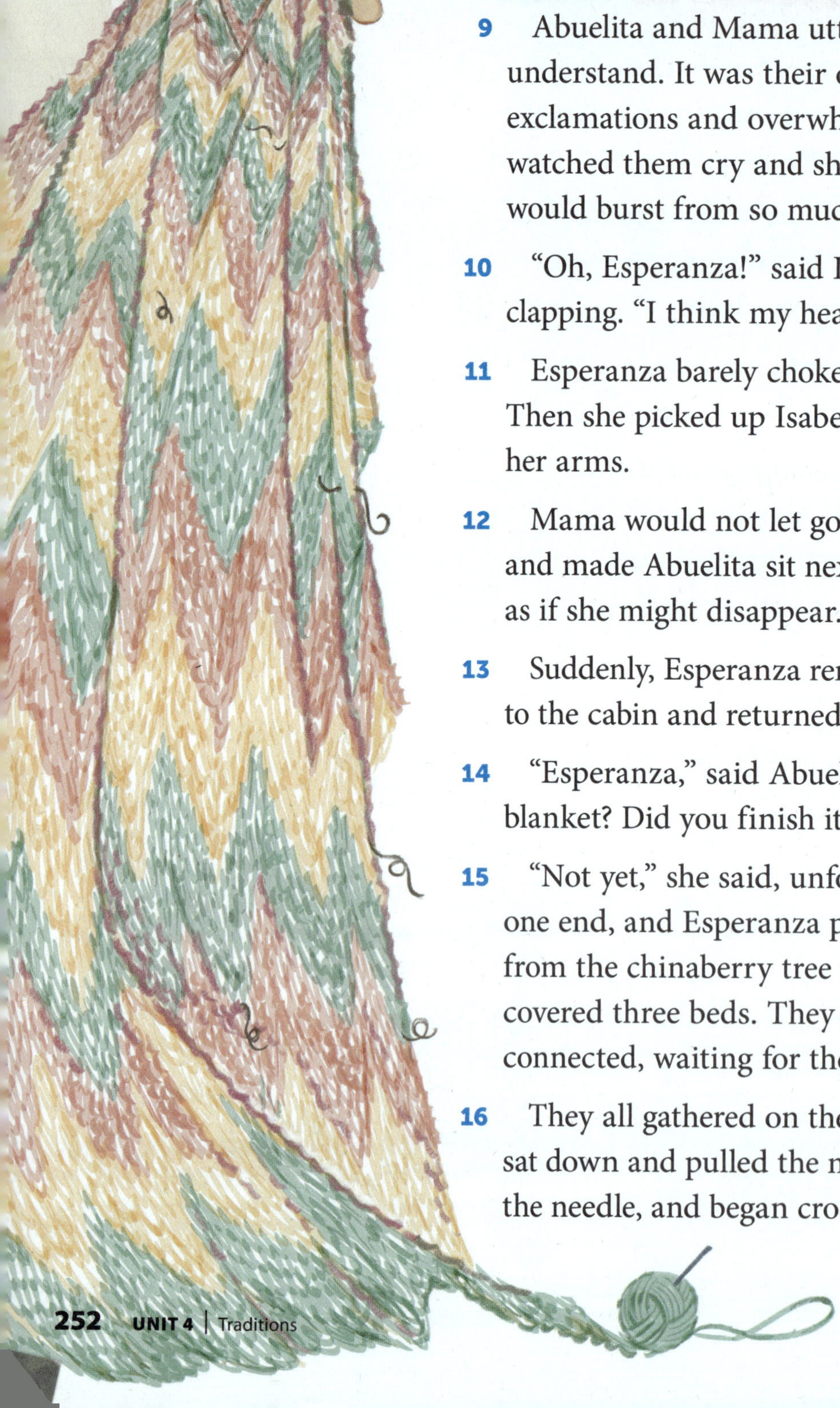

9 Abuelita and Mama uttered no words that anyone could understand. It was their own language of happy exclamations and overwhelming emotions. Esperanza watched them cry and she wondered if her own heart would burst from so much joy.

10 "Oh, Esperanza!" said Isabel, jumping up and down and clapping. "I think my heart is dancing."

11 Esperanza barely choked out the whisper, "Mine, too." Then she picked up Isabel and spun her around in her arms.

12 Mama would not let go of Abuelita. She scooted over and made Abuelita sit next to her and held on to her arms as if she might disappear.

13 Suddenly, Esperanza remembered her promise, ran back to the cabin and returned, carrying something in her arms.

14 "Esperanza," said Abuelita, "Could that possibly be my blanket? Did you finish it?"

15 "Not yet," she said, unfolding the blanket. Mama held one end, and Esperanza pulled the other end. It reached from the chinaberry tree to the mulberry. It could have covered three beds. They all laughed. The yarn was still connected, waiting for the last row to be finished.

16 They all gathered on the quilt and at the table. Esperanza sat down and pulled the massive blanket next to her, took the needle, and began crocheting the final stitches.

SPOTLIGHT BENCHMARK: ELA.4.V.1.3 Use context clues, figurative language, word relationships, . . . and/or background knowledge to determine the meaning of multiple-meaning and unknown words and phrases, appropriate to grade level.

Respond to Text

Reread/Think

Reread Part 3 of *Esperanza Rising*. Choose the best response to each question.

1. PART A

Read this sentence from paragraph 7, describing Mama's reaction to Abuelita.

> She stared at Abuelita with no reaction, as if she was not really seeing her at all.

What does the sentence tell the reader about Mama?

Ⓐ She does not remember who Abuelita is.

Ⓑ Her lounge has been set up in a dark place.

Ⓒ She cannot believe Abuelita is really there.

Ⓓ Her illness has made it difficult for her to see.

PART B

Which detail from the text **best** supports the answer to Part A?

Ⓐ Mama saying "no words that anyone could understand" to Abuelita (paragraph 9)

Ⓑ Mama holding on to Abuelita's arms "as if she might disappear" (paragraph 12)

Ⓒ Mama laughing because the blanket "could have covered three beds" (paragraph 15)

Ⓓ Mama and the others gathering "on the quilt and at the table" (paragraph 16)

2. What is the meaning of <u>overwhelming</u> as it is used in paragraph 9?

Ⓐ hard to describe

Ⓑ hard to hold back

Ⓒ hard to notice

Ⓓ hard to make sense of

Reread/Think

3. Which **two** details should be included in a summary of Part 3 of *Esperanza Rising?*

Ⓐ Mama rests on a lounge near the vineyard.

Ⓑ Abuelita strokes Mama's hair while she sleeps.

Ⓒ Esperanza has almost finished the blanket.

Ⓓ Mama mistakes Abuelita for Esperanza.

Ⓔ Abuelita finally comes to visit her family.

Write

In paragraph 9, Esperanza wonders "if her own heart would burst." In paragraph 10, Isabel says that her "heart is dancing." What does the figurative language in these phrases tell you about their "overwhelming emotions"? Use details from the text to support your response.

WRITING CHECKLIST

- ☐ I analyzed figurative language to find meaning.
- ☐ I used details from the text to support my ideas.
- ☐ I used complete sentences.
- ☐ I used correct spelling, punctuation, and capitalization.

Respond to the Focus Question

What customs and ideas do people pass down from generation to generation?

Reread/Think

Look back at the three parts of the story. What customs and ideas does Abuelita teach Esperanza? Look for important details about what Abuelita passes on to Esperanza. Record them in the chart below.

Details
Customs:
Ideas:

Talk

As a team, share and discuss your ideas from your chart.

What details and evidence in the text show that Esperanza has learned something from Abuelita?

- A custom Abuelita teaches Esperanza is ___.
- One idea Abuelita teaches Esperanza is ___.
- I think Esperanza has learned these customs and ideas because ___.

Write

Think about your family or community. What is one custom or idea that is passed down from one generation to the next? Explain why these customs and ideas are important for new generations to learn and know.

Different Perspectives

FOCUS QUESTION

What happens when people in a family have different perspectives?

NOTICE AND WONDER

Look at the three texts you will read in this lesson. What do you notice? What do you wonder? Discuss your ideas with a partner.

SHARING PERSPECTIVES

Your *perspective* is your way of looking at the world. It can describe your attitude and ideas about a big topic or an everyday situation. People see things differently; they have different perspectives.

Think about a time when you had a different perspective from someone else. Tell your partner about your experience. What was the situation? What were the perspectives? Did either of your perspectives end up changing?

The situation was ___.

I thought ___ because ___.

But the other person thought ___ because ___.

from *Merci Suárez Changes Gears*

by Meg Medina

Count Me In

by Lee Lewis

from *Any Day with You*

by Mae Respicio

from Merci Suárez Changes Gears

by Meg Medina

After school, Merci rides her brother Roli's bike. She goes to meet her abuelo, Lolo, at the bakery where Tía Inés works.

1 I biked over to El Caribe as soon as I got home from school. It's peaceful in here today, nothing like Sunday mornings, when the line snakes all the way out the door and people shout out their orders to Tía for takeout coffee, **pastelitos**, and warm loaves of bread. Everybody knows this is the best bakery between Miami and Tampa, so it gets crazy.

pastelitos = Cuban pastries

2 Tía Inés is busy refilling the cups of toothpicks that are decorated with mini Cuban flags. "She can't stay long, **viejo**," she tells Lolo. "Merci has to help Abuela with the boys today."

viejo = an older person

3 We both stare at her.

4 I should mention here that 1) no one ever asks me if I want to babysit the twins, 2) Roli almost always gets out of it thanks to his tutoring job and working on his college applications, and 3) I get paid exactly zero for keeping them from swallowing pennies and running blindly into traffic. How am I supposed to buy a bike when nobody pays me for anything?

Stop & Discuss

What does Tía Inés want Merci to do, and how does Merci feel about it?

Discuss your ideas with a partner using evidence from the text.

5 "I wish you'd find somebody else, Tía," I say. "There are kids at school who took that Red Cross class and actually want to babysit. I can get you names. Hire them. I won't be able to watch them once soccer season starts, anyway."

6 She frowns at me. "Who in their right mind would hire a stranger to watch their kids when they have relatives around?"

7 I sigh. It's no use fighting. When it comes to helping, the motto around here is *family or bust*.

8 "Can't I at least have a snack before I go?" I say. "I've had a long day, in case you're interested. And I'll need my strength for the twins."

9 She sizes me up and slides over a small guava square, still warm, on a plate. "Ten minutes, then out you go."

Stop & Discuss

Check all that are true.

- ☐ Merci tries to convince Tía Inés to change her mind.
- ☐ Merci refuses to babysit.
- ☐ Merci agrees to babysit.

Use evidence from the text to support your ideas.

SPOTLIGHT BENCHMARK: ELA.4.R.1.3 Identify the narrator's point of view and explain the difference between a narrator's point of view and character perspective in a literary text.

Explain Point of View and Perspective

- A **narrator** is the person who tells a story.
- In a story written from a **first-person point of view**, the narrator is a character in the story. They describe what they observe, think, and feel.
- Narrators who tell the story from a first-person point of view can describe what other characters say and do but not what other characters think and feel.
- In a story, each character has their own **perspective**, or way of looking at things.

Reread/Think

Reread paragraphs 1–6 of *Merci Suárez Changes Gears.*

Who is the narrator? ______________________________

How do you know? ______________________________

What does Merci think about babysitting the twins? What does Tía Inés think? Complete the chart with text evidence that shows each character's perspective. Label whether the evidence shows what a character says or thinks.

Text Evidence (what a character says or thinks)	**Character's Perspective**
Merci	
Tía Inés	

Talk

Use the details in your chart to discuss both characters' perspectives. What do Merci and Tía Inés think about babysitting the twins? How do we know?

> Merci's/Tía Inés's perspective is ___. I know this because ___.

> The narrator describes more about ___'s ideas because ___.

> If Tía Inés were the narrator, the story would be different because ___.

Write

Identify the narrator and the point of view. Then describe two characters' perspectives on babysitting the twins. Explain which character you learn more about, and why.

WRITING CHECKLIST

- ☐ I identified the narrator and the point of view.
- ☐ I described two characters' perspectives on babysitting the twins.
- ☐ I explained which character I learn more about, and why.
- ☐ I used correct spelling, punctuation, and capitalization.

SESSION 3 READ

Count Me In

by Lee Lewis

1 Alanna and her friends were piled on the couch in their pajamas, buzzing with excitement. Alanna was turning ten and having her very first sleepover.

2 There was a knock. Alanna's mom opened the door, and there, to her surprise, was Gran, holding a beautifully wrapped gift balanced on top of a huge rectangular box.

3 "Gran!" Alanna sprang off the couch and rushed to the door, happy to see her grandmother there.

4 "Happy birthday, Alanna!" Gran said warmly. Alanna loved her grandmother's soft Irish accent.

5 Alanna pointed to her friends. "Gran, this is Quinn, Nichole, and Meng. They're spending the night."

6 "It's great to meet you all," Gran said, stepping inside with her packages. "Now, who's ready for her present?"

7 Alanna loved Gran, mostly because Gran was, well, Gran, but also because Gran gave the *best* presents.

8 Gran handed the boxes to Alanna. "This is a very special present, part of something that meant a lot to your mother when she was your age, and something you might like too, Alanna."

9 Alanna glanced up at her mom and could see the look of surprise on her face.

10 "Well, go ahead and open it!" Gran said.

Stop & Discuss

What do you know so far about the present?

Underline the phrases that give clues.

So far, I know that the present ___.

One clue is ___. Another clue is ___.

11 Alanna tore the wrapping paper off the smaller box and opened it, revealing soft black shoes with *very* long laces. "Oh! Irish dance shoes?" she said, a little puzzled.

12 "They are," said Gran. "Those are soft shoes, of course. And this goes with them as well." She opened the bigger box. Alanna's breath caught at the sight of the dress inside, deep blue, the color of the ocean, with **elaborate** stitching in silver and gold thread running down the middle of the dress and tracing the bottom of the flared skirt.

13 "Wow," Meng murmured as Alanna lifted the dress. It was so beautiful!

14 Alanna's mom pulled Gran aside. "I wish you had asked me first," she whispered.

15 "Ahhh," Gran replied with a wave of her hand. "Let the girl try it for herself now."

16 Alanna's eyes widened at these words. Did she hear her mom and Gran correctly? "Wait, did Mom dance in this dress?" she asked.

17 "She did," Gran said, "until she discovered softball, that is. Her dress has been packed away since then, and I wanted you to have a chance to try it on. Step dancing is a traditional Irish dance, a part of our heritage."

elaborate = highly detailed or having many parts

Stop & Discuss

What does Alanna find out about the dress?

Discuss your ideas with a partner.

18 "Show us some moves, Mrs. Ross!" Nichole said.

19 Alanna's mom blushed, politely refusing, but as the girls continued begging, she gave in. With her arms at her sides, she extended one perfectly pointed foot and sprang to her tiptoes. While her upper body remained still, she kicked and skipped quickly and lightly, always high on her toes. Memories of dance performances played in her mind. She had forgotten how much she loved dancing these steps!

20 The girls applauded wildly. Alanna had just seen a totally different side of her mom, who was sparkling with joy. And Alanna wondered how dancing might transform *her.*

reel = a traditional Irish dance

21 Next, Alanna's mom showed them a **reel**, lilting the same singsong words that her own teacher had used to help her remember the step. Then she stood back to let the girls practice. Quinn, Meng, and Nichole began to hop and skip, excited to try out the step. Alanna joined them, with a wide grin—and beautifully pointed toes.

Stop & Discuss

What happens when Alanna's mom dances?

Discuss your ideas with a partner.

SPOTLIGHT BENCHMARK: ELA.4.R.1.3 Identify the narrator's point of view and explain the difference between a narrator's point of view and character perspective in a literary text.

Explain Point of View and Perspective

- In a story written from a **third-person point of view**, the narrator is not a character in the story.
- Narrators who tell a story from a third-person point of view can describe what more than one character thinks and feels on the inside. They can show more about different characters' perspectives.

Reread/Think

Reread paragraphs 14–21 of "Count Me In."

Is this story told from a first-person or third-person point of view? ____________

How do you know? ____

What is each character's perspective on Irish dance? Complete the chart.

Text Evidence (says, does, thinks, or feels)	Character's Perspective
Gran	
Mrs. Ross	
Alanna	

SESSION 4 PRACTICE

Talk

Use information from the chart to discuss what each character thinks about Irish dance. How does the narrator show different characters' perspectives?

I know ___'s perspective is ___ because ___.

When Alanna/Mrs. Ross ___, it shows that ___.

In this story, the narrator shows ___'s perspective by describing what they say/do/think/feel.

Write

Identify the narrator's point of view in "Count Me In." Then explain how the narrator shows different characters' perspectives on Irish dance.

WRITING CHECKLIST

- ☐ I described the narrator's point of view.
- ☐ I described how the narrator shows different characters' perspectives.
- ☐ I used correct spelling, punctuation, and capitalization.

from Any Day with You

by Mae Respicio

Kaia and her family live in California. She is upset that her great-grandfather, Tatang, is moving back to the Philippines. They walk on the beach to talk.

1 “What did I tell you before? This isn’t goodbye.”

2 “No, but you’re still leaving.”

3 “Shall I tell you a story?” [Tatang] asks.

4 “I don’t feel like one now.”

5 “Can we play the noticing game?”

6 I shake my head. But he closes his eyes.

7 For a long moment I stare at him, the smile around his eyes still coming through even though they’re shut. I close mine too.

8 The things I notice: my hair blowing across my forehead, the crash of waves. Everything like normal.

9 "I'm picturing my happiest memory," Tatang says. "Can you picture yours?"

10 Each perfect day of my life has had the same things: sunshine, waves, and my family near. How will I ever have that again without Tatang? Everything's changing.

11 "Open your eyes," Tatang says. When I do, he's looking at me. "You were able to see something in your past but standing right here, someplace else. We can be aware of the past, the future, and the present, all at once. Do you know what that means?"

12 "What?" I say.

13 "It means that I am always with you."

SPOTLIGHT BENCHMARK: ELA.4.R.1.3 Identify the narrator's point of view and explain the difference between a narrator's point of view and character perspective in a literary text.

Respond to Text

Reread/Think

Reread the passage from *Any Day with You*. Choose the best response to each question.

1. Fill in **one** bubble in each row to show whether the statement is about Kaia, Tatang, both characters, or neither character.

	Kaia	Tatang	Both Characters	Neither Character
The narrator tells what this character says.	Ⓐ	Ⓑ	Ⓒ	Ⓓ
The narrator tells what this character dreams.	Ⓔ	Ⓕ	Ⓖ	Ⓗ
The narrator tells what this character thinks.	Ⓘ	Ⓙ	Ⓚ	Ⓛ
The narrator is this character.	Ⓜ	Ⓝ	Ⓞ	Ⓟ

2. Read paragraph 11 from *Any Day with You*. Fill in the bubble **before** the sentence that shows the narrator of the story.

Ⓐ "Open your eyes," Tatang says. Ⓑ When I do, he's looking at me. Ⓒ "You were able to see something in your past but standing right here, someplace else. Ⓓ We can be aware of the past, the future, and the present, all at once. Ⓔ Do you know what that means?"

SESSION 5 PRACTICE

Reread/Think

3. In paragraph 11, Tatang says, "You were able to see something in your past but standing right here, someplace else." What does he mean?

Ⓐ Kaia imagined an event that happened in the same spot.

Ⓑ Kaia wondered what it would be like to live far away.

Ⓒ Kaia pictured details about another day in her life.

Ⓓ Kaia dreamed of a place she had never seen before.

Write

Identify the narrator's point of view in *Any Day with You*. Then explain how the narrator shows each character's perspective on Tatang leaving.

WRITING CHECKLIST

- ☐ I identified the narrator's point of view.
- ☐ I described how the narrator shows the characters' perspectives.
- ☐ I used complete sentences.
- ☐ I used correct spelling, punctuation, and capitalization.

Respond to the Focus Question

What happens when people in a family have different perspectives?

Reread/Think

Choose one story to reread. Think about each character's perspective on the same situation.

TEXT: ______________________________

How do the characters see the same situation differently? How do you think their ages and life experiences shape their perspectives? What could they learn from each other?

____

____

____

____

____

Talk

As a group, discuss the perspectives of two characters from the same story. What does each character want? Why? What could they learn from each other?

Take turns pretending to be the characters and acting out the same situation in different ways:

- arguing
- working together to create a new solution
- learning from each other

Write

Rewrite one story in the lesson from the point of view of another character in the story. Use first-person pronouns like *I, me,* and *mine* and describe the character's thoughts and feelings. You can also create a new ending or write about what happens next with the characters.

Building Traditions

TALK ABOUT WHAT YOU KNOW

Use the pictures to recall the texts that you read in this unit. Turn and talk with a partner about what you know and have learned about traditions. Use the sentence frames to help you.

Traditions are important to people because ___.

One example of a tradition is ___.

Older people share traditions with younger people because ___.

LESSON 12

Storytelling Through Art

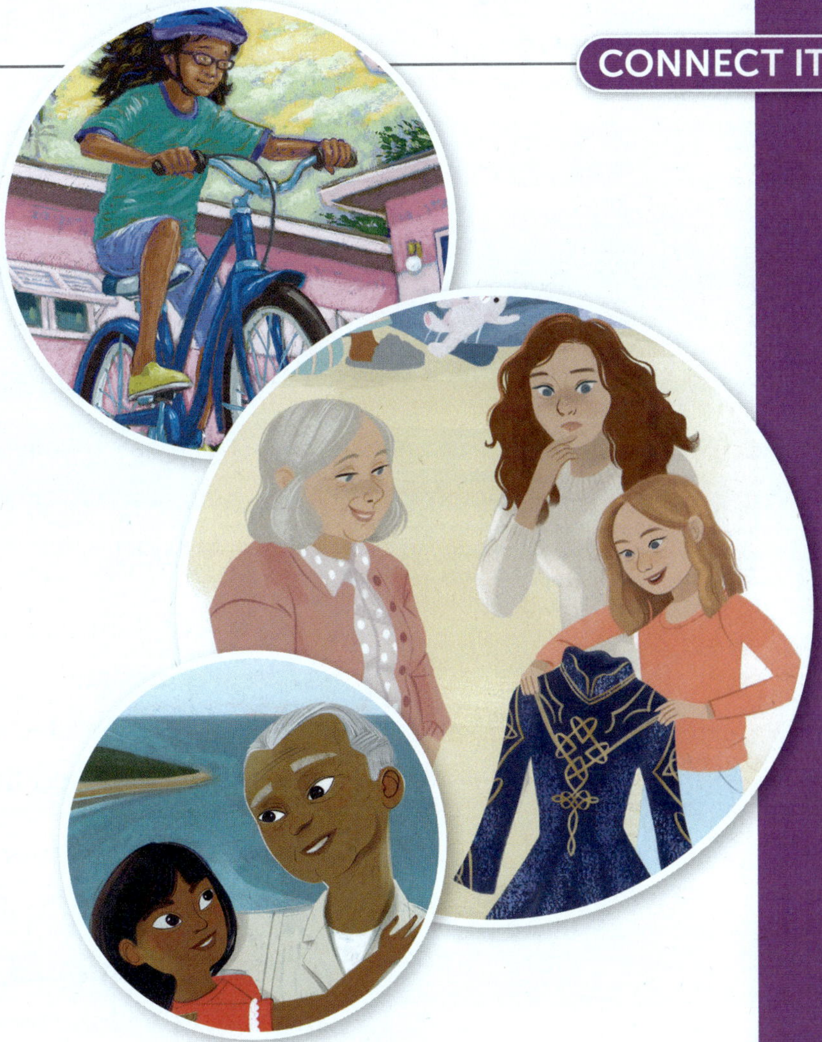

LESSON 13

Generation to Generation

LESSON 14

Different Perspectives

CONNECT TO TRADITIONS

What traditions do you know about from your own community or school? Discuss these questions with a partner:

- What is the tradition?
- Why is it important to people?
- How is it similar to a tradition you have read about in this unit?

SESSION 2 READ

from

The Year of the Rat

by Grace Lin

Pacy describes celebrating Chinese New Year with her parents, her sisters Lissy and Ki-Ki, her friend Melody, and Melody's family.

1 This year, Chinese New Year was on a Saturday, so we could stay up late. After dinner, we all gathered in the family room. As Dad made a warm fire in our fireplace, Ki-Ki almost closed her eyes from sleepiness.

2 "Uh-oh," Lissy said. "Wake up, Ki-Ki! You have to welcome in the New Year!"

3 "Yes," Melody's dad said. "We have to keep you up all night. The longer you stay awake, the longer lives we will have."

4 "Then you better do something to keep us awake," Melody said. "Do something so we're not bored."

5 "Oh, you want us to entertain you, huh?" Dad laughed. "Okay, let's see. I can sing. Do-re-mi . . ."

6 "NO!" we all said together.

Stop & Discuss

Why do the kids want their parents to entertain them?

Find the most important reason and underline it in the text.

7 "How about if you all write down your New Year's **resolutions**?" Dad said. "You can think about what you want to accomplish in the New Year."

resolutions = promises to yourself to achieve your goals

8 "You're supposed to do that for the American New Year," Lissy objected. "Not Chinese New Year."

9 "So?" Dad said. "We celebrate both. We can make up our own traditions."

10 Even though it seemed a little bit like school, it didn't sound so bad. So, I got paper and pencils for everyone. . . . [W]e sat down and started to write. . . .

11 Pacy's Resolutions

1. Write and draw another book, like I did before, and be an author and illustrator
2. See and ride a unicorn, though a white horse would be okay, too
3. Have lots of money and be rich
4. Become famous
5. Have good luck in EVERYTHING

Stop & Discuss

How does Pacy feel about writing down resolutions? Which of them seem likely to happen? Which do not?

Support your answer with details from the text and your own experience.

12 When Mom and Dad read my resolutions, they laughed.

13 "Well, these are very unusual resolutions," Dad said, "though I guess most people would like to share your last resolution."

14 "Americans write resolutions," Mom said. "Chinese and Taiwanese people write wishes. I think some of the things on your list are more like wishes."

15 "Is there a big difference?" I asked.

16 "Well, a resolution is something you can try to accomplish," Mom said. "For a wish to come true, it needs someone else to make it happen."

17 "Resolutions are better," Dad said. "You're more powerful. You don't have to depend on anyone. A wish is left to fate, but a resolution is a change you make yourself. You can change your destiny with your resolution."

Stop & Discuss

According to Pacy's mother, what is the difference between a resolution and a wish?

Support your answer with details from the text.

To make a resolution come true, you ___.

To make a wish come true, you ___.

18 I didn't really understand what Dad was talking about—fate and destiny and resolutions? I did like the idea of being powerful, but I also really liked the idea of someone else making my wishes come true—that seemed a lot easier. I looked at Melody's list. Hers were a lot like mine, except for one.

19 **Melody's Resolutions**

1. Read 100 Books
2. Get Good Grades
3. Win the Lottery
4. Be the Luckiest Person in the World
5. Stay in New Hartford

20 "Why did you write 'stay in New Hartford'?" I asked. New Hartford was the name of our town, the one we lived in now.

21 Melody looked sad. "I wasn't supposed to tell you because we aren't supposed to have sad feelings on New Year," she said. "But my mom told me we might be moving."

22 "Moving!" I said. "You can't move! You just got here."

23 "I know," she said. "I don't want to. But my Dad's company wants to give him a job in California."

24 "California is on the other side of the country!" I said. "That's too far. You can't go."

25 "Well, my mom said maybe," Melody said. "So, maybe we won't. Let's hope for good luck."

Stop & Discuss

What news does Melody share in this part of the story? How does Pacy react?

Explain your answer to a partner, using details from the text.

Respond to Text

Reread/Think

Reread *The Year of the Rat*. Choose the best response to each question.

1. What does Pacy's father think about Pacy's resolutions?

Ⓐ He thinks they are easy to do.

Ⓑ He thinks they are not normal or common.

Ⓒ He thinks they are similar to her friend's resolutions.

Ⓓ He thinks they are not the same resolutions as she made last year.

2. **PART A**

What does the word destiny mean in paragraph 17?

Ⓐ a person's future

Ⓑ what a person looks like

Ⓒ events in the past

Ⓓ special pictures or objects

PART B

Which word from paragraph 17 helps the reader understand the meaning of destiny?

Ⓐ wish

Ⓑ resolution

Ⓒ change

Ⓓ fate

3. Which word from paragraphs 15–17 uses a suffix that means "having a lot of" something?

Ⓐ difference (paragraph 15)

Ⓑ resolution (paragraph 16)

Ⓒ someone (paragraph 16)

Ⓓ powerful (paragraph 17)

4. What does Pacy mean in paragraph 22 when she says to Melody, "You just got here"?

Ⓐ She is excited that Melody might move far away to California.

Ⓑ She is surprised that Melody sat down and stood up again right away.

Ⓒ She feels like Melody has lived in her town for only a short time.

Ⓓ She thinks that Melody just arrived at her house for Chinese New Year.

5. Which sentence describes who is telling the story and what their point of view is?

Ⓐ Pacy is telling the story from a first-person point of view.

Ⓑ Melody is telling the story from a third-person point of view.

Ⓒ The characters take turns telling the story from a first-person point of view.

Ⓓ A narrator outside the story is telling the story from a third-person point of view.

6. Which detail would be **most** important to include in a summary of *The Year of the Rat*?

Ⓐ Pacy's dad builds a fire in the fireplace.

Ⓑ Melody's dad hopes to keep everyone up all night.

Ⓒ Pacy writes that she wants lots of money.

Ⓓ Melody announces that she might have to move.

SESSION 3 PRACTICE

Write

What is Pacy's perspective on resolutions and wishes? How is it similar to or different from her dad's perspective? Use details from the text to support your response.

WRITING CHECKLIST

- ☐ I explained how the perspectives of Pacy and her father are similar or different.
- ☐ I used details from the text to support my response.
- ☐ I used complete sentences.
- ☐ I used correct spelling, punctuation, and capitalization.

Make Connections

Reread/Think

Think about the traditions you have read about in this unit. Answer the questions below using examples from the texts.

With your team: What traditions did you read about? ______

______

______

With a partner: Why do people continue traditions? ______

______

______

How do people add something new to traditions? ______

______

______

On your own: Which tradition are you most interested in? Why? ______

______

______

______

Talk

As a team, discuss your ideas about why people continue traditions and how they add to them. Then share the tradition you are most interested in, and why.

People continue traditions like ___ because ___.

Sometimes people change traditions because ___. For instance, ___.

I think the tradition ___ is interesting because ___.

Sports

LESSON 15

Changing the Game

284

LESSON 16

Crossing the Finish Line

300

UNIT 5

LESSON 17
Heart of the Game
316

CONNECT IT
What Makes a Sport a Sport?
332

Changing the Game

FOCUS QUESTION

When should a sport change?

NOTICE AND WONDER

Look at the three texts you will read in this lesson. What do you notice? What do you wonder? Discuss your ideas with a partner.

FAIRNESS IN SPORTS

Discuss with a partner why fairness in sports is important. What is needed to make sure sports are fair? Write some things that can bring fairness to sports.

fairness in sports

Fairness is important in sports because ___.

For a sport to be fair, there must be ___ because ___.

Bigger than the Rules

by Timothy Tocher

Title IX: A Win for Equality

by Sharon Wexler

The Fabulous Fastball

by Layne DeMarin

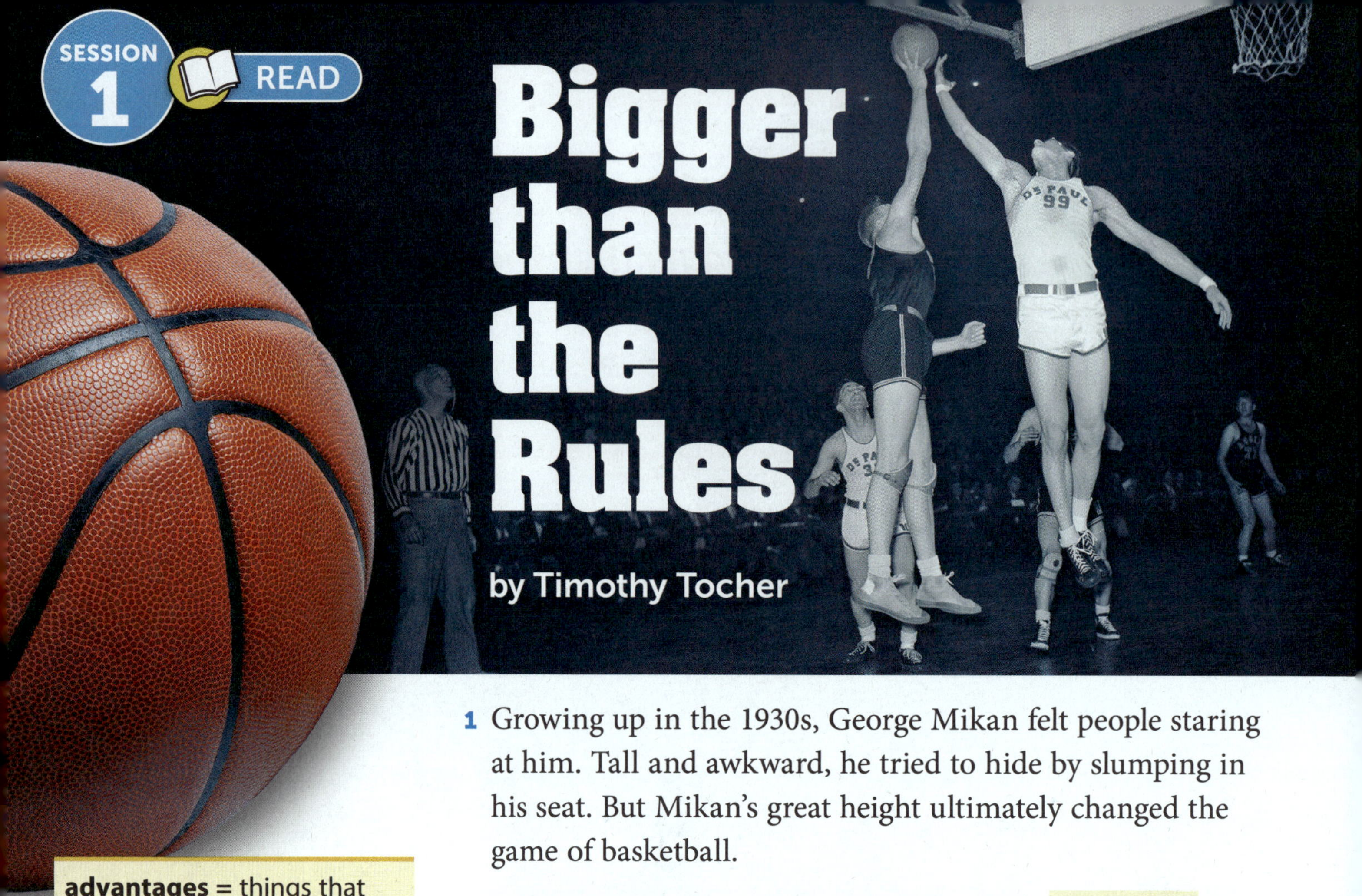

Bigger than the Rules

by Timothy Tocher

1 Growing up in the 1930s, George Mikan felt people staring at him. Tall and awkward, he tried to hide by slumping in his seat. But Mikan's great height ultimately changed the game of basketball.

2 Mikan's unusually tall height led to unfair **advantages** in basketball games. At age 14, Mikan was already 5 feet 10 inches tall when he joined a youth basketball team. Six months later, he had grown another 6 inches! By the time he was 16 years old, he was 6 feet 8 inches tall. Basketball coaches thought the perfect height for a player was 6 feet tall. But, being super tall gave Mikan an advantage—it helped him block **opponent**s' shots.

3 While height advantages weren't against the rules, they negatively affected the game. In college, Mikan would reach up to block an opposing player's shot just as the ball was about to go through the hoop. Other teams and their fans hated this action. They called it "goaltending." There weren't rules against it, but it seemed wrong to do. It made games less exciting because fewer points were scored. As a result, the sport stopped attracting new fans.

advantages = things that help one person or group more than another

opponent = a player on the other team

Stop & Discuss

What was goaltending? Why was it a problem?

Discuss your response with a partner.

When Mikan would goaltend, he would ___.

Other teams and fans thought it was unfair because ___.

4 The fans' and players' frustration around Mikan's goaltending reached a breaking point. After Mikan blocked 17 shots in one game, members of the National Collegiate Athletic Association (NCAA) met, and they agreed that to keep the game fair, goaltending should not be allowed. They made a new rule that no player could block a shot on its way down into the basket.

5 The NCAA made another change due to Mikan's height, but this change was on the court itself. The *lane* is a painted area around the basket where a player trying to make a shot can stay for only three seconds at a time. This area used to be 6 feet wide. But Mikan, with his long arms and strong jumping, could easily reach the basket from the edges of the lane. So, to make things fair, the lane was widened to 12 feet. But Mikan simply learned to shoot baskets from farther back. The rule change made Mikan a better player. It also made the game more exciting, which attracted more fans.

6 George Mikan's great height was a true game changer. It changed the rules of the sport, resulted in a wider lane on the court, and brought excitement back to the game. George Mikan's great height helped shape the game of basketball as we know it today.

Mikan's goaltending meant it was hard for anyone to get a shot in.

The wider lane made it harder for Mikan to make shots.

Stop & Discuss

What effect did the rule changes have on the game?

Discuss your response with a partner.

SESSION 2 PRACTICE

SPOTLIGHT BENCHMARK: ELA.4.R.2.4 Explain an author's claim and the reasons and evidence used to support the claim.

Explain an Author's Claim

- Authors may make a claim in a text to try to persuade readers to agree with their ideas about the topic.
- A **claim** is a statement that something is true even though other people might not agree. To convince readers that a claim is true, authors support their claims with reasons and evidence.
- A **reason** explains why a claim is correct or true.
- **Evidence** includes facts or examples that support the reasons.

Reread/Think

Reread "Bigger than the Rules." Write the author's claim. Then complete the chart with the reasons and evidence used to support that claim.

Claim: ______________________________

Reasons	Evidence
Paragraph 2 Mikan's height led to unfair advantages.	• The ideal height for a player was 6 feet tall. Mikan was 6 feet, 8 inches tall.
Paragraph 4	
Paragraph 5	

Talk

Review your chart with a partner. Then discuss how the author supports the claim with reasons and evidence. Make sure you explain a different reason than your partner.

The author's claim is ___.

One reason that supports the claim is ___.

Evidence that supports the reason is ___.

Write

State the author's claim in "Bigger than the Rules." Then describe at least two reasons and supporting evidence that the author uses to support the claim.

WRITING CHECKLIST

- ☐ I explained the author's claim.
- ☐ I included at least two reasons and evidence that support the claim.
- ☐ I used complete sentences.
- ☐ I used correct spelling, punctuation, and capitalization.

SESSION 3 READ

TITLE IX A WIN FOR EQUALITY

by Sharon Wexler

Patsy Mink

1 Let's take a step back in time. The year is 1968. A girl is about to start school, and she loves basketball. Her dream is to play on the school team, but she's not allowed to try out. Why? Her school has one basketball team, and it's for boys only.

2 Until the 1970s, schools often had several sports teams for boys, such as basketball, soccer, and wrestling. But for girls, there was often only one choice: field hockey. Then, in 1972, things changed. Someone named Patsy Mink fought for a new law called Title IX. Patsy Mink's efforts changed girls' and women's opportunities for the better.

A New Law

3 Patsy Mink, a member of the U.S. Congress from Hawaii, noticed how schools treated girls unfairly. She decided to do something about it. Her goal was for girls to have the same chance as boys to get involved in school activities, including sports. Mink **proposed** Title IX, which passed in 1972. The law said that if a school receives government money for a program, then that program must be offered to all students.

proposed = formally suggested for debate

Stop & Discuss

What did the Title IX law state?

Underline details in the text that tell what the law was meant to change.

Sports for Everyone

4 Because of Title IX, schools must now have a girls' team and a boys' team for each sport they offer, or they must let all students participate on the same team. As a result, girls and young women today have a real chance at developing their athletic skills and exploring their interests. Just ask the 2,400 young women currently playing high-school football in the United States. Title IX helped prove that there is no such thing as a "boy" sport or a "girl" sport. Students today can try out for any sport offered at their school, **regardless** of their gender.

regardless = without thought

A Win for Women and Girls

5 Title IX has created more opportunities for women. For example, it has helped talented female athletes earn college scholarships. For many years, athletic scholarships for girls were very uncommon. But now, if a girl wants to become a professional athlete, a scholarship may help her pay for college *and* give her a chance to continue training.

6 Title IX has also allowed many girls to discover the fun and team spirit of sports at school. For example, in 1972, only 700 girls in the United States played high-school soccer. Today, close to 400,000 girls play on their high-school teams every year. That's almost equal to the number of boys who play each year!

Stop & Discuss

What effects did Title IX have on school sports?

Discuss your response with a partner.

One effect of Title IX was ___. Another effect was ___.

equality = the same rights for all people

7 Title IX has created opportunities beyond sports. Remember, the law isn't only about sports or just about girls; It's about gender **equality**. The law says that *any* school program must be open to *all* students. Before Title IX, classes like automobile repair or cooking were offered only to boys or only to girls. But today, no student can be kept from taking a class because of gender. Just as Mink had hoped, her efforts led to more opportunities for girls and women.

Stop & Discuss

In addition to sports, how did Title IX affect students in school?

Discuss your response with a partner.

Because of Title IX, all students, regardless of gender, get to participate in all sports and activities.

Explain an Author's Claim

- When authors make a claim, they support their claim with reasons and evidence.
- Evidence can include facts and examples.

Reread/Think

Reread "Title IX: A Win for Equality." Complete the chart below with reasons and evidence. Identify each type of evidence as a fact or an example.

Claim: ____________________

Reason	Evidence
Paragraph 4	There are now around 2,400 female students playing high-school football in the U.S. **Type of Evidence:** fact
Paragraph 5	**Type of Evidence:**
Paragraph 6	**Type of Evidence:**
Paragraph 7	**Type of Evidence:**

Talk

Review your chart with a partner. Then discuss how the reasons and evidence help you understand the author's claim.

The author's claim is ___.

One reason that supports the claim is ___.

Evidence that supports the reason is the fact/example ___.

Write

State the author's claim in "Title IX: A Win for Equality." Which reason and supporting evidence do you find most convincing? Explain why that reason and evidence stand out for you.

WRITING CHECKLIST

- [ ] I stated the author's claim.
- [ ] I identified the reason and evidence that I find most convincing.
- [ ] I used complete sentences.
- [ ] I used correct spelling, punctuation, and capitalization.

THE FABULOUS FASTBALL

by Layne DeMarin

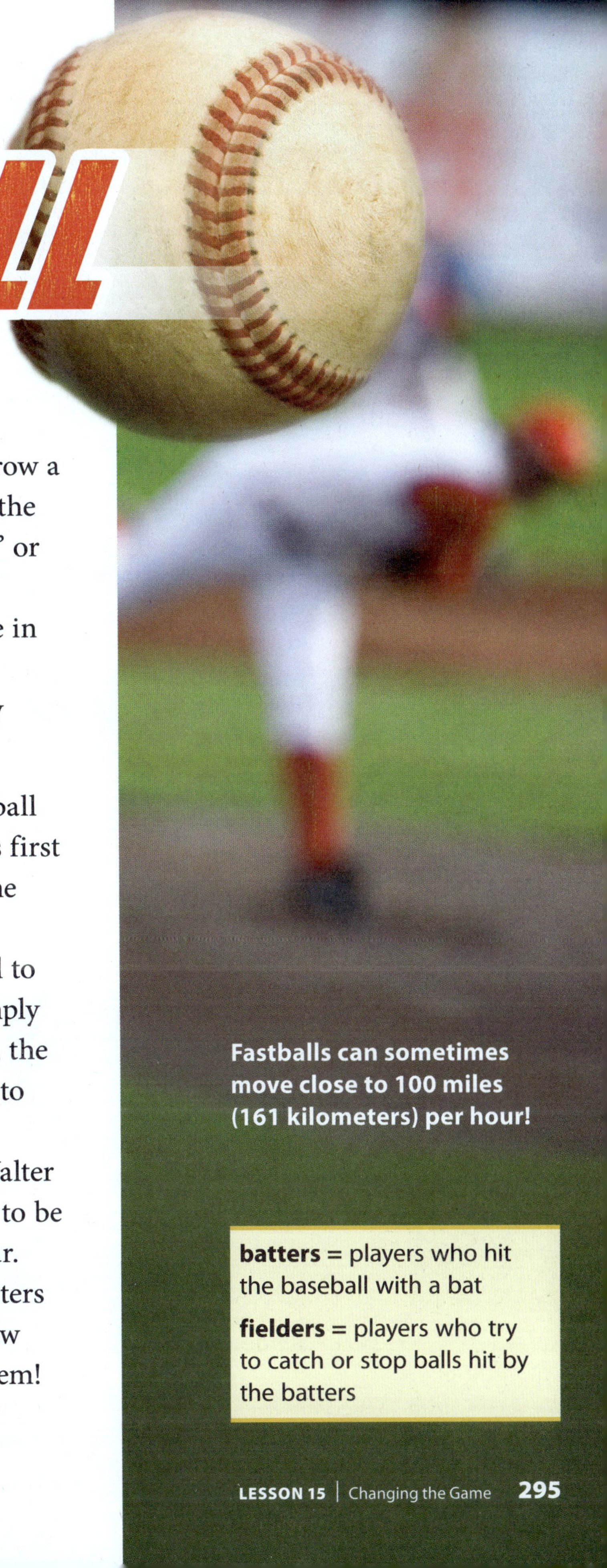

1 In baseball, a good pitcher knows how to throw a heater. What does that mean? It means that the pitcher can throw a ball so fast that it's "hot" or "on fire." Believe it or not, very fast pitches, called fastballs, haven't always been welcome in baseball. But over the years, fastballs have changed the way baseball is played, and they have made the game even better.

2 Fans would agree. Fastballs have made baseball more exciting to watch. When the game was first invented, people thought the fun would come from watching **batters** hit the ball and then waiting to see if **fielders** could catch the ball to get the batters out. The pitcher's job was simply to toss the ball to the batter. For this reason, the first rules actually made it *easier* for batters to hit the ball. But over time, pitchers started throwing the ball harder. In 1914, pitcher Walter Johnson threw a fastball that was estimated to be moving at 97 miles (156 kilometers) per hour. These pitches were more challenging for batters to hit. But fans loved watching pitchers throw fastballs—and watching batters try to hit them!

Fastballs can sometimes move close to 100 miles (161 kilometers) per hour!

batters = players who hit the baseball with a bat

fielders = players who try to catch or stop balls hit by the batters

TWO-SEAM FASTBALL

FOUR-SEAM FASTBALL

SPLIT-FINGER FASTBALL

3 Fastballs have also improved the skill level of the game. Pitchers realized that throwing fast was a skill they could improve with practice. In fact, a pitcher could learn to control the path of the ball by gripping and releasing it in a particular way. Today, the best pitchers know how to throw different types of fastballs, such as the two-seam, the four-seam, and the split-finger. Batters, too, have needed to improve their skills to hit fastballs. Batters must be able to identify the type of pitch thrown and react to it in a very short amount of time to hit the ball.

4 Pitchers have set some amazing records. The first pitcher to throw a ball over 100 miles (161 kilometers) per hour was Bob Feller in 1946. People are often watching to see who, if anyone, will break the current fastball record. As of 2021, the fastest pitch on record flew through the air at just over 105 miles (169 kilometers) per hour in 2010. This speed is almost as fast as the fierce winds of a tornado!

5 Fastballs are still changing the sport of baseball. Pitchers have become so good at throwing fastballs and striking out batters that **officials** are considering new rule changes. But even if some things change, the fastball is here to stay. Fans love the excitement, and the players keep getting better and better—all big wins for baseball!

officials = persons in charge of a sports game

SPOTLIGHT BENCHMARK: ELA.4.R.2.4 Explain an author's claim and the reasons and evidence used to support the claim.

Respond to Text

Reread/Think

Reread "The Fabulous Fastball." Then choose the best response to each question.

1. What claim does the author make in the text?

   Ⓐ Games take less time to play because of fastballs.

   Ⓑ Fastballs have made the sport of baseball better.

   Ⓒ The record for the fastest pitch will never be broken.

   Ⓓ Fastballs have had little effect on the way fielders play.

2. Which of the following is a reason that supports the author's claim?

   Ⓐ No one is likely to be able to break the current fastball record.

   Ⓑ Batters need to be able to identify the type of fastball thrown.

   Ⓒ Fastballs make baseball more exciting for fans to watch.

   Ⓓ Pitchers need to be able to throw a fastball to win.

3. Which detail from the text supports the idea that fastballs have improved players' skill levels?

   Ⓐ "Believe it or not, very fast pitches, called fastballs, haven't always been welcome in baseball." (paragraph 1)

   Ⓑ "But fans loved watching pitchers throw fastballs—and watching batters try to hit them!" (paragraph 2)

   Ⓒ "Today, the best pitchers know how to throw different types of fastballs, such as the two-seam, the four-seam, and the split-finger." (paragraph 3)

   Ⓓ "People are often watching to see who, if anyone, will break the current fastball record." (paragraph 4)

SESSION 5 PRACTICE

Reread/Think

4. Read the sentence from paragraph 5.

> Pitchers have become so good at throwing fastballs and striking out batters that officials are considering new rule changes.

What is the meaning of considering in this sentence?

Ⓐ making

Ⓑ fighting over

Ⓒ releasing

Ⓓ thinking about

Write

State the author's claim in "The Fabulous Fastball." Which reason and evidence do you find most convincing? Use details from the text to explain why that reason and evidence stand out for you.

WRITING CHECKLIST

- ☐ I identified the author's claim.
- ☐ I used text details to explain which reason and evidence were most convincing.
- ☐ I used complete sentences.
- ☐ I used correct spelling, punctuation, and capitalization.

Respond to the Focus Question

When should a sport change?

Reread/Think

Choose one text from this lesson to reread. What is one change in sports that you learned about in the text? When did the change happen, and why?

TEXT: ______________________________

____

____

Talk

Share your answer with the group.

One change I learned about in this text was ___.

As a group, discuss the following questions. Take notes in the chart.

How did sports change? What helped people realize it was time for a change?

Text	The Change	Reason for Change
"Bigger than the Rules"		
"Title IX: A Win for Equality"		
"The Fabulous Fastball"		

Write

Which change to sports do you think was most important? Why do you think so? Use details from your charts, discussions, and the texts to support your response.

SESSION 1 TALK ABOUT THE TOPIC

Crossing the Finish Line

FOCUS QUESTION

How can sports bring out the best in people?

NOTICE AND WONDER

Look at the map of the New York City Marathon route. What do you notice? What do you wonder? Discuss your ideas with a partner.

MAKE CONNECTIONS

A marathon is a 26.2-mile (42.2-kilometer) road race in which people compete by running or using a wheelchair. Circle the words you know below. Explain how they could be connected to the topic of marathons.

inspire

achieve

goal

determination

___ is related to marathons because ___.

___ said ___ is related to marathons because ___.

Finishing Strong
by Jill Korey O'Sullivan

Team Hoyt
by Angela Brown

You Can't Stop Tegla Loroupe!
by Alice Cary

SESSION 1 READ

Finishing Strong

by Jill Korey O'Sullivan

Spectators are an important part of the New York City Marathon.

1 Running a marathon is very difficult. But people run them anyway. Why? Some of these runners want to achieve a goal they once thought was impossible. Other runners want to build their confidence. If they can run a marathon, they feel as if they can do anything.

2 Despite their goals, runners sometimes want to give up, especially in the final miles of the race when they are exhausted. But at the New York City Marathon, one thing that keeps these tired runners going is the incredible support of the cheering crowd. In fact, throughout the race, more than one million spectators ring bells, shout words of encouragement, and hold up signs. This support helps push runners to complete the 26.2-mile run.

3 The average runner completes the race in about 4 hours and 30 minutes. By late afternoon, most of the marathon's 50,000 racers have crossed the finish line. At 7:25 p.m., well after dark, the official race clock stops. Most of the crowds have disappeared by then, and workers start cleaning up. But for some 100 racers, the finish line is still many miles away.

Stop & Discuss

What is it like to run the New York City Marathon?

Support your ideas with details from the text.

Running the marathon is ___. It helps when ___.

Stephanie Pennington (left); Hannah Gavios (right, center)

4 In the past, continuing the race into the evening hours was a lonely experience. The runners often crossed the finish line with no one to cheer them on. Then, in 2015, after finishing her first marathon, Stephanie Pennington decided that no racers should cross the finish line without a celebration. She came up with the awesome idea of using social media to bring together crowds for the late-hour finishers. These spectators, inspired by the racers' determination and hard work, are committed to celebrating the success of every racer. Pennington's group, known as Project Finish, stays and cheers wildly until the last runner crosses the finish line. Completing 26.2 miles is a huge accomplishment!

5 Project Finish makes all the difference to racers like Hannah Gavios. In 2016, Gavios injured her **spinal cord**. Doctors said she might never walk again. But Gavios didn't give up. She spent two years in **physical therapy**, always challenging herself to get stronger. Finishing the New York City Marathon became her goal.

spinal cord = nerve tissue in the spine that sends messages between the brain and body

physical therapy = medical care that helps people recover from injury

6 In 2018, Gavios did it—she completed the whole marathon on crutches. After crossing the finish line in just over 11 hours, Gavios expressed sincere thanks to the supporters. She said, "[It] just means so much to me that you [all] stayed."

7 The Project Finish supporters show what is most important about the race. It isn't about winning. It's about having the determination to finish.

Stop & Discuss

How does Project Finish support racers? Why do they do this?

Underline the sentence that tells what they do.

SPOTLIGHT BENCHMARK: ELA.4.R.2.3 Explain an author's perspective toward a topic in an informational text.

Explain an Author's Perspective

- The **topic** of an informational text is what the text is about. The **author's perspective** is the author's attitude about the topic, or how they feel about it.
- The words an author uses to describe people, events, and ideas can show the author's perspective.
- An author may use language that shows a positive or negative attitude. As you read, look for words and phrases that show the author's attitude.

Reread/Think

Read the text in the chart. Underline the words from the text that show the author's perspective, or attitude. Then explain the author's perspective.

Text Which words show the author's perspective?	**Author's Perspective** What do the author's words show about their attitude toward the topic?
Paragraph 2 "one thing that keeps these tired runners going is the incredible support of the cheering crowd."	The cheering crowd gives the runners energy to finish.
Paragraph 4 "She came up with the awesome idea of using social media to bring together crowds for the late-hour finishers."	
Paragraph 7 "The Project Finish supporters show what is most important about the race. It isn't about winning. It's about having the determination to finish."	

Talk

Choose a quotation from the chart. Tell your partner how the words the author uses helps show her perspective toward Project Finish.

> The word(s) ___ show(s) that the author thinks ___ about ___.

> The author thinks Project Finish is ___ because ___.

Write

What is the author's perspective toward Project Finish? Use details from the text to support your response.

____

____

____

____

____

____

____

____

____

____

____

____

____

____

WRITING CHECKLIST

- ☐ I stated the author's perspective on Project Finish.
- ☐ I used details from the text to support my response.
- ☐ I used complete sentences.
- ☐ I used correct spelling, punctuation, and capitalization.

Team Hoyt

by Angela Brown

Dick (left) and Rick (right) Hoyt competing in one of their first marathons

1 Dick and Rick Hoyt, known as "Team Hoyt," were an unforgettable father-and-son pair. They competed in marathons and other athletic contests all around the world. Together, they participated in more than 1,100 races. Rick, who cannot fully control the movement of his arms or legs, was pushed or pulled by his father, Dick, in specially designed wheelchairs, bikes, or boats. They made an amazing team!

2 Rick Hoyt was born in 1962 with cerebral palsy, a disability that affects muscles and movement. The doctors told his parents that Rick would never be able to walk or speak. Although Rick wasn't able to verbally communicate his thoughts or feelings when he was very young, his **devoted** parents saw how carefully he listened. They knew their son wanted to learn.

devoted = loving and involved

3 When Rick was 10 years old, engineering students created a computer that he could use to type out his thoughts and communicate with others. This technology allowed Rick to connect with family and friends in ways that were not possible before. He was finally able to share his interests and feelings—and his sense of humor.

benefit = raise money to help

4 When Rick was 15, he heard about a five-mile charity run to **benefit** an athlete who was paralyzed. He convinced his father that they should join the run. With Dick pushing Rick's wheelchair, Team Hoyt came in second to last. But they were happy to have simply finished.

Stop & Discuss

Why did Team Hoyt begin racing?

Underline two sentences that tell you.

5 That night, Rick typed this message into his computer: "Dad, when I'm running, it feels like I'm not disabled."

6 That was all the motivation his father needed. Dick dedicated himself to competing with Rick. He worked hard to improve his own fitness. Team Hoyt was off and running!

7 Their years of training paid off. Team Hoyt's first big race was the Boston Marathon. After that, they were unstoppable. Over the course of 35 years, Team Hoyt participated in hundreds of events, including an impressive *six* long-distance triathlons. The triathlon may be the most challenging of all sporting events. It includes a 2.5-mile (4-kilometer) swim, a 112-mile (180.3-kilometer) bike ride, and a 26.2-mile (42.2-kilometer) marathon.

8 Although Team Hoyt won many medals and honors, the goal was never to win but to finish. Rick says that even when things went wrong, "We still continued and finished the race. Dad and I are not quitters. . . . To me, finishing is so important."

9 Why is finishing so important to Rick? Rick feels that having the determination to get to the end of a race is a symbol for something greater. It's about believing in yourself and believing in others. Rick knows he has achieved many of his dreams because of his parents' love and support.

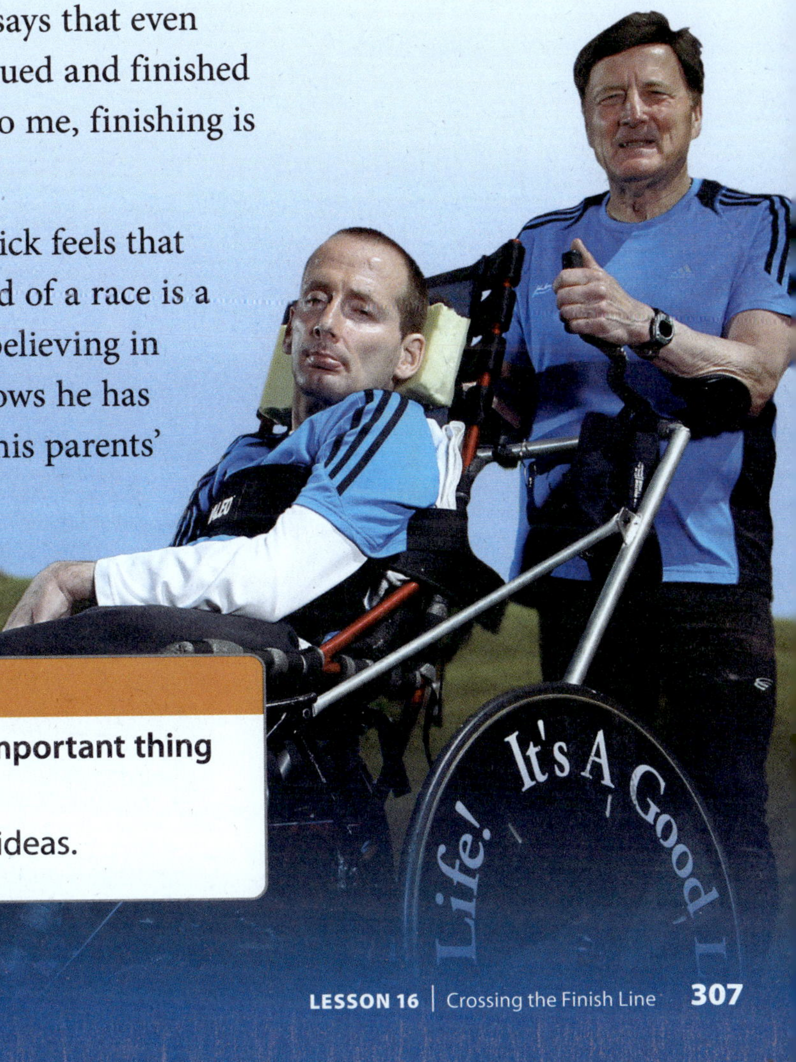

Stop & Discuss

What does Rick Hoyt think is the most important thing about racing?

Use details from the text to support your ideas.

motivated = made someone want to do something

10 Dick Hoyt died in 2021 at the age of 80. Few who saw Team Hoyt will ever forget his devotion to Rick. "He's the one who has **motivated** me," Dick once said, "because if it wasn't for him, I wouldn't be out there competing."

tirelessly = with energy, without getting tired

11 Rick has also had an incredible impact outside of athletic competitions. After earning a college degree in special education at Boston University, he worked **tirelessly** with university researchers on new technologies for people with disabilities. Along with software engineers, Rick has tested and helped develop several devices to assist people with physical challenges.

12 Rick has a simple message: "Yes, you can." What Rick and Dick wanted most is to encourage people—with or without disabilities—to work for and achieve their goals. In Rick's words, "You can do anything you want to do as long as you make up your mind—you can do it."

Stop & Discuss

What is the message Rick wants to share? Why does Rick want to share this message?

Discuss the message and what it means.

The Hoyts inspired each other and many others.

Explain an Author's Perspective

Look for words in a text that show the author's perspective, or attitude, toward the topic.

Reread/Think

Reread paragraphs 7 and 11. Complete the chart with text from each paragraph that shows the author's perspective about the Hoyts. Underline words that show the author's perspective. Then explain the perspective.

Text **Which words show the author's perspective?**	**Author's Perspective** **What do the author's words show about their attitude toward the topic?**
Paragraph 1 "Dick and Rick Hoyt, known as 'Team Hoyt,' were an unforgettable father-and-son pair." "They made an amazing team!"	The Hoyts were a great and memorable team.
Paragraph 7	
Paragraph 11	

SESSION 4 PRACTICE

Talk

What does the author think about Dick and Rick Hoyt? How do her words show her perspective? Share the ideas from your chart with a partner.

> The word ___ has a positive/negative feeling.

> Words like ___ show that the author believes or feels ___ about ___.

Write

What is the author's perspective toward Team Hoyt? Use details from the text to support your response.

____

____

____

____

____

____

____

____

____

____

____

____

____

____

WRITING CHECKLIST

- ☐ I described the author's perspective toward Team Hoyt.
- ☐ I included details from the text to support my response.
- ☐ I used complete sentences.
- ☐ I used correct spelling, punctuation, and capitalization.

You Can't Stop Tegla Loroupe!

by Alice Cary

Tegla Loroupe has loved running since she was a child.

1 When 21-year-old Tegla Loroupe (lah-ROO-pee) won the 1994 New York City Marathon, many people were surprised. Why? Loroupe was the first African woman to win in New York—and the youngest winner in the marathon's history. But the most impressive surprise? This was her first marathon ever! Loroupc, though, has been surprising people with her talent for most of her life.

2 Growing up in Kenya, Loroupe loved to race. Her dream was to become a professional runner, but she had to overcome others' negative attitudes about her goal. Her father called the sport "unladylike." When she was 12, he even told her to stop running. But students were required to play sports at her school, so Loroupe ran anyway. She astonished people by winning many races at school.

"I don't run for myself. I run for others," says Loroupe.

3 By age 13, Loroupe had claimed a well-deserved spot on Kenya's national athletics team. However, her community was unsupportive. Many people thought a person needed long legs to be good at running, and Loroupe was just 4 feet, 11 inches (1.5 meters) tall at the time. But that didn't stop a determined Loroupe. Her mother told her to believe in herself, saying, "One day you will be the best."

4 Her mother was right. Between 1994 and 2002, Loroupe won several major marathons all over the world. She also ran in three Olympics. For a while, she held the impressive title of fastest female long-distance runner in the world.

5 Loroupe is an inspiration to all Kenyan girls who want to follow their dreams. "I don't run for myself," she once said. "I run for others." She also hopes that professional athletes from Africa who compete around the world will return—just like she has—to help encourage young people.

Respond to Text

Reread/Think

Reread "You Can't Stop Tegla Loroupe!" Choose the best response to each question.

1. PART A

What is the author's perspective in paragraphs 1 and 2?

Ⓐ The author thinks Loroupe was too young to run in a marathon.

Ⓑ The author admires Loroupe's hard work, dedication, and speed.

Ⓒ The author agrees that running is an "unladylike" activity.

Ⓓ The author believes it is a good idea for schools to require sports.

PART B

Which detail from the text **best** supports the answer to Part A?

Ⓐ "When 21-year-old Tegla Loroupe won the 1994 New York City Marathon, many people were surprised." (paragraph 1)

Ⓑ "Loroupe, though, has been surprising people with her talent for most of her life." (paragraph 1)

Ⓒ "Growing up in Kenya, Loroupe loved to race." (paragraph 2)

Ⓓ "Her dream was to become a professional runner, but she had to overcome others' negative attitudes about her goal." (paragraph 2)

2. Read this sentence from paragraph 5.

> Loroupe is an <u>inspiration</u> to all Kenyan girls who want to follow their dreams.

What does the word <u>inspiration</u> show about what the author thinks about Loroupe?

Ⓐ She has amazing talent.

Ⓑ She is a good influence on others.

Ⓒ She will probably win many more races.

Ⓓ She is not well known in many countries.

Reread/Think

3. What does the word unsupportive mean in paragraph 3?

Ⓐ cheering on

Ⓑ not knowing about

Ⓒ not providing help

Ⓓ giving assistance

4. What is the central idea of the text?

Ⓐ Tegla Loroupe is an amazing athlete who makes others want to succeed.

Ⓑ Tegla Loroupe started running when she was in school in Kenya.

Ⓒ Tegla Loroupe was told by many people that she should not run.

Ⓓ Tegla Loroupe was the first African woman to win the New York City Marathon.

Write

What is the author's perspective on Tegla Loroupe? Use details from the text to support your response.

WRITING CHECKLIST

- ☐ I described the author's perspective on Tegla Loroupe.
- ☐ I used details from the text to support my response.
- ☐ I used complete sentences.
- ☐ I used correct spelling, punctuation, and capitalization.

Respond to the Focus Question

How can sports bring out the best in people?

Reread/Think

Reread one text from the lesson. Then answer the question below.

TEXT: ______________________________

What did you learn from the text you reread about how sports can bring out the best in people?

____

____

____

____

____

____

Talk

Discuss the following questions about the people featured in this lesson's texts.

How did sports bring out the best in each person?

Which person or group do you think is most inspiring? Why?

Sports brings out the best in ___ when ___.

The person/group that is most inspiring is ___.

They are inspiring because ___.

Write

In this lesson, you read about people who participate in marathons and the people who support them. Who do you think is most inspiring? Why?

Heart of the Game

FOCUS QUESTION

How do sports make us feel?

NOTICE AND WONDER

Look at the titles of the poems you will read in this lesson. What do you notice? What do you wonder? Discuss your ideas with a partner.

WORD WEB

What are some words that describe how playing sports makes people feel? Add these words to the word web below. Then discuss your choices with the people in your group.

The sport ___ can make you feel ___. I think so because ___.

The Goal

by Janet Costa Bates

Notes from the Court

by R. J. Rocky

Basketball Rule #2 from *The Crossover*

by Kwame Alexander

Elm Park School, 7:00 A.M. from *Girls Got Game: Sports Stories and Poems*

poem by Christa Champion; edited by Sue Macy

The Goal

by Janet Costa Bates

1 Turn and glide
Grasp your stick
Guide the puck
To the net real quick
Now shoot

2 Left foot, right foot
Dribble that ball
Down the green field
Give it your all
Now kick

3 Strike one, strike two
Reset your stance
Be cool, be calm
You have another chance
Now swing

Stop & Discuss

What does each stanza describe? How do you know?

Point to words and phrases that give you clues. Discuss with a partner.

4 Stand tall, stand proud
This is your art
Run across the mat
Perform with your heart
Now flip

5 No matter your sport
Make it your **quest**
Win or lose
To be your best
Now play!

quest = a journey to reach your dreams or goals

Stop & Discuss

What message does the speaker want to share with the reader?

Talk about the message with a partner.

The message in the poem is ___.

SESSION 2 PRACTICE

SPOTLIGHT BENCHMARK: ELA.4.R.1.4 Explain how rhyme and structure create meaning in a poem.

Analyze Poetry

- Every poem has certain **elements**, or parts, that authors use to create the look, sound, and meaning of a poem.
- A poem's **structure** includes lines of text. The length of the lines can vary. The lines may be grouped into **stanzas**, or sections.
  - — The structure may include **repetition**, or the repeating of words and phrases. It may also include **alliteration**, or the repeating of sounds at the beginning of nearby words. For example, *buzzing bees* or *cats and kittens*.
  - — The structure may also include **rhyme**, or words that end in the same or similar sound. Rhyming words are sometimes used in a predictable pattern.
- As you read a poem, notice how all of its parts contribute to its meaning.

Reread/Think

Reread "The Goal." Then use the chart below to record information about the poem's line structure, including stanzas, repetition, alliteration, and rhyme.

Stanza and Line Structure	Repetition and Alliteration	Rhyme
Stanza 1: 5 short lines, no end punctuation	• Grasp, Guide	stick, quick
Stanza 2:		
Stanza 3:		
Stanza 4:		
Stanza 5:		

Talk

How do the elements of the poem "The Goal" work together to create meaning? Look carefully at the lines, repetition, alliteration, and rhyme and explain how they contribute to your understanding.

An example of repetition/rhyming words is ___. This creates an effect of ___.

An example of alliteration is ___. This helps me understand ___.

Write

How do all of the elements, or parts, of the poem work together in "The Goal?" Think about the lines, stanzas, rhyme, repetition, and alliteration. How does each part add to the meaning of the poem? What is the overall message of this poem?

WRITING CHECKLIST

- [ ] I explained how the lines, stanzas, rhyme, repetition, and alliteration add to the meaning.
- [ ] I explained the message of the poem.
- [ ] I included examples from the poem.
- [ ] I used complete sentences.
- [ ] I used correct spelling, punctuation, and capitalization.

Notes from the Court

by R.J. Rocky

1 Our sneakers *squeeeak*, drum, and creak.
Squeak, drum, creak. Screech, drum, squeak.
But I slow the dribble
at the top of the key,
and the sneaker song softens to a hum beat.
The slow dribble echoes—a bass drum solo.
I watch the defense roll like boulders down a hill
then stop.
Solid.
Unbreakable.

Stop & Discuss

What happens in stanza 1 of the poem?

Support your response with details from the poem.

2 But I am a roar—
a sonic-boom-boulder-busting force!
I ricochet right, left, into the cracks,
and the sneaker song surges like
cymbals crashing.
When I float the shot, it arcs to the rim
like a winged wish . . .

3 Bam. Blocked. Shocked!
My shot's denied.
I deflate and want to fizzle—flop on the
court and cry. But the game still flies,
no time for sighs. I am up and running.
Showing my team, *pass to me!* Because
I'm ready for another, and another, and
another TRY!

Stop & Discuss

What happens in stanzas 2 and 3 of the poem?

Support your response with details from the poem.

In stanza 2, the speaker ___.
In stanza 3, the speaker ___.

BASKETBALL RULE #2

(Random text from Dad)

from *The Crossover*

by Kwame Alexander

Hustle dig
Grind push
Run fast
Change pivot
Chase pull
Aim shoot
Work smart
Live smarter
Play hard
Practice harder

Stop & Discuss

What is the message of this poem?

Share your ideas with a partner.

Analyze Poetry

Poetic elements work together to create feelings, effects, and meaning in a poem.

- Another poetic element is **rhythm**, or a pattern of sounds similar to a musical beat.
- The use of repetition, alliteration, and rhyme can help create a poem's rhythm. The rhythm adds to the meaning of the poem.

Reread/Think

Reread "Notes from the Court" and "Basketball Rule #2." Then use the chart below to record information about the elements that help to create rhythm in both poems.

	Repetition and Alliteration	Rhyme	Rhythm
NOTES FROM THE COURT			
Stanza 1	sneaker song softens	squeak, creak	Squeak, drum, creak Screech, drum, squeak
Stanza 2			
Stanza 3			
BASKETBALL RULE #2			
Whole Poem			

SESSION 4 PRACTICE

Talk

What did you notice about the use of rhyme, repetition, alliteration, and rhythm in "Notes from the Court" and "Basketball Rule #2"? How do these elements contribute to the meaning of each poem?

The rhyming words ___ and ___ contribute to the meaning of the poem by ___.

The repeated sounds/ words ___ add to the meaning of the poem by ___.

The rhythm in ___ helped me understand that ___.

Write

Choose either "Notes from the Court" or "Basketball Rule #2." Describe the poem to a friend who has never heard it. Explain what you like about it and how the rhyme, rhythm, and repetition add to the meaning of the poem.

WRITING CHECKLIST

- [ ] I described how the poem uses structure, rhyme, repetition, alliteration, and rhythm.
- [ ] I explained what the poetry elements help me understand about the poem.
- [ ] I used correct spelling, punctuation, and capitalization.

Elm Park School, 7:00 A.M.

from *Girls Got Game: Sports Stories and Poems*

poem by Christa Champion;
edited by Sue Macy

1 better than gym class
better than recess
better than pizza for lunch—

2 not even ice cream
with fudge sauce
can top it—

3 nothing is sweeter
and no one
can stop it—

4 whenever I want
I can just stop
and pop it—

5 it's fresh
and it's smooth
on the playground it rules—

6 it just doesn't get
any better
than this—

7 my jump shot
as it drops
through the net
with a swish.

SPOTLIGHT BENCHMARK: ELA.4.R.1.4 Explain how rhyme and structure create meaning in a poem.

Respond to Text

Reread/Think

Reread "Elm Park School, 7:00 A.M." Choose the best response to each question.

1. What does the repetition of the phrase better than in the first three lines add to the poem?

Ⓐ It creates an image of the title of the poem.

Ⓑ It gives the name of the speaker's favorite thing.

Ⓒ It tells where the events of the poem take place.

Ⓓ It shows how much the speaker likes something.

2. How are stanzas 2–4 connected to one another?

Ⓐ They all talk about recess games.

Ⓑ They all begin with the same word.

Ⓒ They all end with a phrase that rhymes.

Ⓓ They all describe a favorite dessert.

3. Read these lines from stanza 5 of the poem.

> it's fresh
> and it's smooth
> on the playground it rules—

What is the meaning of the word rules as it is used in stanza 5?

Ⓐ to state a law or direction

Ⓑ to be seen as cool or excellent

Ⓒ to govern or lead

Ⓓ to make something impossible

SESSION 5 PRACTICE

Reread/Think

4. How is stanza 7 different from the other stanzas in the poem?

Ⓐ It is the only stanza with four lines.

Ⓑ It is the only stanza that has rhythm.

Ⓒ It uses more rhyming words than the other stanzas.

Ⓓ It uses more repeating sounds than the other stanzas.

Write

How do all the poetic elements of "Elm Park School, 7:00 A.M." work together? Explain how the line length, repetition, alliteration, and rhythm all contribute to the meaning of the poem.

WRITING CHECKLIST

- ☐ I explained how the poem uses structure, rhyme, repetition, alliteration, and rhythm.
- ☐ I included examples from the poem.
- ☐ I used correct spelling, punctuation, and capitalization.

Respond to the Focus Question

How do sports make us feel?

Reread/Think

Choose one poem from this lesson to reread.

POEM: ______________________________

What is the poem's message about sports? What words and phrases in the poem reveal the feelings that a player might feel?

____

____

____

Talk

Discuss your poem with two students who chose different poems than you. Explain the message of the poem you selected. Listen as they describe the message of theirs.

The message of ___ is ___.

The poet shares this message by ___.

Name:	Name:

Write

Write a poem about your favorite sport or another activity you enjoy. In your poem, describe what you do and the feeling you get from the activity. Include as many elements of poetic structure as you can, such as line length, rhyme, rhythm, repetition, and alliteration.

What Makes a Sport a Sport?

TALK ABOUT WHAT YOU KNOW

Use the pictures to recall the texts that you read in this unit. Turn and talk with a partner about what you already know about sports. Use the pictures and the sentence frames to help you.

Sports have changed over time because ___.

Sports can bring people together by ___.

Sports make people feel ___.

LESSON 15

Changing the Game

LESSON 16

Crossing the Finish Line

LESSON 17

Heart of the Game

A SPORT SORT

Circle the activities you think are sports. Then add your own examples of sports. At the bottom of the page, write your definition of a sport.

running	**basketball**	**board games**	______________
swimming	**chess**	**fishing**	______________

My definition of *sport*: ____

____

SESSION 2 READ

From Football

What Sports Are and Are Not

by Kathryn Hulick

1 It's the Super Bowl, the most exciting football game of the year. All around the United States, fans cheer in joy or groan in disappointment at every play. You know football is a sport, but what, exactly, makes it a sport? You may be surprised that sports aren't so easy to define.

2 Some activities are obviously sports. Many dictionaries define sports as activities involving physical effort, skill, and competition for entertainment. So, most people would agree that football and gymnastics are sports. These athletes must move and think quickly—very important skills. Teams compete against each other on the field, or individuals compete for high scores from the judges.

3 But it's not always easy to tell whether an activity is a sport. For example, when you play a board game with a friend, you are competing. But playing does not take much physical effort, and you sometimes need more luck than skill to win. So, board games have some but not all of the qualities of sports.

Stop & Discuss

What does the author think about football and board games?

Use details from the text to support your answer.

The author thinks football is ___ because ___.

She thinks a board game is ___ because ___.

to Fishing

4 Some activities are sports some of the time but not at other times. If you go swimming for fun in a lake, you are not playing a sport. This activity takes physical skill, but you aren't competing against anyone. If you were on the swim team, then swimming would be a sport because competition *is* involved. Similarly, driving a car to the store is not a sport. There's little physical effort involved and no competition. But race car driving *is* a sport. Drivers must use physical effort to control cars at high speeds. And the competition is **fierce**. Fishing is another good example. When a person goes fishing to catch food to eat, it's not a sport. But a fishing competition is a sport. **Participants** usually get points for the number, type, and weight of the fish they catch.

fierce = very strong

participants = people who join in an activity

5 Activities can also become sports over time. Some activities that were never considered sports before have become very sport-like because people enjoy watching them. For example, dancing, marble racing, and obstacle courses have become competitive sports that are fun to watch.

6 Still, there are some activities that you might *think* are sports, but that doesn't mean they are. For example, chess players or robotics team members develop many skills and must face challenges, just like athletes who compete in sports like softball or hockey. But are chess and robotics real sports? Who's to say? Defining sports is not a simple task.

Stop & Discuss

When does the author think swimming is a sport? When does the author think swimming is not a sport? Why?

Use details from the text to explain the author's ideas.

SESSION 2 READ

Chess: Board Game or Sport?

by Helen Walz

effort = hard work

1 The player moves her queen across the chess board. "Check!" she announces. The other player must protect his king or lose the game. Most people think chess is just a game, but it's more than that. Believe it or not, it meets all the definition of a sport; it requires skill, competition, physical **effort**, and physical training. In fact, chess actually *is* a sport.

2 Like other sports, chess involves skill and competition. Players spend hours practicing every day for years to become competitive players. Professional players each have a rank that rises or falls with each match. Big chess matches even have announcers who report the moves for fans watching from all around the world.

Stop & Discuss

What does the author think about chess? Why?

Use details from the text to discuss the author's ideas.

3 Chess also requires more physical effort than you may realize. Even though chess players sit down during matches, very long or challenging games can be tough on the body. In two hours of playing chess, one top chess player, called a chess grandmaster, burned 560 calories. This amount is equal to about one hour of playing tennis!

4 Like other athletes, chess players train their bodies for competition. Being physically fit helps the players stay alert and focused during a match. Chess trainers recommend that players eat healthy foods and exercise **regularly** to prepare for long matches. Fabiano Caruana, one of the top-ranked chess players in the world, is a great example. On a normal day of chess training, he runs for five miles and swims for an hour. He also plays tennis and basketball. "Physical fitness and brain **performance** are tied together," says Maurice Ashley, a chess grandmaster.

regularly = at certain times

performance = how well something works

5 More and more people now consider chess to be a sport. For example, in 1999, the Olympic Committee recognized chess as a sport. While no chess matches have been played at the Olympic games yet, it is only a matter of time.

Stop & Discuss

What is one reason the author thinks chess is a sport?

Underline at least one reason in the text and discuss the evidence that supports it.

Respond to Text

Reread/Think

Reread "From Football to Fishing" and "Chess: Board Game or Sport?" Then choose the best response to each question.

1. Which **two** statements describe the perspective of the author of "From Football to Fishing"?

Ⓐ It's difficult to figure out whether an activity is a sport.

Ⓑ Deciding which activities should be called sports is simple to do.

Ⓒ If an activity is a sport, it is always a sport.

Ⓓ Activities can become sports in certain situations or over time.

Ⓔ We should all agree on what makes an activity a sport.

2. Which statement **best** describes the perspective of the author of "Chess: Board Game or Sport?"

Ⓐ Chess is an easy game because players compete while sitting down.

Ⓑ Chess is a challenging game that requires a lot of training.

Ⓒ Chess is an exciting game because players exercise during a match.

Ⓓ Chess is a relaxing game that people play only for fun.

3. Read the sentence from paragraph 4 of "Chess: Board Game or Sport?"

> Chess trainers recommend that players eat healthy foods and exercise regularly to prepare for long matches.

What is the meaning of recommend as it is used in the sentence?

Ⓐ command

Ⓑ argue

Ⓒ suggest

Ⓓ complain

4. Fill in the bubble **before** the sentence from "Chess: Board Game or Sport?" that states the author's claim.

Ⓐ The player moves her queen across the chess board. Ⓑ "Check!" she announces. Ⓒ The other player must protect his king or lose the game. Ⓓ Most people think chess is just a game, but it's more than that. Ⓔ Believe it or not, it meets all the definition of a sport; it requires skill, competition, physical effort, and physical training. Ⓕ In fact, chess actually *is* a sport.

5. The author of "Chess: Board Game or Sport?" says that playing chess requires physical effort. Which detail supports this idea?

Ⓐ One top chess player trains by running five miles every day.

Ⓑ Chess trainers recommend that chess players eat healthy foods.

Ⓒ One top chess player burned hundred of calories during a match.

Ⓓ Chess players practice for years to become good enough to compete.

6. Fill in **one** bubble in each row to show whether each statement describes the perspective of the author of "From Football to Fishing," the author of "Chess: Board Game or Sport?," or both authors.

	Author of "From Football to Fishing"	Author of "Chess: Board Game or Sport?"	Both Authors
Chess is a competition.	Ⓐ	Ⓑ	Ⓒ
Physical fitness is linked to mental skill.	Ⓓ	Ⓔ	Ⓕ
Activities that were not sports can become sports.	Ⓖ	Ⓗ	Ⓘ

SESSION 3 PRACTICE

Write

State the author's claim in "Chess: Board Game or Sport?" Then describe at least two reasons and supporting evidence that the author uses to support the claim.

WRITING CHECKLIST

- ☐ I stated the author's claim.
- ☐ I described at least two reasons that support the claim.
- ☐ I provided evidence to support each reason.
- ☐ I used complete sentences.
- ☐ I used correct spelling, punctuation, and capitalization.

Make Connections

Reread/Think

Think about the texts you have read about sports. Also think about your own experiences. Why are sports important to people? Give three different reasons and use evidence from two texts and your own life to explain your ideas.

Why are sports important?	Evidence from the texts and my own life
1.	
2.	
3.	

Talk

Meet as a small group to discuss this question:

Why are sports important to people?

Sports can help people ___.

Sports can make people feel ___.

Sports can inspire people by ___.

Humans and Energy

LESSON 18

First Fires

344

LESSON 19

Sources of Energy

360

UNIT 6

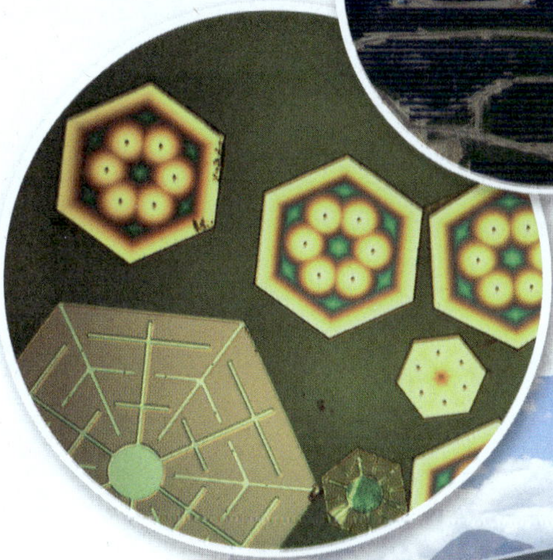

NOTICE AND WONDER

Look at the myths you will read in this lesson. What do you notice? What do you wonder? Discuss your ideas with a partner.

WHAT IS A MYTH?

Pick one of the words below and explain how it connects to myths. Add other words you know that connect to myths.

gods	explanation	nature	story
trickster	storyteller	tradition	ancient

The word ___ is connected to myths because ___.

Another word connected to myths is ___.

Maui and the Flaming Fingernails

by Amira Shea

Coyote Steals Fire: A Shoshone Tale

by The Northwestern Band of the Shoshone Nation

Prometheus's Gift

by Caleb Stanley

MAUI AND THE FLAMING FINGERNAILS

by Amira Shea

Maui is a hero and trickster in tales of the Maori people of New Zealand. He is a demi-god: part-god, part-human.

1 Long ago, the Maori people kept their fires always burning, because, if their fires went out, they would not know how to start them. Only the gods knew that secret.

2 Maui wanted to help the people. *If I could learn to make fire,* he thought, *things would be much better.*

3 So he formed a plan. That night while everyone was sleeping, Maui put out every fire in the land.

4 The next day his mother, Hina, commanded him to go see his grandmother, the goddess Mahuika, keeper of fire, and bring fire back to the people.

5 So Maui went to the burning mountain where Mahuika lived. The goddess, glowing orange, red, and yellow, listened to her grandson's plea. Then she plucked out one of her fingernails. Sparks flickered and popped inside it. "Use this to relight the fires," she said.

6 Maui nodded, but on the way home, he dropped the flaming nail into a stream, extinguishing its tiny flame. Then he returned to Mahuika.

7 "Grandmother," he cried, "the fire you gave me got wet!"

8 *Surely,* he thought, *she will teach me the secret of fire now.*

Stop & Discuss

What is Maui's plan?

Discuss details that help you understand what Maui wants and how he plans to get it.

* * *

9 Instead of teaching Maui the secret of fire, Mahuika gave him a second fingernail. He doused that one, too, went back, and got another nail. Maui did this over and over. Finally realizing that she had been tricked, Mahuika grew angry. She threw her next-to-last fingernail to the ground, starting a fire.

10 Maui tried to outrun the blaze. He changed himself into a hawk, but up in the sky the heat burned his wings. Then he dove into the ocean, but boiling water forced him out again. He begged the gods for rain, and they answered him with water that drowned the fire.

11 But Maui was not safe. Mahuika, still furious, chased the hawk back to the sky. Plucking out her last fingernail, she threw it at him. The flaming nail missed Maui and fell on five trees. The trees were pleased to receive Mahuika's gift of fire, and they held the sparks within their branches to keep fire safe from wind and rain.

12 Maui discovered that he could start a fire by rubbing together sticks from the trees. So, he brought home many branches and showed the people how to make their own fires. And that is how Maui brought back fire to the Maori people.

Stop & Discuss

Maui's plan works perfectly.

- ☐ agree
- ☐ disagree

Use details from the text to explain your answer.

SESSION 2 PRACTICE

SPOTLIGHT BENCHMARK: ELA.4.V.1.3 Use context clues . . . and/or background knowledge to determine the meaning of multiple-meaning and unknown words and phrases. . . .

Determine Word Meanings

- A story may include words you do not know. Context clues can help you understand the meanings of these words.
- **Context clues** are words, phrases, or sentences around a word that help you figure out the meaning of the word.
- Sometimes you can make an inference about a word's meaning. An **inference** is a conclusion based on details in the text and your own background knowledge.

Reread/Think

Reread "Maui and the Flaming Fingernails." Find each word in the story. Use context clues and your own background knowledge to figure out the meaning of each word.

Word	Context Clues	What I Know	Meaning
plea (paragraph 5)	Mahuika "listened to her grandson's plea."	Hina tells Maui to go see Mahuika and bring back fire. He must be asking her for fire.	a request
plucked (paragraph 5)			
extinguishing (paragraph 6)			
doused (paragraph 9)			

Talk

Choose a word from your chart to discuss with a partner. Tell about about the context clues and any inferences you used to figure out the meaning of the word.

> I figured out that ___ means ___.

> The context clues I used were ___. The background knowledge I used was ___.

Write

What does the word doused mean in paragraph 9? Explain how you used context clues to make an inference about the meaning. Then tell how the word helps you understand the story.

WRITING CHECKLIST

- ☐ I explained the meaning of the word doused.
- ☐ I explained how I used context clues to make an inference about the meaning of the word.
- ☐ I explained how the word helps me understand the story.
- ☐ I used complete sentences.
- ☐ I used correct spelling, punctuation, and capitalization.

Coyote Steals Fire:
A Shoshone Tale

by The Northwestern Band of the Shoshone Nation

Coyote, also known as Itsappe, is a trickster character in many Shoshone stories.

1 Every winter, Grandmother came to the *Moson Kahni* valley to gather with her people. There were hot springs here, and fish, game, and plenty of shelter. It was the old ones' time. Grandmother was a storyteller.

2 "Grandmother, tell us how *Itsappe*—Old Coyote—stole fire!"

3 "Oh, that's a good story. But remember, if you fall asleep during the story, we all go to bed."

4 "*Haa*" and "*hoo*," agreed the children.

Stop & Discuss

What do the children want Grandmother to do? What do you think will happen next?

Underline details that support your ideas.

* * *

5 Coyote was walking along and was tired of being cold. He called the animals together.

6 "Let's go to the desert lands in the south," he said, "and steal the people's fire."

7 "*Haa*" and "*hoo*," said the animals.

8 Coyote chose Packrat, Stinkbug, and Porcupine to go with him. The friends walked a long time. They watched the landscape change from pine to **piñon**, mountain to desert.

piñon = pine tree found in dry areas

9 Nearing the camp of the people in the south, Coyote searched for a disguise.

impress = to amaze or get attention from

10 "Those people don't need to know who I am," he said.

11 He tore off long shreds of juniper bark to make a wig. Packrat said he looked good.

12 They found the people dancing the round dance, so Coyote and his partners happily joined in. The girls thought Coyote was handsome in his wig, and that Porcupine's quill dress was very pretty. Stinkbug jumped up and down to **impress** them, but they didn't think he was good looking. They danced all night.

Stop & Discuss

Why does Coyote want fire? How does he try to get it?

Underline details in the text that explain Coyote's plan.

13 At dawn Coyote danced closer and closer to the flames, till suddenly . . . he set his wig on fire! Then the people said, "It's *Itsappe!* He's stealing our fire!" The animals ran for the hills, with the people right behind them.

14 First they caught the slow ones—Stinkbug and Porcupine. Packrat and Coyote ran and ran, but the people followed fast. When he couldn't run one more step, Coyote tossed the burning wig to Packrat. Then the people caught Coyote. Packrat kept running with the fire under his belly. He watched the landscape change from piñon to pine, desert to mountain.

coal = a piece of wood that is burning slowly

15 Finally, Packrat reached his nest, and by then the fire was a little red **coal**. He blew on it gently, added twigs, and soon he had a fire to share with all the animals.

16 They divided the fire in the four directions.

* * *

17 "Is everyone still awake?"

18 "*Haa*" and "*hoo*."

19 "*Kaan kwaisi yukwamitto'i,*" Grandmother said. "That's the end of the story."

Stop & Discuss

How does Packrat help Coyote?

Explain how Packrat helps Coyote in your own words.

Packrat helps Coyote by ___.

SPOTLIGHT BENCHMARK: ELA.4.V.1.3 Use context clues . . . and/or background knowledge to determine the meaning of multiple-meaning and unknown words and phrases. . . .

Determine Word Meanings

- A story may contain **multiple-meaning words**, or words that have more than one meaning. For example, the word *bark* can describe the outside of a tree or the noise a dog makes.
- When you read a word that has more than one meaning, context clues can help you figure out which meaning makes sense in the text.

Reread/Think

Reread "Coyote Steals Fire." Find each word from the chart and write a context clue that supports its meaning. Explain its meaning as it is used in the story.

Word	Context Clues	Meaning
springs (paragraph 1)	"Grandmother came to the *Moson Kahni* valley to gather with her people. There were hot springs here"	places where water comes up from under the ground
game (paragraph 1)		
round (paragraph 12)		
caught (paragraph 14)		

SESSION 4 PRACTICE

Talk

Choose a word from your chart to discuss with a partner. Explain how you used context clues to decide which meaning of the word is used in the story.

> In the story, the word ___ means ___.

> I know this because the context clues say that ___.

Write

Explain how you used context clues to decide which meaning of caught is used in paragraph 14. Then tell how this word helps you understand the story.

WRITING CHECKLIST

- ☐ I identified the meaning of caught used in the story.
- ☐ I supported my response with context clues.
- ☐ I explained how the word helps me understand the story.
- ☐ I used complete sentences.
- ☐ I used correct spelling, punctuation, and capitalization.

Prometheus's Gift

by Caleb Stanley

This story is a retelling of a Greek myth.

1 Long ago in ancient Greece, two families of gods, Titans and Olympians, lived in the mountains in splendid marble and gold palaces. Warmed by crackling fires, they ate honey-flavored food and drank sweet nectar. Yet, humans did not have these comforts and were miserable. They ate raw food and slept in cold, dark caves.

2 One Titan, Prometheus, felt sorry for humans. He traveled to Mount Olympus to speak with Zeus, ruler of the Olympians. "I wish to share fire with humans," Prometheus declared.

3 "Impossible!" Zeus shouted. "With fire, humans would become strong and independent."

fennel = a plant with feathery leaves

4 Determined, Prometheus formed a plan. While Zeus was asleep, Prometheus stole a glowing spark from Zeus's lightning bolt, hid it in a hollow stalk of **fennel**, and then gave it to humans. Prometheus showed humans how to use fire for warmth, cooking, and light.

5 Gazing down from Mount Olympus, Zeus spotted small bonfires blazing across the earth like scattered fireflies. "How dare Prometheus defy me!" he roared.

6 Furious, Zeus chained Prometheus to a large rock to punish him. For one thousand years, Prometheus suffered scorching sun, drenching rains, and howling winds. Eventually, Heracles, famous for his strength, freed him.

7 Prometheus's gift forever brightened the lives of humans.

SPOTLIGHT BENCHMARK: ELA.4.V.1.3 Use context clues . . . and/or background knowledge to determine the meaning of multiple-meaning and unknown words and phrases. . . .

Respond to Text

Reread/Think

Reread "Prometheus's Gift." Choose the best response to each question.

1. Read the sentence from paragraph 2.

"I wish to share fire with humans," Prometheus declared.

What does declared mean?

Ⓐ bragged

Ⓑ said with certainty

Ⓒ whispered

Ⓓ said nervously

2. In paragraph 3, what does the word independent help the reader understand about Zeus and his fear about giving humans fire?

Ⓐ The humans will not need him.

Ⓑ The humans will help the Titans.

Ⓒ The humans will injure themselves.

Ⓓ The humans will attack the Olympians.

3. Which meaning of spotted is used in paragraph 5 of the story?

Ⓐ saw or noticed

Ⓑ covered in spots

Ⓒ places or locations

Ⓓ gave money to

SESSION 5 PRACTICE

Reread/Think

4. PART A

How does Zeus discover that Prometheus stole fire?

Ⓐ Zeus sees Prometheus stealing a spark of lightning.

Ⓑ Zeus sees humans making their own fires.

Ⓒ Zeus sees Prometheus show humans how to use fire.

Ⓓ Zeus sees many small fires across the earth.

PART B

Fill in the bubble **before one** sentence from the text that supports the answer in Part A.

Ⓐ While Zeus was asleep, Prometheus stole a glowing spark from Zeus's lightning bolt, hid it in a hollow stalk of fennel, and then gave it to humans. Ⓑ Prometheus showed humans how to use fire for warmth, cooking, and light. Ⓒ Gazing down from Mount Olympus, Zeus spotted small bonfires blazing across the earth like scattered fireflies. Ⓓ "How dare Prometheus defy me!" he roared.

Write

Explain how you can make an inference using context clues to determine the meaning of defy in paragraph 5. What does this word help you understand about the story?

____

____

____

____

____

____

____

____

WRITING CHECKLIST

- ☐ I explained the meaning of defy.
- ☐ I supported my inference with context clues.
- ☐ I explained how the word defy helps me understand the story.
- ☐ I used correct spelling, punctuation, and capitalization.

Respond to the Focus Question

What do myths tell us about the importance of fire?

Reread/Think

Choose one myth from this lesson to reread. Then answer the question.

TEXT: ______________________________

What does the myth tell us about the importance of fire?

____

____

____

____

____

Talk

Discuss the questions below.

Why do some characters want to share fire and others do not?

Why do some characters use tricks instead of asking or fighting for what they want? Is tricking ever OK?

What is similar about all the myths? What is different about the myths?

Some characters want to share fire because ___.

Some characters use tricks because ___.

Write

Write your own myth about fire that follows a similar pattern of events as the myths in this lesson. Explain how a trickster character gets fire from someone powerful and shares it with others.

Sources of Energy

FOCUS QUESTION

Why have people used energy from different sources?

NOTICE AND WONDER

Look at the titles and images of the three texts you will read in this lesson. What do you notice? What do you wonder? Discuss your ideas with a partner.

TALK ABOUT WORDS

Circle the terms below that you know. Pick one term and tell a partner what you know about it.

energy renewable resources

fuel nonrenewable resources

waste fossil fuels

I think the word ___ means ___ because ___.

One example of ___ is ___.

First Came Fire: A Story of Energy and Fuel

by Jessica Miller

What Makes It Go?

by Stephanie Peters

Cool Solutions: Trash to Gas

by Danielle Jansen

First Came Fire

A Story of Energy and Fuel

by Jessica Miller

source = where something comes from

dung = animal waste

1 People have used fire for thousands of years to cook food, stay warm, and light up the dark. Fire is a powerful **source** of energy. But to make fire and use its energy, you need a fuel. So, for as long as people have been using fire, they have been looking for fuel.

2 People found that certain types of materials, such as wood, oil, and cow **dung**, could be burned as fuel for a fire. For a long time, wood was the main source of fuel for many people. But as more and more trees were cut down, people searched for other fuels and, finally, found something deep underground: coal.

Stop & Discuss

Why did people look for fuels?

Underline details that tell why people looked for fuels. Discuss the details with your partner.

FUEL USE

More than 400,000 years ago

People begin to control fire and use it for heat, light, and cooking. People use fuel such as wood and dried dung.

More than 3,000 years ago

Coal is first used in China.

1500s

Coal replaces wood as fuel in parts of Europe. As time goes on, coal is used by more and more people.

1821–1859

First successful natural gas well is dug (1821) and first oil well is drilled (1859) in the United States.

3 Coal is a fuel that looks like hard black lumps of rock. It formed over millions of years from dead plants that got buried under layers of dirt and rock. Pound for pound, coal gives off more energy when it is burned than wood does, and it burns longer, too. Coal continues to be used to heat homes, power engines, and generate, or make, electricity.

4 Natural gas and petroleum are other fuels that formed over millions of years from living things that died. In the 1850s, people in the United States started using petroleum, also called oil. Gasoline, which powers many cars and trucks, is made from oil.

5 Over time, scientists have learned that fuels such as coal and oil have **disadvantages**. Burning them pollutes the air, and they can't be replaced once they're used up. So, more and more people are turning to different sources of energy to power their homes, vehicles, and machines.

disadvantages = problems; things that cause difficulty

Stop & Discuss

How is coal helpful? How is it harmful?

Underline one way coal is helpful and one way it is harmful.

1880s

First electricity plants are built. The plants are fueled by coal. Electricity is used for lighting and for powering trains and other vehicles.

TOP ENERGY SOURCES IN THE U.S. IN 2019

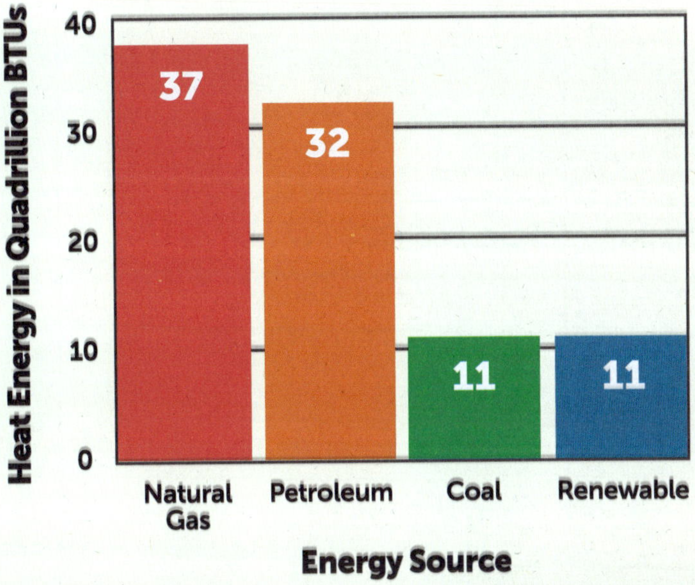

SESSION 2 PRACTICE

SPOTLIGHT BENCHMARK: ELA.4.R.2.1 Explain how text features contribute to the meaning . . . in texts.

Use Text Features

- **Text features** are parts of a text that stand out from the main body of the text. They can help you understand the main text and provide more details about the topic.
- **Visuals** such as photos, illustrations, graphs, and timelines help you picture information.
  - — A **graph** shows the relationship between numbers or amounts of something.
  - — A **timeline** shows a sequence of events over time.
  - — A **caption** is a short description explaining what a visual shows.

Reread/Think

How have wood, coal, and oil been used as fuel over time? Reread "First Came Fire: A Story of Energy and Fuel" and complete the chart with information from both the main text and the text features.

Fuel	Information from Main Text	Information from Text Features
wood	Paragraph 2: For a long time, wood was the main source of fuel for fire.	Timeline: Wood was used more than 400,000 years ago as fuel for fire.
coal	Paragraphs 2 and 3:	Timeline: Graph:
petroleum (oil)	Paragraph 4:	Timeline: Graph:

Talk

Discuss with your partner how text features helped you better understand how people have used wood, coal, and petroleum. Use each row of your chart to explain what you learned from both the main text and the text features.

> The ___ helped me better understand ___ because it includes ___.

> Long ago, ___. Now ___.

Write

How has coal been used over time? Use information from the main text and text features to support your response.

____

____

____

____

____

____

____

____

____

____

____

____

____

WRITING CHECKLIST

- ☐ I explained how coal has been used over time.
- ☐ I included information from the main text and text features.
- ☐ I used complete sentences.
- ☐ I used correct spelling, punctuation, and capitalization.

SESSION 3 READ

WHAT MAKES IT GO?

by Stephanie Peters

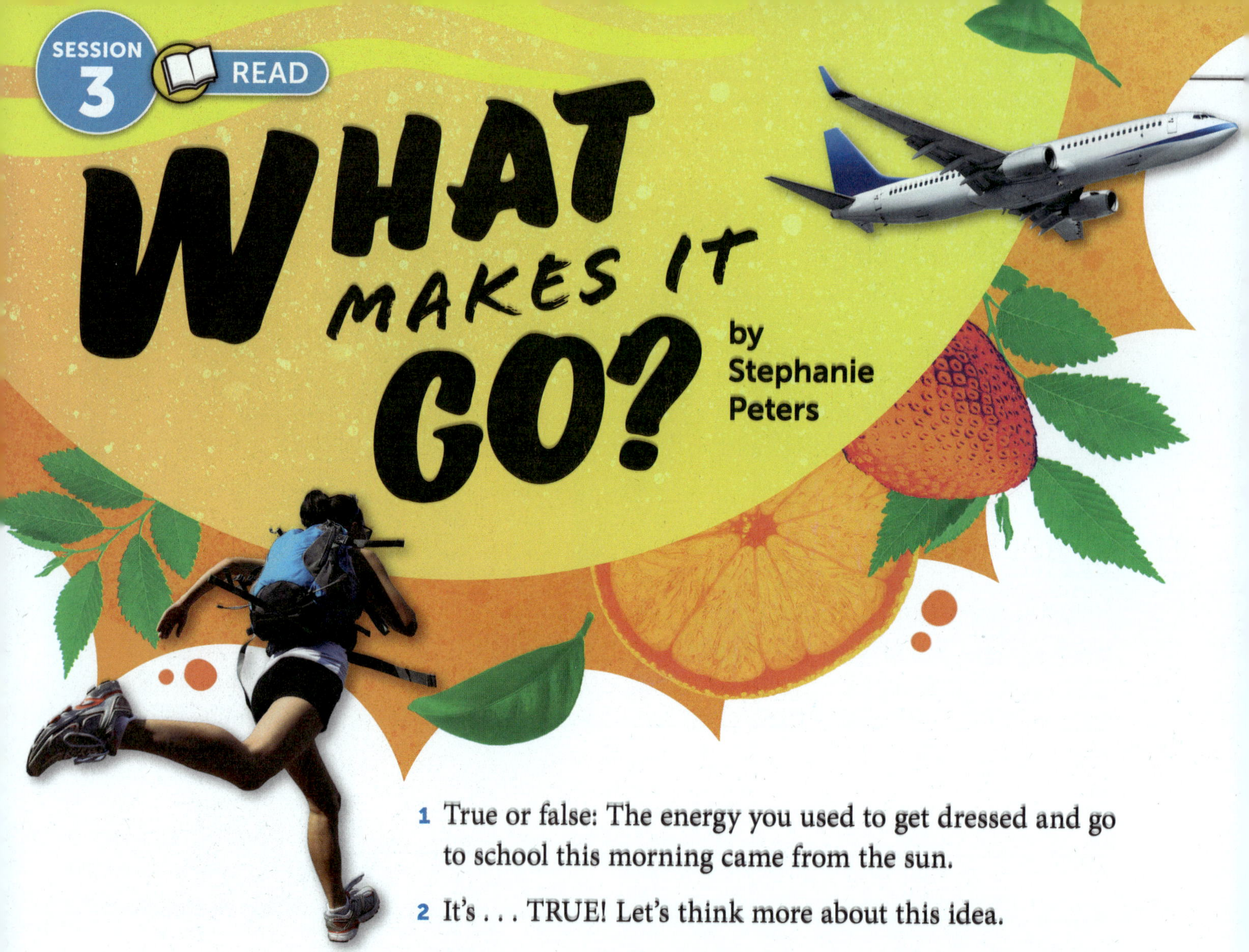

1 True or false: The energy you used to get dressed and go to school this morning came from the sun.

2 It's . . . TRUE! Let's think more about this idea.

3 Suppose you had orange juice and cereal for breakfast. The fruit in your juice and the grains in your cereal come from plants. The plants grew with energy from the sun. When you eat plants or food made from plants, your body turns that food into energy it can use to do things like get dressed.

4 But your body is not the only thing that uses energy from the sun. The bus or car you rode in to get to school also runs on energy from the sun. So do trains, ships, and airplanes. Do these vehicles use sunbeams for fuel? Not at all. Rainbows? Cool idea, but nope. To understand the sun's **role** in making the fuels of today, we need to know what was happening on Earth about 300 million years ago.

role = job that something does

Stop & Discuss

What uses energy from the sun?

Underline two examples of things that use energy from the sun.

From Ancient Plants to Power Plants

5 Back before dinosaurs lived, plants grew all over Earth. These plants used energy from the sun to make food for themselves. But once the plants and other living things died, sand and clay covered them, slowly turning to rock. Over time, more and more layers of rock formed over the dead things. The crushing weight of all this rock squeezed the dead material. Over millions of years, heat and pressure turned the dead material into fossil fuels.

power plants = places that use equipment and natural materials to make electricity

6 Fossil fuels come in three forms: a black rock called coal, a black or brownish liquid called petroleum (oil), and a clear gas called natural gas. (If fossil fuels are rocks, liquid, and gas, why are they called *fossil* fuels? Well, just like fossils, they formed from plants and other living things that died long ago.)

7 Some **power plants** use fossil fuels to make electricity, and people still burn fossil fuels to heat their homes. Gasoline, which is made from oil, powers most of the cars, buses, trains, and airplanes we use to travel. All the fossil fuels we burn come from plants that grew millions of years ago using energy from the sun.

Stop & Discuss

Which statement would the author agree with?

- ☐ Fossil fuels form slowly, but people use them a lot.
- ☐ Fossil fuels form quickly, and people use them a little.

Explain your choice to a partner.

HOW FOSSIL FUELS FORMED

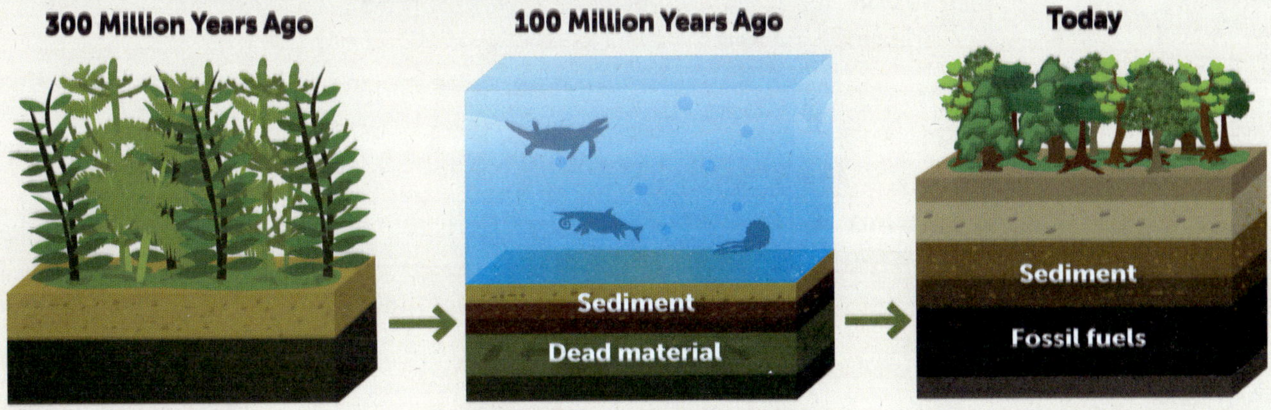

Plants used energy from the sun to grow. Eventually, they died.

Over millions of years, water and layers of sediment buried the dead plant material.

Heat and pressure turned the dead material into fossil fuels such as coal.

Fuel for the Future

8 Today, more than 80% of the world's energy still comes from fossil fuels. But petroleum, coal, and natural gas will not last forever, and they take millions of years to be replaced. They are nonrenewable resources. They also create pollution, which harms human health and the environment. So, people must find **alternative** sources of energy.

alternative = different

9 Renewable resources are one option. Renewable energy sources, such as **solar energy**, wind energy, and hydropower (water power), create less pollution and will not run out. When it is cloudy or calm, we don't have to wait long for more sun and wind. At least not as long as the millions of years it would take for dead animals or plants to turn into oil or coal!

solar energy = energy from the sun

10 People have explored different ways to use energy from natural resources for centuries. And every new discovery has affected the way people live. What will the energy of the future be?

RENEWABLE RESOURCES

ENERGY SOURCE	DESCRIPTION
 Solar	• Energy from sunlight • Can be turned into electricity or heat • Heats buildings, warms water, powers vehicles and tools
 Wind	• Energy from moving air (wind) • Can be used to generate electricity • Wind turns the blades of a turbine. The turbine spins a generator, which generates electricity.
 Hydropower	• Energy from moving water • Can be used to produce electricity • Flowing water turns a turbine to spin a generator, which generates electricity.

Stop & Discuss

What is the difference between renewable and nonrenewable resources?

Use details and examples from the text and chart to support your answer.

Renewable resources are different because ___.

Use Text Features

- Text features include words, images, or both.
  - — A **heading** is a word or phrase at the beginning of a section. The heading tells what the section is about.
  - — A **diagram** is a picture that shows what something looks like or how it works.
  - — A **label** is a word or phrase on a visual that tells what the visual shows.
  - — A **chart** often has rows and columns that organize information in a way that makes it easier to understand.

Reread/Think

What do the text features in "What Makes It Go?" help you understand about different energy sources? Complete the chart with information from the main text and the headings, diagram, and charts on pages 367 and 368.

Energy Sources	Information from Main Text	Information from Text Features
Fossil Fuels	Paragraphs 5 and 6: • Sand and clay covered dead plants and other living things and turned them to rock.	Heading: • Says that the section is about getting power from ancient plants. Diagram: • Illustrations, arrows, labels, and captions show how fossil fuels formed.
Renewable Resources	Paragraph 9:	Chart:

SESSION 4 PRACTICE

Talk

How do the text features help you better understand the differences between fossil fuels and renewable resources? Share the information from your chart with a partner.

> Something I learned from a text feature is ___.

> The text feature helped me better understand ___ by showing ___.

Write

What are some differences between fossil fuels and renewable resources? Use information from the main text and the text features to support your response.

WRITING CHECKLIST

- ☐ I explained the differences between fossil fuels and renewable resources.
- ☐ I included information from the main text and the text features.
- ☐ I used complete sentences.
- ☐ I used correct spelling, punctuation, and capitalization.

COOL SOLUTIONS: TRASH TO GAS

by Danielle Jansen

1 Lunch is almost over. You crunch into the last morsel of your apple. Then you toss your apple core into the trash bin. In a week or two, this trash will be dumped in a landfill, where the trash will remain.

2 In the United States, people throw away tons and tons of waste every year, and most of it goes to landfills. Can you guess the most common type of waste at landfills? It's not plastic, and it's not paper—it's food!

3 Food is a kind of organic waste. Organic waste is plant or animal material that breaks down over time. This waste takes up a lot of space in landfills, but imagine if it could be turned into something useful instead of sitting in a landfill, left there to rot.

banned = stopped allowing

4 Sweden has thought of one solution. In 2005, the country **banned** organic waste in landfills. What does Sweden do with all this organic waste, then?

SESSION 5 READ

HOW BIOGAS IS MADE

Organic waste is collected and prepared. → The organic waste goes in a big tank where bacteria break it down. → As bacteria break down the organic waste, biogas is produced. → Biogas is turned into fuel that powers vehicles.

5 The waste is taken to a plant, which is a place where something is produced. At the plant, waste is broken down by tiny living things called bacteria. When bacteria do this, they produce biogas. Biogas can be used as a fuel to power cars, buses, and other vehicles. In fact, biogas powers more than 200 city buses in Sweden!

6 But people don't stop at recycling food waste. Some have also developed plants that reuse animal manure from farms or human waste (poop) that gets flushed down the toilet. Why *poop*? Well, when poop breaks down, it can also create biogas!

7 Here's how it works: The waste that people flush down the toilet travels to a treatment plant. There, the waste is separated from water. Machines take this waste, remove and clean the water, and then release the water into the sea. What's left is lots of thick, muddy stuff called sludge. As the sludge breaks down, it makes biogas. The treatment plant uses biogas to make fuel for vehicles.

8 People are still looking for new ways to use waste. Maybe one day, all our trash will skip the landfill and become fuel.

Respond to Text

Reread/Think

Reread "Cool Solutions: Trash to Gas." Choose the best response to each question.

1. Which information is included in the diagram on page 372?
   - Ⓐ Organic waste takes up a lot of space in landfills.
   - Ⓑ Machines separate human waste from water.
   - Ⓒ Biogas can be used as a fuel to power cars, buses, and other vehicles.
   - Ⓓ The waste people flush down the toilet travels to a treatment plant.

2. What does the word common mean as it is used in paragraph 2?
   - Ⓐ belonging to all
   - Ⓑ appearing a lot
   - Ⓒ simple
   - Ⓓ general

3. Fill in the bubbles to show whether each detail describes information in the main text, in the diagram, or in both.

	Main Text	Diagram on Page 372	Both
Sweden does not allow organic waste in landfills.	Ⓐ	Ⓑ	Ⓒ
Organic waste is collected and placed in a big tank.	Ⓓ	Ⓔ	Ⓕ
Bacteria break down the waste, producing biogas.	Ⓖ	Ⓗ	Ⓘ

Reread/Think

4. How does the diagram on page 372 help the reader understand paragraph 5?

Ⓐ It shows the steps organic waste goes through to become biogas.

Ⓑ It shows the amount of organic waste needed to make biogas.

Ⓒ It shows how long it takes to make biogas with organic waste.

Ⓓ It shows how often the big tank is filled with organic waste.

Write

How do details from both the main text and the diagram on page 372 explain how waste is turned into fuel? Use at least **one** example from the text and **one** from the diagram to support your response.

WRITING CHECKLIST

- ☐ I explained how waste is turned into fuel.
- ☐ I included at least one example from the main text.
- ☐ I included at least one example from the diagram.
- ☐ I used complete sentences.
- ☐ I used correct spelling, punctuation, and capitalization.

Respond to the Focus Question

Why have people used energy from different sources?

Reread/Think

Choose one text from the lesson to reread with a partner. Then answer the questions using examples from the text.

TEXT: ______________________________

1. **What is one source of energy that people use, and how have they used it?**

____

____

____

2. **Why have people used energy from that source?**

____

____

____

Talk

Work with a new partner who has reread a different text. Share what you learned from the text that you reread. Use the sentence frames to get started.

People have used energy from ___ to ___.

People have used ___ as a source of energy because ___.

Write

Why have people used energy from different sources? Use information from at least two of the texts in this lesson in your response.

Solar Power

FOCUS QUESTION

Why and how do people use solar power?

NOTICE AND WONDER

Look at the three texts you will read in this lesson. What do you notice? What do you wonder? Discuss your ideas with a partner.

WHAT IS SOLAR POWER?

What does *solar power* mean? Circle the terms that are related to *solar power*. Discuss how the terms are connected to *solar power*.

solar panels

fossil fuels

solar cells

pollution

sun

renewable energy

___ said that *solar power* means ___. I agree/disagree because ___.

I think the term ___ is connected to *solar power* because ___.

Panda Power
by Mary Lindeen

From Race Cars to Solar Cells
by Alicia Terry

Powering a Community
by Theresa Liberatore

PANDA POWER

by Mary Lindeen

Ada Li Yan-tung explains her idea for panda-shaped solar farms.

1 In 2015, Ada Li Yan-tung was a 15-year-old Hong Kong student who noticed a problem. She was worried about how people use energy from burning fossil fuels and how this creates air pollution that hurts the environment. But her friends and other young people were not very interested in using other sources of energy. So, she thought of a creative connection between two very different things: pandas and solar panels.

2 Like millions of other people, Ada and her friends loved watching videos of giant pandas online. Whether eating bamboo or rolling in the snow, these black-and-white bears always seem so cute. They're also a national symbol of China and a global symbol of environmental protection.

3 Solar panels are an alternate energy source. But unlike pandas, they are not cute. And solar farms are big. A solar farm is made up of hundreds or even thousands of solar panels arranged together on open land. The good news is that one 32-acre solar farm can supply electricity to about 1,000 homes. However, these farms take up *a lot* of space. And some people think they're not much fun to look at.

4 Ada wondered if more people would support solar power if solar farms were more meaningful and more interesting to look at. Then she realized that the black and gray solar panels could be arranged to make pictures of pandas!

Stop & Discuss

Why did Ada connect pandas and solar power?

Use details from the text to support your answer.

The first Panda Solar Station was built in Datong, China, in 2017.

5 Ada presented her panda idea at a global **forum**. After the forum, the United Nations Development Programme contacted her and then connected her with a Chinese group interested in building her solar farms.

6 Two years later, China built its first panda-themed solar farm. From the sky, the carefully placed panels show pictures of two smiling pandas. The panels collect energy from sunlight and change it into electricity without burning anything. As a result, they generate renewable energy that creates less air pollution.

7 China has plans to build 100 of these panda solar farms. Meanwhile, Ada is helping other countries plan their own **symbolic** solar power farms. In Australia, for example, the panels form both pandas and koalas. Thanks to her creative solution, Ada Li Yan-tung is raising awareness about solar energy. She is showing one way people can reduce the use of fossil fuels and decrease air pollution.

forum = a meeting where people share ideas

symbolic = a shape or design standing for an idea

Stop & Discuss

Which statement best describes how people feel about Ada's idea?

Underline details in paragraphs 5–7 to support your answer.

- ☐ People like her idea a lot.
- ☐ People wonder if her idea will work.

SPOTLIGHT BENCHMARK: ELA.4.R.2.1 . . . identify the text structures of problem/solution . . . in texts.

Identify Text Structure

- **Text structure** is the way an author organizes information. Paying close attention to the text structure will help you better understand the text.
- A text with a **problem-and-solution text structure** describes a problem and the way it is solved. A text may describe more than one problem or more than one solution.
- Words such as *problem, solution, solve,* and *as a result* may signal a problem-and-solution text structure.

Reread/Think

Identify the text structure of "Panda Power." Then complete the graphic organizer by identifying the problems and how Ada solved them in each part of the text.

Type of Text Structure: ______________________

Problems (Paragraphs 1–3)		Solutions (Paragraphs 3–7)
Paragraph 1 Burning fossil fuels for energy hurts the environment.	→	**Paragraphs 3 and 6**
Paragraph 1	→	**Paragraphs 5 and 7** Ada is raising awareness about solar energy and has interested other countries in building solar farms.
Paragraph 3 Some people do not like solar farms because they're not fun to look at.	→	**Paragraph 4**

Talk

What problems did Ada want to solve in "Panda Power"? How did she solve them? How did signal words help you identify the problems and solutions? Share your ideas with a partner.

One problem was ___. One solution to this problem was ___.

The signal word ___ helped me ___.

Write

Explain how the author uses a problem-and-solution text structure to present the information in "Panda Power." Support your response with two examples of problems and solutions from the text.

WRITING CHECKLIST

- ☐ I described the text structure.
- ☐ I included two examples of problems and solutions.
- ☐ I used complete sentences.
- ☐ I used correct spelling, punctuation, and capitalization.

From Race Cars to Solar Cells

by Alicia Terry

Jose Luis Cruz-Campa built cars as a child.

1 Do you know what you want to be when you grow up? If you're not sure, don't worry. Just by doing activities that you love, you may already be preparing for your career, whatever that may be.

2 Just ask Jose Luis Cruz-Campa. He grew up to become an award-winning **engineer**. As a boy in Mexico City, Mexico, Jose spent hours building race cars with plastic blocks. He wanted to make his cars faster and stronger, but he had a lot of questions about how to do this. So, he experimented. "I would make cars and crash them, put them back together and crash them again," Jose remembers. Each crash helped him learn how to build better cars.

engineer = a person who uses science and math to design and build things

3 When Jose was in high school, he turned his attention to making paper airplanes. Jose and his classmates threw their airplanes out of the school's third-floor windows. They competed to see whose would fly the farthest. "I read books on how paper planes could be folded to fly faster and farther. I'd mix and match designs I found in the books and try them out," he remembers. Since he had worked so hard on his design solutions, Jose's airplanes usually won.

4 Even losses were helpful. "You have to have some experiments fail," Jose explains. Whenever a plane didn't fly well, Jose tried to figure out what went wrong. Once he identified the issue, he was able to make a better paper airplane.

Stop & Discuss

How did Jose's interest in cars and planes help prepare him for a career as an engineer?

Use details from the text to support your answer.

5 As an adult, Jose brought the same skills to his career. He has always been concerned about solving environmental problems, like air pollution. He wanted to work on ways to produce energy without harming the environment. So he chose to work on solar power projects. "We need more energy for our cars, our houses, and our computers," he says. "We can create energy from the sun without burning fossil fuels."

6 Solar panels use sunlight to generate electricity. However, they are large and expensive. Jose has worked on bringing down both the cost and the size. How? Solar "glitter." Jose designs tiny solar cells, called micro solar cells. They are about the size of a piece of glitter and thinner than a strand of hair. Despite their small size, they work really well. They are also less expensive to make than larger solar cells.

Stop & Discuss

What are micro solar cells? Why are they important?

Explain your ideas using details from the text.

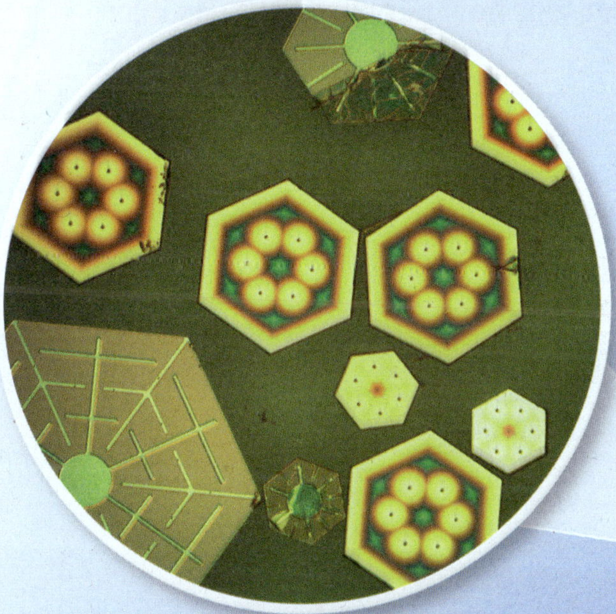

(Above) Micro solar cells as seen through a microscope

(Right) Jose Luis Cruz-Campa holding a container with solar panels made of micro solar cells

charge = to add electricity to; to power

7 Because micro solar cells are so small, someday they could be attached to many different surfaces, like clothing or tents. Then, as people walk or rest, the solar cells could **charge** things like phones, cameras, or flashlights.

8 Ever since he was a boy, Jose has loved finding new ways to do things. "Once you build something [as a scientist]," Jose observes, "you see that what you did helped people have something nice. You might see millions of people using what you made." Jose didn't realize it at the time, but doing what he loved to do—playing and problem-solving—gave him the skills to do what he loves today. "Even thinking about problems," he says, "is fun for me."

Stop & Discuss

How could people use Jose's micro solar cells?

Underline the text that tells how people might use micro solar cells.

People could use micro solar cells to ___.

Micro solar cells are so small they could be attached to your clothes.

Identify Text Structure

- Remember that a problem-and-solution text structure is organized to describe problems and how they are solved.
- Look for clues in the text that signal problems and their solutions. Words such as *issue, question, figure out, reason,* and *resolve* may signal a problem or solution.

Reread/Think

Reread "From Race Cars to Solar Cells." Identify the text structure. Then identify a problem in each of the paragraphs listed below. Finally, write the solution that Jose found for each problem.

Type of Text Structure: ______________________________

Paragraph	Problem	Solution
2	Jose was not sure how to build faster and stronger cars.	He experimented by crashing cars, putting them back together, and crashing them again.
4		
5		
6		

SESSION 4 PRACTICE

Talk

What problems did Jose solve in "From Race Cars to Solar Cells"? Share your ideas with a partner.

One problem Jose had was ___.

Jose solved the problem by ___.

Write

Describe the text structure of "From Race Cars to Solar Cells." How does this text structure help you understand what Jose did as a child and as an adult? Use details from the text in your response.

WRITING CHECKLIST

- ☐ I described the text structure.
- ☐ I explained what Jose did as a child and as an adult.
- ☐ I included evidence from the text.
- ☐ I used complete sentences.
- ☐ I used correct spelling, punctuation, and capitalization.

POWERING A Community

by Theresa Liberatore

The hot, dry lands of the Ute Mountain Reservation are a perfect place to capture solar energy.

1 Imagine living in a town or a city powered only by the sun. This may sound like a dream. But it may be a **reality** for a community in the Southwest.

2 The Ute Mountain Ute Tribe lives in southwestern Colorado, where they have been for thousands of years. Most of the 2,000 members live in a small town. But the tribe's reservation includes almost 1,000 square miles of desert.

3 For years, the Ute tribal leaders have been looking to provide more opportunities for their people. The leaders want to create more jobs and find more ways to support their people within the community. They also want to produce energy without polluting the air.

4 Because of the ideal **conditions** of their land, a solar power project seemed like a natural solution. So, the tribe began to plan. They set a goal to one day power their reservation with 100% renewable energy.

reality = fact; the way something is

conditions = the surroundings and climate of a place

grant = a large amount of money given to a person or group to use for a special purpose or project

5 The project was expensive. So, the tribe had to raise money. They applied for a $1 million **grant** from the government. The Utes received the grant, but the tribe also had to spend $1 million of their own money.

6 The money was used to build a small solar array. A solar array is a group of solar panels that work together to collect the sun's energy. The tribe's solar array, made up of about 3,500 solar panels, produces about 1 megawatt of power. This is enough electricity to power about 1,000 homes. The array was completed in September 2019 and is supplying about 10% of the tribe's electricity.

funding = money

7 Ute leaders believe this solar array is just the beginning. "We see this as a stepping stone to a much larger project," says Scott Clow, the tribe's environmental director.

Workers and volunteers begin construction of the Ute Mountain solar power project.

8 This larger project would be building a huge solar array that could produce 200 to 300 megawatts of power. All that electricity could power every home and building on the reservation, with a lot left over. However, the cost of building a huge array is a problem. The tribe would need $400–600 million of **funding**, which the tribe doesn't have.

9 Still, the Ute Tribe has hopes for the future. Bernadette Cuthair, a community leader who helped plan the first project, says, "Our tribe likes to think outside of the box and take risks." So, using solar arrays for 100% of their energy needs *is* possible. The only question is *when*.

Respond to Text

Reread/Think

Reread "Powering a Community." Choose the best response to each question.

1. How does the author organize the information in paragraphs 3 and 4?

Ⓐ in a descriptive text structure

Ⓑ in a problem-and-solution text structure

Ⓒ in a cause-and-effect text structure

Ⓓ in a sequential text structure

2. Why is the land around the Ute reservation a good place to make a solar power project?

Ⓐ There are many opportunities in southwestern Colorado.

Ⓑ The mountains will make the solar panels closer to the sun.

Ⓒ The community has 2,000 members who live in a small town.

Ⓓ There are almost 1,000 square miles of land in the sunny desert.

3. What does produces mean in paragraph 6?

Ⓐ makes

Ⓑ needs

Ⓒ sells

Ⓓ wastes

Reread/Think

4. According to the article, which is a possible problem with the solar power project?

Ⓐ It will create more pollution.

Ⓑ It will lead to people losing their jobs.

Ⓒ It will cost a lot of money.

Ⓓ It will only work when it is sunny.

Write

Describe the text structure of "Powering a Community." Include examples from the text to support your response.

WRITING CHECKLIST

- ☐ I described the text structure.
- ☐ I included examples from the text to support my response.
- ☐ I used complete sentences.
- ☐ I used correct spelling, punctuation, and capitalization.

Respond to the Focus Question

Why and how do people use solar power?

Reread/Think

Choose one text from the lesson to reread.

TEXT: ______________________________

What did you learn from your text about why and how people use solar power? Write one example of *why* people use solar power. Then write one example of *how* they use it.

1. Why: ______________________________

____

____

2. How: ______________________________

____

____

Talk

Share the example of solar power you wrote about. Then, as a group, discuss which idea about solar power you think is the most interesting, and why. How else could people use this idea?

The example that I wrote about is ___.

I think ___ is the most interesting idea because ___.

People could use ___ to ___.

Write

Which idea about solar power do you think is best? Explain the idea and how people could use it. Use information from the texts in your response.

Smarter Energy

TALK ABOUT WHAT YOU KNOW

Use the pictures to recall the texts that you read in this unit. Turn and talk with a partner about what you already know about humans and energy. Use the sentence frames to help you.

Humans need energy to ___.

In the past, people used energy to ___.

___ and ___ are types of energy.

LESSON 18

First Fires

LESSON 19
Sources of Energy

LESSON 20
Solar Power

WORD SORT

Underline words that name energy sources. Circle words that describe things that use energy. Discuss your thinking with a partner.

fuel		wood	light bulb
solar panel		car	electricity
coal	fire	sun	heater

Teen Inventor Captures the SUN

by Alice Cary

Kelly Charley is a teenage inventor.

1 Wouldn't you love a good excuse to skip your chores? Not Kelly Charley. Living with her mother and sister on her grandparents' farm in Arizona, she willingly helped with many different tasks. One of her most important jobs was heating her family's home.

2 Most winter evenings at about five o'clock, Kelly went outside to chop wood and load the pieces into a wagon. She also filled a bucket with coal and then carried the wood and coal inside. It was hard but necessary work, because her family used this fuel to heat their home.

3 When Kelly was about to enter high school, she began to worry. The school was 90 minutes away from her home, making it too far to travel each day. She would need to board at school during the week. But who, she wondered, would bring in the fuel each evening while she was away? Not only were coal and wood heavy, but when supplies got low her family had to drive more than 100 miles to get more. She hated the idea of her grandparents having to take over her chores.

Stop & Discuss

Why did Kelly worry about going away to school?

Underline details that describe her worries.

4 Even though finding heating fuel each day was a lot of work, Kelly's family had no choice. Their home, like one-third of the homes in the Navajo nation, doesn't have electricity. That means a lot of families face the problem of having to heat their homes with coal and wood.

5 The labor of collecting coal and wood every day wasn't the only problem that concerned Kelly. Burning coal and wood creates dust and smoke and can release harmful chemicals into the air. This pollution can cause breathing problems and lung damage. Kelly was worried about the physical **toll** this type of heating system would take on not only her family's health but also the Navajo community as a whole.

toll = damage or cost

Stop & Discuss

Why was burning coal and wood both necessary and possibly harmful?

Talk with a partner about its good and bad effects.

6 Growing up, whenever Kelly ran into challenges, her mother reminded her, "We can do this. We can do this ourselves." So, Kelly decided to work on a solution to the heating problem. For her science project, she planned to invent a new way to heat her home using solar power.

7 Kelly designed her heating system to be used in a traditional Navajo home, a round building called a hogan. She wanted it to work without any need for electricity or running water. "It was important for me to make my solar heater work with a hogan because I feel like I'm connected to who I am and where I come from," Kelly explained. "I've been able to say thank you back to the ones who have supported me."

antifreeze = a liquid added to water to stop it from freezing

8 Kelly's heater used a solar panel that was placed on the roof. The panel contained tubes of **antifreeze**, which were heated by the sun. These tubes connected to a large bucket of water inside the home. The antifreeze flowed through the tubes to heat the water in the bucket, which made the room warmer.

Stop & Discuss

How did Kelly's mother support her? What was the result of this support?

Underline details in the text.

HOW KELLY'S INVENTION WORKS

1. The solar panel on the roof contains tubes of antifreeze. The sun heats the antifreeze.
2. The heated antifreeze flows through the tubes into a bucket of water in the house.
3. The heated antifreeze heats the water, which heats the house.
4. The antifreeze runs back up to the solar panel on the roof.

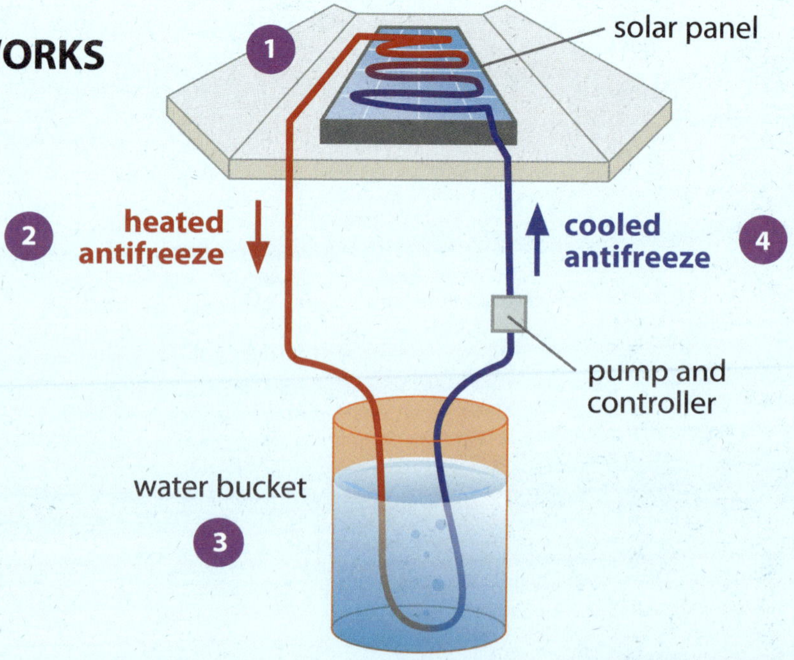

Kelly's heating system begins with a solar panel on the hogan's roof.

9 Kelly worked on improving her invention throughout her four years of high school. She entered her invention in national science contests and won many awards. But Kelly didn't build her solar heater to win awards. "I did all of this because I care and wanted something for my grandparents," she stated. "I was doing this for a purpose, and all those other things just came along with it."

10 By the time she graduated and headed to college, Kelly had decided to study **engineering**. She loved using science to solve problems. "There was a purpose behind what I was doing," Kelly says, "rather than just doing an experiment to do an experiment."

engineering = the work of designing and building machines or structures

11 Of course, no matter where she is or what she is doing, Kelly's Navajo roots will always be close to her heart. "We can still be connected to our culture. We won't have to stick to the old ways, but we don't have to let go of them, either," she said. "We can incorporate new technologies, and we can continue to develop and move forward with our culture." The addition of Kelly's new heating system into her community has brought not only greater ease for the Navajo people but also a healthier environment.

Stop & Discuss

According to Kelly, why did she invent her heater?

Discuss her reasons with a partner.

Kelly invented her heater because ___.

Respond to Text

Reread/Think

Reread "Teen Inventor Captures the Sun." Choose the best response to each question.

1. Read the sentence from paragraph 3.

> She would need to board at school during the week.

What does the word board tell about what Kelly would have to do?

Ⓐ She would need to travel to the school.

Ⓑ She would need to help repair the school.

Ⓒ She would need to build and heat the school.

Ⓓ She would need to stay and live at the school.

2. Which statement **best** describes a problem that Kelly was worried about?

Ⓐ The new heating system made the hogan too warm.

Ⓑ It would take four years for Kelly to finish her invention.

Ⓒ Burning wood and coal could be bad for people's health.

Ⓓ Kelly's grandparents wanted her to win a lot of awards.

3. Read the sentence from paragraph 5.

> The labor of collecting coal and wood every day wasn't the only problem that concerned Kelly.

What does the word labor mean in this sentence?

Ⓐ hard work

Ⓑ danger

Ⓒ high cost

Ⓓ pain

4. What is the purpose of the numbered descriptions in the diagram on page 396?

Ⓐ The descriptions explain why Kelly invented the system.

Ⓑ The descriptions explain how the solar panel was installed.

Ⓒ The descriptions explain how each part of the system works.

Ⓓ The descriptions explain why Kelly put hot water in the bucket.

5. Which **two** details are in the diagram on page 396 and **not** in the main text?

Ⓐ where the pump and controller are located

Ⓑ what the tube connects to inside the house

Ⓒ how the sun heats up the solar panel

Ⓓ how the tube bends to fit within the solar panel

Ⓔ where the antifreeze flows after it is heated

6. In paragraph 11, what does Kelly mean when she says the Navajo people can "incorporate new technologies"?

Ⓐ They can create new technologies by themselves without any help.

Ⓑ They can make new technologies a part of how they already live.

Ⓒ They can teach other people how to build new technologies.

Ⓓ They can be careful about how they use new technologies.

SESSION 3 PRACTICE

Write

What text structure does the author use in "Teen Inventor Captures the Sun"? How does the author use this text structure to organize the information? Use details from the text to support your response.

WRITING CHECKLIST

- ☐ I identified the text structure.
- ☐ I used details from the text to explain how the text structure is used.
- ☐ I used complete sentences.
- ☐ I used correct spelling, punctuation, and capitalization.

Make Connections

Reread/Think

In this unit, you have read about how people have solved problems related to energy. Which text do you think describes the best energy solution? Why do you think it is the best?

Text: ______________________________

My opinion: ______________________________

____

____

Text evidence that supports my thinking:

1. ______________________________

____

____

2. ______________________________

____

____

Talk

Discuss your opinion and the evidence that supports it with your group. Use the sentence frames to get started.

I think ___ because ___.

I agree that ___ because ___.

I disagree that ___ because ___.

Another reason that supports my thinking is ___.

Unit Assessments

Read the story. Then answer the questions that follow.

Drawing Conclusions

by Brooks Benjamin

1 Finn was the first student to get out his science book and **sketchpad**.

2 His class had been learning about biology, the study of living things, in science class since school started. Finn loved Ms. Kashif's class because he got to draw wild creatures, complex food chains, and detailed ecosystems. Finn loved putting his artistic talents to work.

3 "No science books today, everyone," Ms. Kashif said. "We're starting a brand-new unit. I want you to use the materials in the kits I give you to see if you can build a working **electrical circuit**. And here is a hint: Electric currents move through metal, including the metal in wires. Experiment with these items to see if you can get the bulb to light up."

4 Ms. Kashif placed a shoebox in front of Finn. Inside was a pile of junk: pieces of wire, a tiny lightbulb, an old battery, and other random objects.

5 Finn panicked. Why was Ms. Kashif doing this? None of the stuff in the shoebox had anything to do with plants or animals.

sketchpad = a book of blank pages for drawing
electrical circuit = a complete path that electricity travels through

6 He looked around, noticing everyone was already pulling things out of their kits, happily sticking them together like they knew exactly what to do. Finn slumped back in his seat, finding it harder and harder to stay calm.

7 "Everything okay?" Ms. Kashif said, kneeling by his desk.

8 Finn shook his head. "This is science class, but none of these things are living. I thought we were studying *living* things."

9 Ms. Kashif smiled. "Well, there are many different types of science. We're done with the Living Things unit for now, and today we're going to learn about another kind of science."

10 "I don't know about this kind. I'm good at the kind where we get to draw." The worry in Finn's gut grew so hot he was afraid his stomach would catch fire.

11 "Drawing can be a helpful tool for all kinds of science, not just life science."

12 *What is there to draw?* Finn thought. *There's only a pile of junk.*

13 "I'm not sure where to start," Finn admitted.

14 "When you draw, are your pictures always perfect right away?"

15 Finn shook his head. He *always* gave his eraser a good workout when he drew.

16 "The scientific process can be just as messy," Ms. Kashif said. "You'll need to try something and then adjust as you go. There are different skills and strategies people can use to get the bulb to light up. Drawing out your ideas for this could be a great way to begin." She tapped on Finn's sketchpad before walking to the next group of students.

17 Nobody else was drawing. Would he be wasting time? He thought about what Ms. Kashif told him, then flipped open his sketchpad to the first blank page.

18 Finn sketched out his first idea of how he might put the items together, keeping in mind that electric currents move through metal. He drew a little more, tried building it, erased some things, and started over. Every time he thought he had it, the bulb failed to light up. Finn had tried about every way he could imagine . . . except for one.

19 He sketched out his final idea and put the circuit together one more time. As soon as the last wire touched the battery, he let out a sharp gasp.

20 The lightbulb lit up!

21 He looked at Ms. Kashif, his mouth hanging open in a surprised smile. She smiled back, giving him a proud thumbs-up.

22 Maybe his teacher was right. If trial and error is part of both the artistic and scientific processes, then maybe his artistic skills would come in handy in all types of science after all.

Respond to Text

Reread/Think

1. Which sentence **best** summarizes paragraph 2?

Ⓐ Finn learns about food chains and ecosystems in biology.

Ⓑ Finn loves learning about biology because he gets to draw.

Ⓒ Finn draws living things because that is his only artistic talent.

Ⓓ Finn likes Ms. Kashif's class and learning about living things.

2. Read this sentence from paragraph 10.

> "The worry in Finn's gut grew so hot he was afraid his stomach would catch fire."

What does this sentence reveal about how Finn feels?

Ⓐ He is uninterested in building a circuit.

Ⓑ He is nervous about building a circuit.

Ⓒ He is sad to build a circuit.

Ⓓ He is excited to build a circuit.

3. PART A

Which inference about Finn is **best** supported by paragraphs 12–16?

Ⓐ He is upset when he learns the scientific process is messy.

Ⓑ He thinks the materials for the project are not useful.

Ⓒ He does not think drawing will help him solve the problem.

Ⓓ He rarely makes drawings he likes.

PART B

Which detail **best** supports the answer in Part A?

Ⓐ "*What is there to draw?* Finn thought. *There's only a pile of junk.*" (paragraph 12)

Ⓑ "Finn shook his head. He *always* gave his eraser a good workout when he drew." (paragraph 15)

Ⓒ "'There are different skills and strategies people can use to get the bulb to light up.'" (paragraph 16)

Ⓓ "She tapped on Finn's sketchpad before walking to the next group of students." (paragraph 16)

4. PART A

Read this sentence from paragraph 14.

"'When you draw, are your pictures always perfect right away?'"

Why does Ms. Kashif ask Finn this question?

Ⓐ She wants him to remember that his drawing skills need improvement.

Ⓑ She wants to show that drawing is unnecessary for the circuit experiment.

Ⓒ She wants him to stop drawing in class so he can pay attention to the lesson.

Ⓓ She wants to make a connection between the artistic and scientific processes.

PART B

Which detail **best** supports the answer in Part A?

Ⓐ "'This is science class, but none of these things are living.'" (paragraph 8)

Ⓑ "'I'm not sure where to start,' Finn admitted." (paragraph 13)

Ⓒ "'You'll need to try something and then adjust as you go.'" (paragraph 16)

Ⓓ "Nobody else was drawing." (paragraph 17)

5. Which sentence **best** summarizes paragraph 18?

Ⓐ Finn tries to build a working circuit, but he runs out of ideas.

Ⓑ Finn erases many of the sketches in his sketchpad.

Ⓒ Finn remembers that electric currents run through metal.

Ⓓ Finn continues to sketch and build until he has one more idea.

6. Which inference about Finn is **best** supported by paragraphs 19–22?

Ⓐ He is happy the experiment is finished so he can continue to draw.

Ⓑ He realizes people can solve problems in different ways.

Ⓒ He understands science is more important than art.

Ⓓ He decides he likes building circuits more than studying living things.

7. What is the meaning of the phrase trial and error as it is used in paragraph 22?

Ⓐ the act of trying different ideas to find one that works

Ⓑ the process of asking others for help with a problem

Ⓒ the act of appearing in court and being found not guilty

Ⓓ the process of finding one specific way of doing something

8. **PART A**

How does Finn respond to the problem in the story?

Ⓐ Finn tries drawing but decides that it will not help build the circuit.

Ⓑ Finn thinks he cannot use drawing and ignores Ms. Kashif's advice.

Ⓒ Finn does not see anyone else drawing but decides to draw anyway.

Ⓓ Finn uses drawing to complete the circuit to prove Ms. Kashif wrong.

PART B

Which detail **best** supports the answer to Part A?

Ⓐ "He *always* gave his eraser a good workout when he drew." (paragraph 15)

Ⓑ "He . . . flipped open his sketchpad to the first blank page." (paragraph 17)

Ⓒ "As soon as the last wire touched the battery, he let out a sharp gasp." (paragraph 19)

Ⓓ "He looked at Ms. Kashif, his mouth hanging open in a surprised smile." (paragraph 21)

9. Based on the story, which sentence **best** describes Ms. Kashif?

Ⓐ She wants to help Finn improve his drawing and sketching skills.

Ⓑ She wants to stop Finn from interrupting his classmates.

Ⓒ She thinks it is important to know how electric circuits work.

Ⓓ She thinks people can use different strategies to solve a problem.

10. **SHORT RESPONSE** What is the theme of "Drawing Conclusions"? How does the theme develop in the story? Use details from the story to support your response.

____

____

____

____

____

____

____

____

____

____

11. Which detail is **most** important to include in a summary of the story?

Ⓐ Finn's class had been learning about biology.

Ⓑ Finn always uses his eraser when he draws.

Ⓒ Finn successfully puts the electrical circuit together.

Ⓓ Ms. Kashif smiles at Finn after he finishes the circuit.

12. Which detail is **most** important to the plot of the story?

Ⓐ Finn's class has moved from studying living things to building circuits.

Ⓑ Materials include wires, a lightbulb, and a battery.

Ⓒ Finn likes biology because he can draw pictures of living things.

Ⓓ Finn's teacher, Ms. Kashif, suggests that he draw his ideas for a circuit.

Write

EXTENDED RESPONSE What conflict does Finn experience in "Drawing Conclusions"? How does he respond to the conflict, and what does he learn? Include details about the setting, events, and characters in your response.

WRITING CHECKLIST

- ☐ I described the conflict in the story and how Finn responds to it.
- ☐ I included details about the setting, events, and characters to support my response.
- ☐ I used complete sentences.
- ☐ I used correct spelling, punctuation, and capitalization.

Read the passage. Then answer the questions that follow.

Up, Up, and Away!

by Catherine Graham

Launch a simple rocket with these materials. Ask a grown-up to help.

MATERIALS

- 1 empty plastic bottle (quart or liter)
- 1 sheet of paper towel
- 1 thumbtack
- 1/2 cup vinegar
- 1 cork
- 3 4-inch **streamers**
- 1/2 cup water
- 1 tablespoon baking soda

STEP 1 First, transport the materials outside and set them up where there is plenty of space.

STEP 2 Second, inspect the cork and make sure it will fit tightly into the bottle. If it is too tight, ask an adult for assistance in trimming the cork with a knife. If it is too loose, wrap pieces of paper towel around the cork until it will fit snugly in the top of the bottle. Then attach streamers to the top of the cork with the thumbtack and leave the cork to the side. The cork is the rocket.

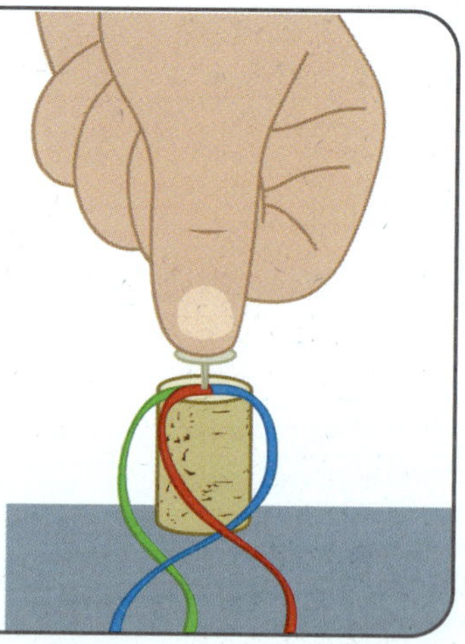

streamers = long pieces of ribbon or paper

STEP 3 After preparing the cork, put water and the vinegar into the bottle.

Optional: Consider using a funnel to limit spilling if you have one available.

STEP 4 Next, cut a 4-inch by 4-inch piece of paper towel, and put the baking soda in the center. Twist the ends of the paper towel to keep the baking soda in.

STEP 5 Then, drop the paper-towel-wrapped baking soda into the bottle and fit the cork into the bottle top. Set the bottle upright far away from people.

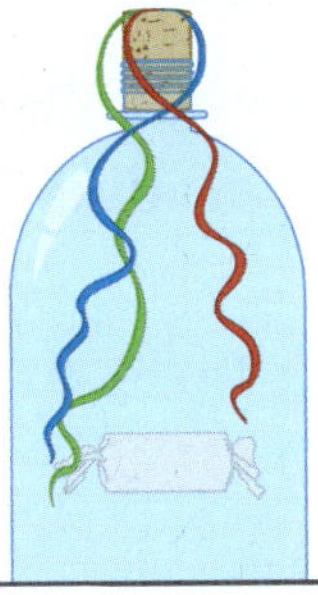

STEP 6 The last step is to WAIT. Do not be impatient. The liquid will soak through the paper towel. Then the vinegar will react with the baking soda and produce **carbon dioxide** gas. As gas forms, pressure will build up inside the bottle. Finally, the cork, or rocket, will fly out of the bottle. Use the ribbons to trace the cork's path as it soars through the sky.

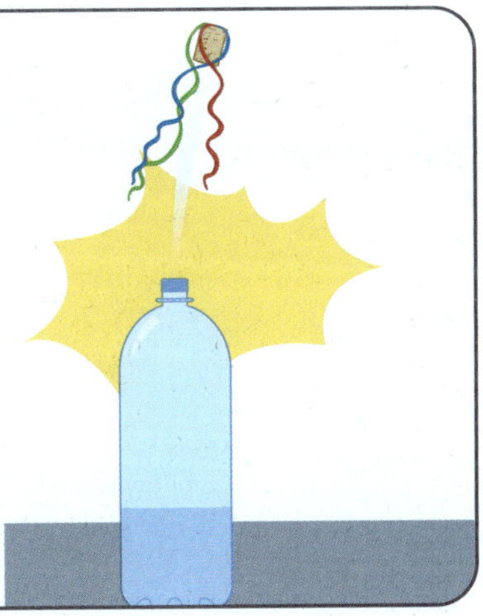

carbon dioxide = gas made up of carbon and oxygen

Respond to Text

Reread/Think

1. Read this sentence from Step 1.

> "First, transport the materials outside and set them up where there is plenty of space."

Using knowledge of word parts, what is the meaning of transport?

Ⓐ keep

Ⓑ gather

Ⓒ make new

Ⓓ carry across

2. Why does Step 5 suggest setting the bottle "upright far away from people"?

Ⓐ to make sure the vinegar does not spill

Ⓑ to make it easier to take a good picture

Ⓒ to stop the cork from hitting someone

Ⓓ to let air flow around and into the bottle

3. The word impatient in Step 6 has the prefix *im-* and the base word *patient*. Based on these word parts, what does impatient **most likely** mean?

Ⓐ willing to wait

Ⓑ waiting for a long time

Ⓒ not willing to wait

Ⓓ making someone wait

4. What is the meaning of the word soars as it is used in Step 6?

Ⓐ flies or glides

Ⓑ drops

Ⓒ explodes

Ⓓ draws a line

5. PART A

Which **best** describes the structure of this passage?

Ⓐ sequential text structure

Ⓑ descriptive text structure

Ⓒ problem-and-solution text structure

Ⓓ compare-and-contrast text structure

PART B

Which sentence contains a signal word or phrase that **best** supports the answer to Part A?

Ⓐ "If it is too tight, ask an adult for assistance in trimming the cork with a knife." (Step 2)

Ⓑ "Next, cut a 4-inch by 4-inch piece of paper towel, and put the baking soda in the center." (Step 4)

Ⓒ "Twist the ends of the paper towel to keep the baking soda in." (Step 4)

Ⓓ "Use the ribbons to trace the cork's path as it soars through the sky." (Step 6)

6. How does the text structure add to the meaning of the passage?

Ⓐ It provides examples of the central idea.

Ⓑ It describes details about a topic.

Ⓒ It tells what to do in a certain order.

Ⓓ It shows how a problem was solved.

7. Fill in **one** bubble in each row to show the order of the actions.

	First	Then	Finally
combine water and vinegar	Ⓐ	Ⓑ	Ⓒ
drop baking soda in the bottle	Ⓓ	Ⓔ	Ⓕ
set up and prepare materials	Ⓖ	Ⓗ	Ⓘ

Read the passage. Then answer the questions that follow.

READY FOR LIFTOFF!

by Beth Bohac and Jim O'Leary

1 Robert Goddard, born in 1882, was always interested in science and technology. His parents gave him a telescope when he was a child, allowing him to view distant stars and planets. He dreamed of sending a rocket into space long before the United States formed the National Aeronautics and Space Administration (NASA) to explore space. Goddard tried new experiments and read everything he could about space. Most of his experiments were failures, and at times he was mocked and misjudged for his ideas. But Goddard never gave up. He was convinced that space travel was possible, and he turned out to be right.

2 On March 16, 1926, Goddard prepared to launch one of his many test rockets. To make the rocket lighter so that it could travel farther, he did something new. Instead of using solid fuel, such as coal, he used liquid fuel. He and his crew lit the **fuse**, and then waited breathlessly. At first nothing happened. Then suddenly the rocket lifted off the pad.

3 The rocket rose only 41 feet into the sky at the speed of 60 miles per hour. The whole flight lasted only two and a half seconds, but it was the beginning of modern rocket science. The idea behind Goddard's invention would someday lift enormous rockets into space.

4 In a liquid-fueled rocket, two liquids mix and start a fire in a small **combustion chamber**. Except for the combustion chamber, the body of a liquid-fueled rocket is thin and light, but it is also strong. Goddard believed that this type of rocket could be produced to reach the moon.

fuse = a cord for lighting explosives

combustion chamber = a container for burning things

5 Goddard's work, however, brought him problems. Newspapers didn't publish stories about his rockets' successful flights. They often wrote about the disastrous ones that malfunctioned. Many people thought his work and interest in space travel were nonsense. People laughed at Goddard and called him the "Moon Man."

6 These stories, however, caught the attention of Charles Lindbergh, a famous pilot. Despite public doubt, Lindbergh understood Goddard's dream. He became Goddard's benefactor, giving him money to help pay for his work. It was expensive to build and rebuild rockets to test. For the first time, Goddard had enough money to work on his experiments full-time.

7 Robert Goddard never gave up on his dream, and his ideas have been a great benefit to astronauts everywhere. Today's spacecrafts use more than 200 parts that are based on his designs. NASA's Goddard Space Flight Center in Maryland is even named after him. Instead of "Moon Man," Robert Goddard is now known as the "Father of Modern Rocketry."

Robert Goddard holds the launch frame for a rocket of his own design, on March 16, 1926.

Respond to Text

Reread/Think

1. Read this sentence from paragraph 1.

> "His parents gave him a telescope when he was a child, allowing him to view distant stars and planets."

Telescope has two word parts, *tele-* and *scope*. *Scope* means "to see." Which **best** describes what a telescope allowed Goddard to do?

Ⓐ see many colors

Ⓑ see small objects

Ⓒ see clearly

Ⓓ see far

2. Read this sentence from paragraph 2.

> "He and his crew lit the fuse, and then waited breathlessly."

Breathlessly has three word parts: *breath, -less,* and *-ly.* Using what you know about word parts, what does the word breathlessly **most likely** mean?

Ⓐ done while holding your breath

Ⓑ done while not talking

Ⓒ done while taking deep breaths or breathing hard

Ⓓ done while not having enough air or oxygen

3. SHORT RESPONSE Read this sentence from paragraph 6.

> "He became Goddard's benefactor, giving him money to help pay for his work."

In the word benefactor, the Greek root *bene* means "well" or "good." What does the word benefactor mean? Explain how identifying word parts helps readers understand the word's meaning in this sentence.

4. PART A

Which sentence **best** states the central idea of the passage?

Ⓐ Goddard's failed rocket launches caused people to call him "Moon Man."

Ⓑ On March 26, 1926, Goddard used liquid fuel to launch a rocket 41 feet into the air.

Ⓒ Goddard's experiments were important to the future of modern rocket science.

Ⓓ Goddard used liquid-filled engines to lift giant rockets into space.

PART B

Which detail from the text **best** supports the answer in Part A?

Ⓐ "To make the rocket lighter so that it could travel farther, he did something new." (paragraph 2)

Ⓑ "The rocket rose only 41 feet into the sky at the speed of 60 miles per hour." (paragraph 3)

Ⓒ "These stories, however, caught the attention of Charles Lindbergh, a famous pilot." (paragraph 6)

Ⓓ "Today's spacecrafts use more than 200 parts that are based on his designs." (paragraph 7)

5. Which **two** details **best** support the central idea of the passage?

Ⓐ Goddard was born in 1882, long before anyone knew anything about space.

Ⓑ Goddard was the first person to use liquid fuel to make a lighter rocket.

Ⓒ Newspapers didn't publish stories about Goddard's rockets' successful flights.

Ⓓ Goddard gained the attention of Charles Lindbergh, a famous pilot.

Ⓔ Goddard is known as the "Father of Modern Rocketry."

6. What can readers infer from paragraphs 5–6?

Ⓐ Not many people originally believed in Goddard's work.

Ⓑ Goddard had a successful career working at NASA.

Ⓒ Goddard preferred the nickname "Moon Man."

Ⓓ Rocket parts have stayed the same since Goddard's time.

Write

EXTENDED RESPONSE Write a summary of the passage. Include the central idea and relevant details.

WRITING CHECKLIST

- ☐ I included the central idea of the text.
- ☐ I included relevant details that support the central idea.
- ☐ I explained who Robert Goddard is and what he did.
- ☐ I used complete sentences.
- ☐ I used correct spelling, punctuation, and capitalization.

Read the story. Then answer the questions that follow.

Waterfront Worries

by Janet Costa Bates

1 *I should have stayed home,* Jaxon thought. He gripped the side of the boat as he boarded it. His class was going on a tour of a lighthouse for their field trip. It was very exciting, except for one thing—the only way to get to the lighthouse was by boat. Jaxon had never been on a boat before, and the thought of traveling across the bay was making his knees weak.

2 *What if the boat springs a leak?* he wondered. *What if, suddenly, a storm pops up, with lightning, thunder, and even hail?*

3 His classmates were all laughing and joking as they grabbed their **life jackets**, but Jaxon wasn't even smiling. He was a stone sinking in a sea of worry. Their tour guide, Chris, introduced herself, shared some safety tips, and told them a little bit about the history of the lighthouse. Jaxon could barely hear her over the moaning and groaning of the boat as it left the dock.

4 When Chris was done speaking, Jaxon walked over and asked quietly, "How do we know nothing will go wrong with the boat?"

life jackets = jackets or vests that keep a person afloat

5 Chris gave Jaxon a **reassuring** smile, and then she pointed to a large tree along the rocky coastline. "This boat is as strong as that oak over there." Then, motioning in the direction toward the lighthouse, she said, "And look out there. You can see the lighthouse from here, and we will be there before you know it."

6 As Jaxon looked out at the lighthouse, he saw the sunlight hop and dance on the water. He took a deep breath—the smell of saltwater and fresh air filled his lungs. The ocean breeze began to melt away Jaxon's fears. He took another deep breath, and the butterflies in his stomach disappeared. Instead of worrying about what could happen, Jaxon began to appreciate what was happening. Surrounded by clear skies and sparkling blue water, Jaxon joined his classmates at the **bow** of the boat to admire the view.

reassuring = comforting

bow = front part of a boat

Respond to Text

Reread/Think

1. What is the meaning of <u>boarded</u> as it is used in paragraph 1?

Ⓐ carried a board

Ⓑ received daily meals

Ⓒ tightly held on to

Ⓓ got into or on

2. **SHORT RESPONSE** Read this sentence from paragraph 3.

> "Jaxon could barely hear her over the moaning and groaning of the boat as it left the dock."

What kind of figurative language is this, and how does it help readers understand the story?

3. PART A

Which detail from the story contains a simile?

Ⓐ "Jaxon had never been on a boat before, and the thought of traveling across the bay was making his knees weak." (paragraph 1)

Ⓑ "His classmates were all laughing and joking as they grabbed their life jackets, but Jaxon wasn't even smiling." (paragraph 3)

Ⓒ "'This boat is as strong as that oak over there.'" (paragraph 5)

Ⓓ "The ocean breeze began to melt away Jaxon's fears." (paragraph 6)

PART B

How does the simile in Part A help readers understand the story?

Ⓐ It explains how Jaxon is feeling.

Ⓑ It describes how steady and safe the boat is.

Ⓒ It shows how excited everyone is to ride the boat.

Ⓓ It tells how Jaxon is affected by the fresh air.

4. PART A

Which detail from the story contains a metaphor?

Ⓐ "His class was going on a tour of a lighthouse for their field trip." (paragraph 1)

Ⓑ "He was a stone sinking in a sea of worry." (paragraph 3)

Ⓒ ". . . then she pointed to a large tree along the rocky coastline." (paragraph 5)

Ⓓ ". . . Jaxon joined his classmates at the bow of the boat to admire the view." (paragraph 6)

PART B

What does the metaphor in Part A help readers understand?

Ⓐ where the field trip takes place

Ⓑ how a character feels

Ⓒ what the setting looks like

Ⓓ how a character acts

5. Fill in the bubble **before one** sentence in paragraph 6 that shows personification.

Ⓐ As Jaxon looked out at the lighthouse, he saw the sunlight hop and dance on the water. Ⓑ He took a deep breath—the smell of saltwater and fresh air filled his lungs. Ⓒ The ocean breeze began to melt away Jaxon's fears. Ⓓ He took another deep breath, and the butterflies in his stomach disappeared.

6. What lesson does Jaxon learn at the end of the story?

Ⓐ Traveling by boat can be quick and easy.

Ⓑ It is important to follow boating safety rules.

Ⓒ Worrying can prevent a person from enjoying themselves.

Ⓓ The ocean can be both beautiful and dangerous.

Read both passages. Then answer the questions that follow.

Passage 1:

from Ferris's GRAND Idea

by Marcia Amidon Lusted

1 Daniel Burnham needed a good idea. He was one of Chicago's best building designers, but he was **stumped**. A huge fair was going to be held in Chicago in 1893. It was called the World's Columbian Exposition, and it needed a special attraction—something that would bring thousands of visitors. Burnham knew this attraction had to be even more amazing than the Eiffel Tower, built a few years earlier in Paris, France. Burnham wanted to show the world that America's **engineers** were more talented than France's. He told a group of engineers at a dinner that "something original, daring, and unique must be designed and built" in order to "out-Eiffel" the 1,063-foot metal tower. The Eiffel Tower was built for the International Exposition held in Paris in 1889.

2 George Washington Gale Ferris, a young engineer from Pittsburgh, Pennsylvania, was at the banquet that night. Ferris remembered an idea he had been working on. He scribbled the design on his dinner napkin. It was something that had never been done before. It would be a giant, rotating wheel, 250 feet wide and 264 feet high. It would hold more than 2,000 people in 36 **coaches** attached to the wheel's rim. Each coach would be as large as a bus and would hold 40 to 60 people. Burnham loved the idea!

stumped = unable to find an answer

engineers = people who design machines or structures

coaches = passenger cars with doors

3 The wheel was not finished in time for the fair's opening day on May 1. But by June the engineers were testing it. On the first day of testing with passengers aboard, crowds of onlookers refused to stand back. Instead, they rushed the wheel and climbed into the coaches for the 20-minute ride. The first ten minutes were spent getting passengers off and on. This was followed by a 10-minute single turn of the wheel. Ferris's grand idea was a huge success. It quickly became the highlight of the fair.

4 A ride on the Ferris wheel cost 50 cents, the same as the price to get into the fair itself. The huge wheel had cost $400,000 to build and operate during the fair. That was an enormous amount of money in those days. But the wheel's total earnings were more than $700,000, making a nice **profit** for everyone involved.

5 After the fair closed in October of 1893, the wheel was taken down. It was used several more times in other places, including at the St. Louis World's Fair in 1904. But two years later it was sold and turned into scrap metal.

6 Today there are Ferris wheels at almost every amusement park and carnival. So if you find yourself sitting at the top of one of these rides, enjoy the view. Then think of George Ferris and the vision he had to put you there.

profit = amount of money gained

Passage 2:

from THE FERRIS WHEEL

by Denton J. Snider, *World's Fair Studies* (1893)

1 After thinking about the matter for a while, and seeing the huge toy revolve several times in a playful way, I **conclude** that my experience of the Fair will not be complete unless I take the trip. I enter the coach and the thing starts, slowly rounding upwards.

2 My imagination starts to work, being set in motion by the Wheel. Can any person help asking repeatedly, "What if?" What if the Wheel should leap from its supports and start rolling down the street like a boy's hoop? What if it should break a **cog** and begin whizzing round and round? What if it should stop when we are at the top and absolutely refuse to budge? How could we ever get down?

3 Thus my imagination calls up all sorts of possibilities, painting them in vivid colors, while the wheel keeps steadily going. The wheel goes round twice, and it is just as well, for I am focused inwardly on my own thoughts at first. But with the second turn, my mind is called outward by the splendid views of the buildings of the Fair, with gleams of the lake beyond, and of the city in the distance. Not the least interesting is the wheel itself, holding us out at arm's-length and giving us a slow toss through the air as a father does his child. Down it brings us once more, and we pick up the ground where we left it a few moments before.

conclude = make up one's mind

cog = a piece on a wheel

Respond to Text

Reread/Think

1. PART A

Based on paragraph 1 of Passage 1, what does Daniel Burnham think about the Eiffel Tower in France?

Ⓐ He thinks the Eiffel Tower is uninteresting and wonders why it has become so famous.

Ⓑ He is impressed by the Eiffel Tower and wants something more amazing built for the World's Columbian Exposition.

Ⓒ He is puzzled by the design of the Eiffel Tower and thinks its design should be simpler.

Ⓓ He believes the Eiffel Tower was poorly designed and that it will be easy to design something better.

PART B

Which detail **best** supports the answer in Part A?

Ⓐ "He was one of Chicago's best building designers, but he was stumped."

Ⓑ "A huge fair was going to be held in Chicago in 1893."

Ⓒ "Burnham knew this attraction had to be even more amazing than the Eiffel Tower, built a few years earlier in Paris, France."

Ⓓ "Burnham wanted to show the world that America's engineers were more talented than France's."

2. Read these sentences from Passage 1.

> "On the first day of testing with passengers aboard, crowds of onlookers refused to stand back. Instead, they rushed the wheel and climbed into the coaches for the 20-minute ride." (paragraph 3)

What can readers infer from these sentences?

Ⓐ People could not wait to ride the Ferris wheel.

Ⓑ People were confused by the Ferris wheel.

Ⓒ People were worried about the Ferris wheel.

Ⓓ People did not care about the Ferris wheel.

3. PART A

In Passage 2, which word **best** describes how the author feels in paragraphs 1 and 2?

Ⓐ joyful

Ⓑ worried

Ⓒ peaceful

Ⓓ tired

PART B

Which detail **best** supports the answer in Part A?

Ⓐ "I conclude that my experience of the Fair will not be complete unless I take the trip." (paragraph 1)

Ⓑ "I enter the coach and the thing starts, slowly rounding upwards." (paragraph 1)

Ⓒ "My imagination starts to work, being set in motion by the Wheel." (paragraph 2)

Ⓓ "What if it should stop when we are at the top and absolutely refuse to budge?" (paragraph 2)

4. Read this sentence from Passage 2.

> "But with the second turn, my mind is called outward by the splendid views of the buildings of the Fair, with gleams of the lake beyond, and of the city in the distance." (paragraph 3)

Based on this sentence, which statement about the Ferris wheel would the author **most likely** agree with?

Ⓐ It makes people feel sick.

Ⓑ It allows riders to enjoy the sights.

Ⓒ It moves around very quickly.

Ⓓ It is the best attraction at the fair.

5. Fill in **one** bubble in each row to choose whether each description is about "Ferris's Grand Idea," "The Ferris Wheel," or both passages.

	Passage 1	**Passage 2**	**Both**
primary source	Ⓐ	Ⓑ	Ⓒ
secondary source	Ⓓ	Ⓔ	Ⓕ
explains the motion of the Ferris wheel	Ⓖ	Ⓗ	Ⓘ
describes the view while riding the Ferris wheel	Ⓙ	Ⓚ	Ⓛ

Write

EXTENDED RESPONSE Compare and contrast "Ferris's Grand Idea" and "The Ferris Wheel." Explain how the primary source and secondary source provide different information about the Ferris wheel. Use details from both passages to support your response.

WRITING CHECKLIST

- ☐ I compared the passages.
- ☐ I explained the types of information in a primary source and a secondary source.
- ☐ I included details from both passages to support my response.
- ☐ I used correct spelling, punctuation, and capitalization.

Read the passage. Then answer the questions that follow.

Treating the Red Fox

by Mark B. Champlin

1 I first spotted the red fox on a June morning. It was crouched beside the tool shed, unhappy and shaking. I approached the animal slowly and saw that its left hind leg was injured.

2 I went inside my cabin and got my medical bag and **veterinary** books for reference. Then, with caution, I returned to the fox. Next, I gently lifted the animal's injured leg and examined it. I concluded that it should be put in a **splint**. Luckily, the fox settled back and let me proceed with my work.

3 With some wood and tape, I prepared a splint for the fox and then attached it to its leg. Then, so the fox could have a safe, comfortable place to rest, I set up a wooden box padded with pillows on my porch. Next to the box, I set bowls of food and water, refilling them daily.

veterinary = related to the medical care of sick animals

splint = support for a broken bone

4 A few weeks later, I saw the fox moving and noticed it no longer had a limp. It looked like the treatment had worked! Now that the limp was gone, it was time to detach the splint from its leg. Not too long after that, the red fox was nowhere to be found. I looked by the tool shed and checked around the yard, but the fox had disappeared.

5 Late one August afternoon, I spied the red fox coming up the path to my cabin. A short distance behind, a silver fox was limping along. Another fox needed kindness and care. I watched as the animals approached the tool shed. The silver fox was fearful, but the red fox seemed to assure it that the area was safe.

6 Finally, the silver fox lay down beside the tool shed. The red fox observed its friend for a few moments, then it turned around and trotted back into the woods. The silver fox gazed up at me. As I had done once before, I entered the cabin, located my medical bag, and returned outside to treat the silver fox.

The red fox shows the silver fox where to get help.

Respond to Text

Reread/Think

1. Which word from paragraph 3 has a prefix that means "before"?

Ⓐ prepared

Ⓑ attached

Ⓒ comfortable

Ⓓ refilling

2. Read this sentence from paragraph 4.

"I looked by the tool shed and checked around the yard, but the fox had disappeared."

Disappeared means "not being seen any longer." It can be broken down into the word parts listed in the left column of the chart. Fill in **one** bubble in each row to show what each word part means.

	happened in the past	**not, opposite of**	**to come into view, become visible**
dis-	Ⓐ	Ⓑ	Ⓒ
appear	Ⓓ	Ⓔ	Ⓕ
-ed	Ⓖ	Ⓗ	Ⓘ

3. Read this sentence from paragraph 4.

"It looked like the treatment had worked!"

The word treatment is made up of the base word *treat* and the suffix *-ment*, which means "the state or act of." Based on these word parts, what does treatment mean?

Ⓐ to cure someone many times

Ⓑ care given to cure an injury

Ⓒ someone who tries to cure an injury

Ⓓ to cause someone to be cured

4. Why does the red fox assure the silver fox in paragraph 5?

Ⓐ The silver fox was scared, but the red fox wanted it to feel safe.

Ⓑ The silver fox was excited, but the red fox wanted it to feel calm.

Ⓒ The silver fox was hungry, but the red fox wanted it to be patient.

Ⓓ The silver fox was angry, but the red fox wanted it to be careful.

5. SHORT RESPONSE Read this sentence from the passage.

"I went inside my cabin and got my medical bag and veterinary books for reference." (paragraph 2)

The base word of reference is *refer*, which means "to seek information, help, or advice." The suffix *-ence* means "the action of." Based on these word parts, what does reference mean? What clues help you figure out this meaning?

ASSESSMENT

Read the story. Then answer the questions that follow.

The Escape

by Villa Getakes

1 The only light in the stone dungeon came from two torches on the walls. I picked at the lock of the prison cell I shared with Kasper. It was still night, but the morning cry of a blackbird urged me to hurry. We didn't have much time before the guards would return to bring us before the evil Prince Robert and his icy heart. My friend Kasper lay groaning on the cold, damp floor by my feet.

2 Kasper clutched his leg and breathed heavily. He looked up at me, grinning weakly, and said, "The pair of us, with our shovels and rakes, we weren't much of a match for those guards and their swords, were we? We were like two leaves against a powerful wind." He laughed, but I could hear the pain in his voice. It hurt me to see my friend Kasper suffering so much.

3 "We've got to get you help," I said as I continued to work on the lock. I picked at it a moment longer, until I finally heard it click and a huge wave of relief washed over me. I pushed the creaking door open and reached down to help Kasper up. But he stopped me.

4 "Carl, I can barely stand, let alone walk," he said. "You might make it by yourself, but you won't have a chance if you are burdened by me."

5 I stood in silence, pondering Kasper's words. I realized that he might very well be right. If I went alone, I could go quickly and get help for Kasper. But what if Kasper did not survive till then? I would be imprisoned in another way. I would be trapped by my own thoughts of the friend I left behind.

6 "To escape alone would be no escape at all," I said firmly. I raised Kasper up, and then, with a grunt of effort, lifted him onto my shoulders. He was heavy, but my heart was light as a feather. Together we escaped into the frosty, moonlit night.

Respond to Text

Reread/Think

1. Fill in the bubbles **before two** sentences that **best** show Kasper and Carl are easily overpowered by the guards.

> ● Kasper clutched his leg and breathed heavily. Ⓑ He looked up at me, grinning weakly, and said, "The pair of us, with our shovels and rakes, we weren't much of a match for those guards and their swords, were we? ● We were like two leaves against a powerful wind." Ⓓ He laughed, but I could hear the pain in his voice. Ⓔ It hurt me to see my friend Kasper suffering so much.

2. What is the meaning of burdened as it is used in paragraph 4?

Ⓐ to be unlucky

Ⓑ having many questions

Ⓒ dealing with something difficult

● given a serious injury

3. What is the meaning of pondering as it is used in paragraph 5?

Ⓐ to repeat slowly and loudly

Ⓑ to think deeply and carefully about something

Ⓒ to put words into action

Ⓓ to try to ignore or forget something

4. **PART A**

What does imprisoned mean as it is used in paragraph 5?

Ⓐ to be stuck in a bad situation

Ⓑ very saddened or upset

Ⓒ kept locked in a jail

Ⓓ accused of doing a crime

PART B

Which detail from paragraph 5 **best** supports the answer to Part A?

Ⓐ "I realized that he might very well be right."

Ⓑ "If I went alone, I could go quickly and get help for Kasper."

Ⓒ "But what if Kasper did not survive till then?"

Ⓓ "I would be trapped by my own thoughts of the friend I left behind."

5. PART A

From what point of view is the story told?

Ⓐ Kasper, first-person point of view

Ⓑ Carl, first-person point of view

Ⓒ Someone outside the story, third-person point of view

Ⓓ Prince Robert, third-person point of view

PART B

Which sentence from the text **best** supports the answer to Part A?

Ⓐ "The only light in the stone dungeon came from two torches on the walls." (paragraph 1)

Ⓑ "Kasper clutched his leg and breathed heavily." (paragraph 2)

Ⓒ "It hurt me to see my friend Kasper suffering so much." (paragraph 2)

Ⓓ "But what if Kasper did not survive till then?" (paragraph 5)

6. Based on paragraph 1, what will happen if Carl and Kasper are brought to Prince Robert?

Ⓐ Prince Robert will let them go free.

Ⓑ Prince Robert will ask for a doctor for Kasper.

Ⓒ Prince Robert will punish them harshly.

Ⓓ Prince Robert will reward them for their good deed.

Write

EXTENDED RESPONSE Identify the point of view from which "The Escape" is told. Then explain what the narrator's perspective is about escaping and how the author shows that perspective.

WRITING CHECKLIST

- ☐ I identified the point of view of the narrator.
- ☐ I used details to describe how the author shows the narrator's perspective.
- ☐ I used complete sentences.
- ☐ I used correct spelling, punctuation, and capitalization.

Walking BIG Bailey

by Clarisse Bartonelli

Read the poem. Then answer the questions that follow.

1 While I am working hard at school,
To master math and this and that,
Bailey **dozes** at home all day
And dreams of chasing a neighbor's cat.

2 Big Bailey shakes himself awake
When through the door I come at three.
A furry rocket knocks me down.
A leash is dropped upon my knee.

3 We're on the street. No time to waste.
He's got a million scents to smell,
And squirrels and birds and cats to chase.
"Come back here, Bailey! NOW!" I yell.

4 Around the block and up the street,
He travels at the speed of sound,
And I, attached to him by leash,
Am led around and 'round and 'round.

5 I must confess I like the speed.
It's fun to travel, zip, and zoom.
But sometimes when I'm out with Bailey,
I wonder, who is walking whom?

dozes = sleeps

Respond to Text

Reread/Think

1. Which two lines in each stanza rhyme?

Ⓐ the first and second lines

Ⓑ the first and third lines

Ⓒ the second and third lines

Ⓓ the second and fourth lines

2. Why does the author **most likely** use the word *'round* instead of *around* in the last line of stanza 4?

Ⓐ to explain the theme of the poem

Ⓑ to keep the rhythm the same as in the other stanzas

Ⓒ to show that the speaker is joking

Ⓓ to suggest that the word has a different meaning

3. **SHORT RESPONSE** Describe two poetic elements, such as structure, rhyme, or rhythm, the author uses in "Walking Big Bailey." How do these elements add to the poem's meaning?

4. PART A

Reread stanza 5.

"I must confess I like the speed.
It's fun to travel, zip, and zoom.
But sometimes when I'm out with Bailey,
I wonder, who is walking whom?"

How does this stanza add to the meaning of the poem?

Ⓐ It shows the speaker is worried about how fast Bailey runs.

Ⓑ It shows the speaker feels Bailey is sometimes in charge.

Ⓒ It shows the speaker does not like walking Bailey.

Ⓓ It shows the speaker wishes Bailey would go faster.

PART B

Which line from the poem **best** supports the answer in Part A?

Ⓐ "When through the door I come at three." (stanza 2)

Ⓑ "We're on the street. No time to waste." (stanza 3)

Ⓒ "He travels at the speed of sound," (stanza 4)

Ⓓ "And I, attached to him by leash," (stanza 4)

Read the passage. Then answer the questions that follow.

Should We Settle the Moon?

by Jo Newbold

1 Humans have a strong curiosity to learn more about the world. This interest has let us go where no one has gone before, such as the Moon. But it's been 50 years since humans have walked on the Moon. This has some people wondering: What's next when it comes to Moon exploration? Should humans one day live there?

2 Some people think that living on the Moon would be exciting, and that the effort and research needed to get us there would be worth it. However, it is impossible for humans to live on the Moon.

3 Humans cannot live on the Moon because it does not have an **atmosphere** with oxygen, the way Earth does. This means there is no air to breathe and that temperatures can vary from a burning 232°F during the day to a freezing –315°F at night. Humans cannot live in an environment with such extreme temperatures. And without an Earth-like atmosphere, **radiation** from the sun would make anyone living on the Moon extremely sick.

atmosphere = gases surrounding a planet
radiation = waves of energy

4 Humans also need water to survive, and the Moon does not have water that is easily **accessible**. Water may be trapped in tiny pockets below the Moon's surface, but astronauts have yet to pull it from the ground. There is also not that much water. Scientists say the **Sahara Desert** has 100 times more water than the Moon does. The lack of large amounts of easy-to-reach water is a serious problem for anyone who hopes to one day live on the Moon.

5 Even if water were easily available, the Moon's regolith makes living there dangerous. Regolith is the name for a powdery dust that covers the surface of the Moon. Because the dust is electrically charged, it sticks to everything. It can get inside a spacesuit, break an engine, and interfere with breathing. After returning from a moonwalk, one astronaut said that "the dust really bothered my eyes and throat. I was tasting it and eating it." Regolith also got inside the spacecraft, making it hard to breathe. If scientists cannot find a way to control regolith, it could destroy the lungs of everyone living on the Moon.

6 Although we do not know what the future will bring, today's technology is not ready to make life on the Moon practical or enjoyable. There are many reasons why it is impossible to settle the Moon. Anyone living there would struggle constantly with the extreme conditions. And it would be frightening to always worry about limited water and dangerous dust. Scientists should stop thinking about how people could live on the Moon and explore other parts of the solar system instead.

accessible = easy to reach

Sahara Desert = the largest sand desert in the world

Respond to Text

Reread/Think

1. What do the words burning, freezing, and extreme in paragraph 3 show about the author's perspective about the Moon's environment?

Ⓐ The Moon's environment interests people who want challenges.

Ⓑ The Moon's environment could be changed so humans can live there.

Ⓒ The Moon's environment is dangerous because it is always dark.

Ⓓ The Moon's environment is unable to support human life.

2. What can readers infer from paragraph 3 about radiation from the sun?

Ⓐ The Moon is the only place where the sun's radiation makes people sick.

Ⓑ The Earth's atmosphere protects people from the sun's radiation.

Ⓒ The sun's radiation can be both helpful and harmful to people.

Ⓓ The sun's radiation also makes people sick on Earth.

3. Which **two** phrases from paragraph 4 **best** show the author's perspective about water on the moon?

Ⓐ "easily accessible"

Ⓑ "below the Moon's surface"

Ⓒ "not that much"

Ⓓ "easy-to-reach"

Ⓔ "problem for anyone"

4. In paragraph 5, what is the author's perspective on regolith?

Ⓐ The author wants astronauts to study regolith for more information.

Ⓑ The author thinks regolith would be challenging to control.

Ⓒ The author likes regolith because it is electrically charged.

Ⓓ The author wants to walk on the Moon to know what regolith is like.

5. What does the word practical mean in paragraph 6?

Ⓐ peaceful

Ⓑ perfect

Ⓒ painful

Ⓓ possible

6. PART A

What claim does the author make in the passage?

Ⓐ It has been too long since people have landed on the Moon.

Ⓑ It is not possible for humans to one day live on the Moon.

Ⓒ The Moon's surface is an interesting place for humans to explore.

Ⓓ New technology makes it possible for humans to live on the Moon.

PART B

Which sentence is a reason that **best** supports the answer to Part A?

Ⓐ "Humans have a strong curiosity to learn more about the world." (paragraph 1)

Ⓑ "But it's been 50 years since humans have walked on the Moon." (paragraph 1)

Ⓒ "Humans cannot live on the Moon because it does not have an atmosphere with oxygen, the way Earth does." (paragraph 3)

Ⓓ "Regolith is the name for a powdery dust that covers the surface of the Moon." (paragraph 5)

7. Which sentence provides evidence to support the idea that the Moon does not have enough water to support human life?

Ⓐ "This interest has let us go where no one has gone before, such as the Moon." (paragraph 1)

Ⓑ "However, it is impossible for humans to live on the Moon." (paragraph 2)

Ⓒ "Scientists say the Sahara Desert has 100 times more water than the Moon does." (paragraph 4)

Ⓓ "And it would be frightening to always worry about limited water and dangerous dust." (paragraph 6)

8. Which sentence is a reason that **best** supports the author's claim?

Ⓐ "Humans have a strong curiosity to learn more about the world." (paragraph 1)

Ⓑ "But it's been 50 years since humans have walked on the Moon." (paragraph 1)

Ⓒ "Some people think that living on the Moon would be exciting, and that the effort and research needed to get us there would be worth it." (paragraph 2)

Ⓓ "Even if water were easily available, the Moon's regolith makes living there dangerous." (paragraph 5)

9. Which statement **best** describes the author's perspective in paragraph 6 about space exploration?

Ⓐ Exploring other parts of the solar system would be difficult and dangerous.

Ⓑ Living on a new world will be important for human survival.

Ⓒ Scientists should explore other parts of the solar system.

Ⓓ Improvements in technology will make living on other planets possible.

Write

EXTENDED RESPONSE State the author's claim in "Should We Settle the Moon?" and describe one reason and the evidence used to support it. Use details from the text to support your response.

WRITING CHECKLIST

- ☐ I stated the author's claim.
- ☐ I described a reason and evidence that support the claim.
- ☐ I used complete sentences.
- ☐ I used correct spelling, punctuation, and capitalization.

Read the story. Then answer the questions that follow.

Out to Win

by Wendy Baryl

1 As the yearly track meet approached, all I could think about was defeating Anna Banks. For the past three years she'd beaten me in the 400-meter run with a smile, always finishing just a step ahead. Anna Banks was my **rival**, and it looked like she enjoyed stomping on my dreams. But this year, I planned to win. In fact, I was obsessed with winning—it was the only thing I could think about. Of course, I did a lot more than just think. I practiced running daily, and each day of practice made me stronger and more **committed** to achieving my goal. My routine was always the same: eat, attend school, run, eat, and sleep.

rival = one who tries to outdo another

committed = willing to work hard

2 On the day of the race, I was eager to compete. I tried to ignore any thoughts of uncertainty as I made my way to the starting line. *TWEET!* The whistle blew and we sprinted forward.

3 Anna and I quickly charged in front of the other racers. At first, I was ahead of Anna, but as the finish line drew closer, she began to gain on me and passed me. As Anna inched ahead, I could feel panic boiling in my stomach. I could not lose again, and I would not lose again.

4 I thought, *This is my chance!* I lunged toward the finish line with a burst of energy, shooting forward with such force my shoe flew off my foot. I pulled a Cinderella—running with one shoe on and one shoe off. I was so focused on the finish line I barely felt the ground scrape against and tear my sock. All my thoughts, all my strength **propelled** me, pushing me forward. I did not spare any energy. The space between us grew smaller, and when we crossed the finish line, we were so close that I wasn't even sure who had won. Then I heard the announcer—it was me!

5 Still breathing hard, Anna rushed over, smiling. She shook my hand and panted, "That was amazing! Great race!" That's when I realized I had been looking at Anna all wrong. She was not some evil person out to destroy me. Anna was an accomplished runner. She had won many races, and she enjoyed racing other hard-working runners to challenge herself. Competing against her had made me a better racer than I ever would have become otherwise. It was time to start thinking of Anna Banks as my muse, not my enemy.

propelled = pushed or moved forward

Respond to Text

Reread/Think

1. Read these sentences from paragraph 1.

"But this year, I planned to win. In fact, I was obsessed with winning—it was the only thing I could think about."

What is the meaning of the word obsessed?

Ⓐ focused on one thing only

Ⓑ disappointed by something

Ⓒ hopeful for a long time

Ⓓ full of confusion about

2. What does the word uncertainty in paragraph 2 help readers understand about the narrator's feelings at the start of the race?

Ⓐ She realizes she is not sure of the race rules.

Ⓑ She feels confident she will win the race.

Ⓒ She worries about what will happen in the race.

Ⓓ She feels annoyed that she is running against her rival.

3. Which meaning of charged is used in paragraph 3 of the story?

Ⓐ filled with electricity

Ⓑ asked for payment

Ⓒ blamed each other

Ⓓ moved forward quickly

4. Which context clue in paragraph 5 **best** helps readers understand what accomplished means?

Ⓐ "Anna rushed over smiling"

Ⓑ "I had been looking at Anna all wrong"

Ⓒ "She was not some evil person"

Ⓓ "She had won many races"

5. **SHORT RESPONSE** In Greek mythology, a muse is a goddess who gives inspiration to others. Use context clues from "Out to Win" to explain why the narrator refers to Anna Banks as "my muse" in paragraph 5. What does this word help readers understand about the story?

Read the passage. Then answer the questions that follow.

Safe Travels for Songbirds

by Nathalie Alonso

1 Every spring, the skies fill up with birds headed north to warm summer **breeding grounds**. The conditions up north are just right for birds to lay eggs and raise their young. There are places to nest and plenty of food for them to eat. In the fall when the weather changes, these birds fly back to their winter homes in the south.

breeding grounds = places where animals have babies

FLYWAYS OF NORTH AMERICA

The migratory routes that birds follow are called flyways. There are four flyway zones across North America.

2 Birds follow the same routes year after year. Many birds, especially songbirds, **migrate** in the darkness of night. Along with a natural instinct and a sense of where to go, the birds use the moon and the stars like a map. They also use information from the position of the setting sun and landforms to help guide their way.

3 Migrating birds often travel thousands of miles. They face many dangers, such as big storms and predators, along the way. One of the biggest threats is from bright **artificial** lights that shine from towns and cities in or near the birds' path of travel. Although the lights themselves do not harm the birds, the birds are drawn to them. This causes them to wander away from their routes and circle or get lost. Tired and confused, many birds end up crashing into windows. As a result, every year, thousands of birds die or suffer injuries and cannot complete their journeys.

migrate = travel from one place to another

artificial = made by human beings; not natural

4 The good news is that there are steps people can take to make the night sky safer for birds. For example, people can help by dimming or turning off outdoor lights when the night sky is darkest, usually after 11:00 p.m. One way to do this is to install motion sensors or an automatic shut-off that helps make sure that lights are on only when they are needed.

5 There are other ways to help, too. People can help migrating birds by making sure their outdoor lights point down at the ground and not up toward the sky. This is especially important to do in the spring and fall when many birds migrate.

6 Finally, making sure that indoor lights cannot be seen from the outside also helps to darken the night sky. These small steps can help make a big difference for millions of birds. Although we cannot remove all the dangers birds face in their travels, we can help solve one problem with the flip of a light switch.

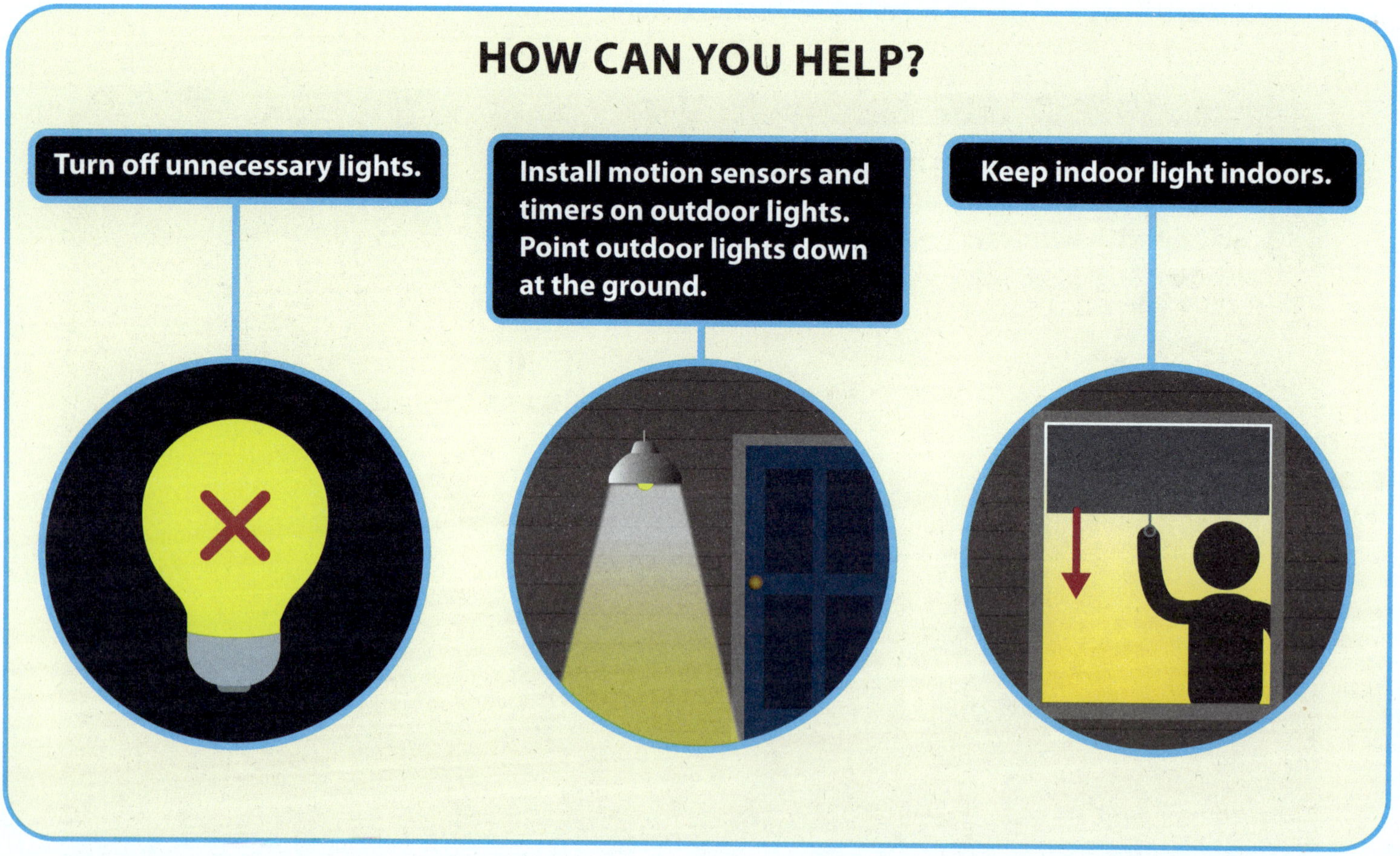

Respond to Text

Reread/Think

1. What inference can readers make about why many birds head south for the winter?

Ⓐ As the weather gets colder, less food is available in the north.

Ⓑ Birds fear big storms and predators in the north.

Ⓒ The breeding grounds become too overcrowded in the north.

Ⓓ The city lights are too bright in the north.

2. Fill in **one** bubble in each row to show whether each detail describes information in the main text, information in the map on page 462, or information in both the main text and the map.

	Main Text	Map	Both
Birds follow routes when they migrate.	Ⓐ	Ⓑ	Ⓒ
There are four flyway zones in North America.	Ⓓ	Ⓔ	Ⓕ
Many birds migrate in the darkness of night.	Ⓖ	Ⓗ	Ⓘ

3. Which information in the main text does the illustration on page 463 help readers understand?

Ⓐ Migrating birds often travel thousands of miles on their routes.

Ⓑ Thousands of birds cannot complete their migration each year.

Ⓒ Bright lights cause birds to stray from their routes and get lost or confused.

Ⓓ Keeping indoor lights indoors can make the night sky safer for birds.

4. How does the illustration on page 463 help readers understand paragraph 3?

Ⓐ It shows how birds can easily avoid cities and towns in their path.

Ⓑ It shows the types of predators that birds can face while migrating.

Ⓒ It shows how some lights shine out and into the birds' paths.

Ⓓ It shows how injured birds cannot complete their journeys.

5. Read this caption from the illustration on page 463.

"Artificial lights confuse birds, causing them to circle until dawn or collide with windows and buildings."

What does the word collide mean as it is used in this sentence?

Ⓐ crash

Ⓑ fly

Ⓒ hurt

Ⓓ land

6. Read this sentence from paragraph 6.

"Finally, making sure that indoor lights cannot be seen from the outside also helps to darken the night sky."

How does the diagram on page 464 help readers apply this information?

Ⓐ It shows someone closing a curtain to keep light in.

Ⓑ It shows an outdoor light pointed down instead of up.

Ⓒ It shows someone looking out the window.

Ⓓ It shows that all lights should be turned off when birds migrate.

7. PART A

According to the text, which is a problem for migrating birds?

Ⓐ Breeding grounds in the north are disappearing.

Ⓑ Birds cannot see landforms in the dark.

Ⓒ Skies are often too cloudy to see the moon and stars.

Ⓓ Bright lights from cities make birds lose their way.

PART B

According to the text, which is a possible solution for the problem identified in Part A?

Ⓐ dimming or turning off outdoor lights

Ⓑ creating new paths for birds to follow

Ⓒ making more areas for birds to build nests

Ⓓ changing the time of year when birds migrate

Write

EXTENDED RESPONSE Identify the text structure the author uses to organize information in "Safe Travels for Songbirds." Include examples from the text to support your response.

WRITING CHECKLIST

- ☐ I explained how the author organized the information.
- ☐ I included examples from the text to support my response.
- ☐ I used complete sentences.
- ☐ I used correct spelling, punctuation, and capitalization.

Glossary of Terms

Academic Talk Words and Phrases

A

account a written or spoken retelling of an event or topic

actions things that a person or character does

alliteration repetition of initial consonant sounds to create a special effect

analyze to closely and carefully examine a text or a part of a text

antonym a word that means the opposite of another word

argument a presentation of a claim, reasons, and evidence to try to persuade others

B

base word a complete word that has no prefixes or suffixes added to it

C

caption a phrase or sentence next to a picture in a text that explains something about the picture

cause a reason, event, or action that makes something else happen

cause and effect a relationship between events in which one event—the cause—brings about, or causes, another event—the effect

cause-and-effect text structure a text organization that describes events, what made them happen, and how they affect people or other events

central idea something important that an author wants readers to know about a topic; often called a *main idea*

chapter a section or part of a story or book

character a person, animal, or made-up creature in a story or play

chart an image that shows or organizes information so that it is easier to understand

chronological text structure a text organization in which events are described in the order in which they happen

chronology the order in which events happen

claim a statement an author believes is true or correct even though other people may not agree

compare to describe how two or more things are similar

compare-and-contrast text structure a text organization that describes the similarities and differences between two or more things

conclusion an opinion about something that is reached after carefully thinking about it

conflict challenges that a characters faces; a disagreement that people, characters, or organizations have with one another

context clues words, phrases, or sentences near an unknown word or phrase in a text that help you determine the meaning of the unknown word or phrase

contrast to describe how two or more things are different

D

describe to tell what something is like; to explain something

descriptive text structure a text organization that presents information in sections, with each section explaining information about the topic

details facts, examples, or other pieces of information in a text

determine to find out or figure out something

develop to build on

diagram a drawing or picture that explains what something looks like or how something works

dialogue the words the characters say in a story or play

E

effect something that happens as a result of something else

event something that happens in a story or in the natural world

evidence facts, figures, and details used to support a central idea or claim

explain to describe or give details about something so it can be understood

Glossary of Terms (continued)

F

fact a detail that is proved to be true

figurative language a word or phrase that means something different from its regular or literal meaning; figurative language is often used to make a comparison or create a certain feeling or image in the reader's mind

first-person point of view when the narrator of a story is a character in the story who describes events using the pronouns *I, me,* or *we*; a first-person narrator can describe their own thoughts and feelings but not what other characters think or feel

free verse a poem that does not have a pattern of rhyme or strong rhythm

G

glossary a list at the back of a book of important words from the text and their meaning

H

haiku a poem that has three lines and a set pattern of syllables: 5 syllables (first line), 7 syllables (second line), 5 syllables (third line)

heading a word or phrase at the beginning of a section of a text that tells what the section is about

historical relating to events from the past

historical fiction a story set in the past that presents characters and situations that reflect history

hyperbole figurative language that uses exaggeration to make a point

I

idea a thought, opinion, or belief that someone has about something

identify to recognize and name something

idiom a phrase that has a different meaning than the meaning of the individual words

illustration a picture in a text that gives information about the text

image a drawing, photograph, map, or chart that shows information about something in a text or story

imagery language that appeals to the five senses

infer to reach a conclusion about a text based on text clues and what you already know

inference a conclusion, or an idea you have about a text, based on details in the text and what you already know

inform to share facts about a topic

information facts and details about someone or something

L

label a word or phrase that gives more information about an image

lesson something learned in a text or story or through experience

limerick a funny, five-line poem that has a set pattern of rhyme and rhythm

literal having the usual or most basic meaning of a word's dictionary definition

literary elements the major parts of a story, including characters, setting, plot, and theme

M

main idea something important that an author wants readers to know about a topic; often called a *central idea*

map a picture or drawing of an area that shows its cities, roads, rivers, mountains, and other features

metaphor a type of figurative language that compares two things without using the word *like* or *as*

motivations the reasons why characters act, think, or feel the way they do

multiple-meaning word a word that has more than one definition

myth an ancient story told by a people or culture that explains their origin and history

N

narrator the person or character who tells a story

Glossary of Terms (continued)

O

opinion an author's feeling or belief about a topic

P

paragraph a group of sentences about a particular idea or topic

personification a type of figurative language that gives human qualities or characteristics to other animals or objects

perspective (informational texts) an author's thoughts, feelings, and attitude about a topic

perspective (literary texts) a character's thoughts, feelings, and attitude about the events in a story

persuade to present information to try to convince others to agree with an idea

photo or photograph a picture made using a camera

phrase a short group of words that has meaning but does not form a complete sentence

play a story that is performed on stage by actors

plot the sequence of events in a story

poem a piece of writing in which the words are chosen for their beauty and sound; the words are often arranged in short lines

poetic elements the parts of a poem that work together to give it meaning

point of view in literary texts, the type of narration used (as in first-, second-, or third-person narration)

predict to say what you think will happen in the future

prefix a word part that comes at the beginning of a word and changes the word's meaning

primary source a text or record created by someone who witnessed an event or took part in it

problem a challenge that the main character or characters face

problem-and-solution text structure a text organization that describes one or more problems and solutions

purpose reason

Q

quote the exact words that an author wrote or a speaker said; these words go inside quotation marks

R

reason an explanation why an idea or point is correct or true

relationship the way in which two or more people, events, or things are connected

relevant related to a topic or idea

repetition the use of repeated words or sounds in a piece of writing to show that something is important or to create a certain effect

resolution the part of a story when the main conflict or problem is solved or when the main goal is reached; the resolution happens at the end of a story

respond to make a reply; to answer; to react

result something that happens or exists because of something else that happened before

rhyme the repeated use of words that end in the same or similar sounds

rhymed verse a poem that has rhyming lines

rhyme scheme a pattern of rhymes in a poem

rhythm the regular pattern of sounds in a poem or beats in a piece of music

root a word part that has meaning and can be combined with other roots, prefixes, or suffixes to form words

S

scene a part of a play in which all the action takes place in the same setting; one or more scenes make up each act of a play

secondary source an account of an event that is written by someone who did not experience it

section a particular part of something, such as a paragraph or a chapter of a book

sensory details details that describe the way something looks, sounds, feels, smells, or tastes

sequence the order in which events or steps in a process happen

Glossary of Terms (continued)

setting where and when a story or play takes place

sidebar a short text, often boxed, placed near the main text that gives more information about the topic

signal words words or phrases that show the connection between ideas or events

simile a type of figurative language that compares two things using the word *like* or *as*

solution the answer to a problem or the way the main characters resolve the conflict of a story

source a text or image that gives information about a specific subject area or topic; a source may be printed or digital

stanza several lines of a poem that are grouped together to form one part of the poem

structure (literary texts) the particular way an author organizes a text, such as parts of a story or stanzas of a poem

suffix a word part that comes at the end of a word and changes the word's meaning

summarize to briefly retell in your own words the most important ideas, events, and details in a text

summary a short retelling of a text that includes the central idea and relevant details of a text, or the theme and important events of a story

support to help explain or provide evidence for a idea

synonym a word that has the same or similar meaning as another word

T

table of contents a list at the front of a book of the sections or chapters of the book in the order in which they appear

text evidence a detail, fact, or example in a piece of writing that can be used to support an idea

text features special parts of a text that help you find certain information or learn more about a topic; titles, headings, illustrations, charts, graphs, and glossaries are examples of text features

text structure (informational texts) the way an author organizes the ideas and information in a piece of writing; text structures include description, problem and solution, chronological, compare and contrast, cause and effect, and sequence

theme an important message or lesson that an author wants to share about life

third-person point of view when the narrator of a story is not a character in the story and describes events using pronouns such as *he*, *she*, and *they*; a third-person narrator can describe what different characters think and feel

timeline a chart or image that shows the dates of important events in the order they happened, sometimes with additional details about the events

title the name of a text

topic the general subject of a text

trait a quality or characteristic that a person or character in a story has, such as courage, pride, or honesty

V

visual an image or picture that appears with a text; visuals can include illustrations, photos, charts, diagrams, and timelines

Credits

Text Credits

UNIT 1:

Jewell Parker Rhodes, excerpt from *Black Brother, Black Brother*. Copyright © 2020 by Jewell Parker Rhodes. Reproduced with permission of HarperCollins Publishers and Little, Brown and Company.

Sherri Winston, excerpt from *President of the Whole Fifth Grade*. Copyright © 2010 by Sherri Winston. Reprinted by permission of Little, Brown, an imprint of Hachette Book Group, Inc.

Greg van Eekhout, excerpt from *Cog*. Copyright © 2020 by Jack Greg van Eekhout. Reproduced with permission by HarperCollins Publishers.

Adapted from "The Flying Test" by Sara Matson, *Cricket* 2017 © by Cricket Media, Inc. Reproduced with permission.

Brenda Woods, excerpt from *Zoe in Wonderland*. Copyright © 2016 by Brenda Woods. Used by permission of Nancy Paulsen Books, an imprint of Penguin Young Readers Group, a division of Penguin Random House LLC. All rights reserved.

Jason Reynolds, excerpt from *Look Both Ways: A Tale Told in Ten Blocks*. Copyright © 2019 by Jason Reynolds. Reprinted with the permission of Atheneum Books for Young Readers, an imprint of Simon & Schuster Children's Publishing Division, and Knights Of. All rights reserved.

UNIT 2:

Adapted from "Stephanie's Strange Mixture" by Tracy Vonder Brink, *Spider* 2019 © by Cricket Media, Inc. Reproduced with permission.

"Meet Stevie" by Corinne Purtill, *TIME for Kids* 2019 © by Cricket Media, Inc. Reproduced with permission.

Adapted from "Fail Better: Gitanjali Rao" by Amanda Baker, *Ask* 2019 © by Cricket Media, Inc. Reproduced with permission.

Adapted from "Behind the Design Process with DIY Girls InvenTeam" by Johanna Arnone, *CricketMedia* 2019 © by Cricket Media, Inc. Reproduced with permission.

Eric Cook, excerpt from *Prototyping*. Copyright © 2015 by Eric Cook. Reproduced with permission by Cherry Lake Publishing

UNIT 3:

"Marie Maps the Sea" by Liz Huyck, *Ask* 2019 © by Cricket Media, Inc. Reproduced with permission.

"Stepping into History" by Shay Maunz, *TIME for Kids*, May 3, 2019 © by Cricket Media, Inc. Reproduced with permission.

Buzz Aldrin, excerpt from *Reaching for the Moon*. Illustrated by Wendell Minor. Text copyright © 2005 by Buzz Aldrin. Illustrations copyright © 2005 by Wendell Minor. Used by permission of HarperCollins Publishers.

Text excerpt and cover snapshot from *Chasing Space*, Young Readers' Edition by Leland Melvin, Laurie Calkhoven. Text Copyright © 2017 by Leland Melvin. Used by permission of HarperCollins Publishers.

"Drawing Under Ice" by Kirsten Carlson, *Muse* 2019 © by Cricket Media, Inc. Reproduced with permission.

UNIT 4:

"Hawaiian Language and Hula," *Faces* 2017 © by Cricket Media, Inc. Reproduced with permission.

Adapted from "Story Painter: Cy Thao and a Hmong Experience" by Missy McDonald, *AppleSeeds* 2006 © by Cricket Media, Inc. Reproduced with permission.

Pam Muñoz Ryan, excerpt from *Esperanza Rising*. Copyright © 2000 by Pam Muñoz Ryan. Reprinted by permission of Scholastic Inc.

Meg Medina, excerpt from *Merci Suárez Changes Gears*. Copyright © 2018 by Meg Medina. Reproduced with permission by Candlewick Press.

Mae Respicio, excerpt from *Any Day with You*. Copyright © 2020 by Mae Respicio. Used by permission of Wendy Lamb Books, an imprint of Random House Children's Books, a division of Penguin Random House LLC. All rights reserved.

Grace Lin, excerpt from *The Year of the Rat*. Copyright © 2008. Reprinted by permission of Little, Brown, an imprint of Hachette Book Group, Inc.

UNIT 5:

"Bigger than the Rules: How One Tall Kid Changed the Way We Play Basketball" by Timothy Tocher, *Ask* 2017 © by Cricket Media, Inc. Reproduced with permission.

Kwame Alexander, "Basketball Rule #2" and "The Last Shot" from *The Crossover*. Copyright © 2014 by Kwame Alexander. Reprinted by permission of Houghton Mifflin Harcourt Publishing Company and Andersen Press. All rights reserved.

Christa Champion, excerpt from *Girls Got Game: Sports Stories and Poems* (Edited by Sue Macy). Copyright © 2001 by Christa Champion. Reproduced with permission by Henry Holt and Co.

UNIT 6:

Northwest Band Shoshone Nation, excerpt from *Coyote Steals Fire*. Copyright © Northwest Band Shoshone Nation. Reproduced with permission by Utah State University Press.

Adapted from Mulder, Michelle. *Brilliant! Shining a Light on Sustainable Energy.* Victoria, BC, Canada: Orca Book Publishers, 2016

UNIT ASSESSMENT:

"And Away We Go: Rockets" from *Kids Discover*, March 2012, vol. 22, issue 3. Reproduced with permission.

Beth Bohac and Jim O'Leary, "Ready for Liftoff!" from *Cricket* © by Cricket Media, Inc. Reproduced with permission.

Marcia Amidon Lusted, "Ferris's Grand Idea" from *Cricket* © by Cricket Media, Inc. Reproduced with permission.

Illustration Credits

pp. cvr, 2 (bl), 8 (cr), 43 (c), 48-50, 75 (cl): Craig Phillips

pp. cvr, 2 (tr), 8 (br), 43 (b), 53-54, 75 (c): Berat Pekmezci

pp. cvr, 4 (bl), 160 (l), 163-165, 168- 170, 173-174: Adam Gustavson

pp. cvr, 6 (b), 283 (tl), 317 (t),318-319, 333 (t): Danny Allison

pp. cvr, 2 (cl), 9 (l), 58–61, 64–66, 69–70, 75 (r): Toni Chambers

pp. cvr, 135, 136–137, 145, 146: Peter Bull Art Studio

pp. cvr, 5 (c), 222 (r), 240–243, 246–248, 251–252, 273 (l): Teresa Martinez

pp. cvr, 342 (tl), 345 (t), 346-347, 392 (tr): Jensine Eckwall

pp. cvr, 342 (bl), 345 (b), 355-356, 392 (bl): Alida Massari

pp. 2 (tl), 8 (tc), 11 (t), 12-13, 74 (tl): Robert Paul Jr.

pp. 2 (br), 8 (cl), 11 (c), 16-18, 74 (cl): Kim Holt

pp. 5 (br), 223 (r), 274–277: Donald Wu

pp. 7 (bl), 342 (cl), 345 (c), 350-352, 392 (cr): Coyote Steals Fire: A Shoshone Tale. Retold and illustrated by the Northwestern Band of the Shoshone Nation. Copyright 2005. Reproduced by permission of the publisher, Utah State University Press.

pp. 8 (bl), 11 (b), 21-22, 74 (bl): Chelen Ecija

pp. 8 (tc), 27 (t), 28-29, 74 (tl): John Joven

pp. 8 (c), 27 (c), 32-34, 74 (br): Sachiko Yoshikawa

pp. 8 (cl), 27 (b), 37-38, 74 (bc): Anastasia Magliore Williams

pp. 8 (tr), 43 (t), 44-45, 75 (tl): Raymond Sebastien

pp. 9 (r), 76-77, 78-79: Chellie Carroll

pp. 152-155: Parwinder Singh

pp. 223 (tl), 257 (t), 259: Meg Medina, excerpt and cover from Merci Suarez Changes Gears. Copyright © 2018 by Mae Medina. Reproduced with permission by Candlewick Press.

pp. 223 (cl), 257 (c), 262-264: Brenna Vaughan

pp. 223 (bl), 257 (b), 267-268: Kristin Sorra

pp. 223 (tr), 283 (cl), 285 (cl, cr), 321 (c, bl) 322-328, 333 (cr): Francesca D'Ottavi

p. 227 (b): Eric Larsen

pp. 283 (bl), 285 (bl), 317 (br), 327-328, 333 (br): Cliff Nielsen

pp. 404-406: Simone Douglas

pp. 426-427: Kelly McMorris

pp. 448, 458: Curriculum Associates

pp. 463-464: DoubleInk Publishing Services

Photography Credits

p. cvr (wind turbines): Rawpixel.com/Shutterstock

p. cvr (hill): Michael Warwick/Shutterstock

p. cvr (bus): Scharfsinn/Shutterstock

pp. cvr (map), 4 (t), 180-181 (bg), 181 (r): World Ocean Floor Panorama, Bruce C. Heezen and Marie Tharp, 1977. Copyright by Marie Tharp 1977/2003. Reproduced by permission of Marie Tharp Maps LLC and Lamont-Doherty Earth Observatory.

pp. cvr (chess), 6 (t), 285 (br), 336: Lottie Davies/ Photodisc/Getty Images

pp. cvr (solar farm), 7 (cl), 343 (br), 377 (b), 387, 388, 393 (br): Avery White

pp. cvr (phone), 94 (r): haroldguevara/ Shutterstock

pp. cvr (shuttle, astronaut), 110 (br), 161 (cl, bl, br), 195 (c), 201 (b), 195 (t, c, br), 196 (t), 197 (t), 200-201 (bg), 200 (t), 201 (c), 202 (t, b), 206 (c), 207, 208, 213 (cl, cr, br), 215, 217, 419, 420: NASA

pp. cvr (LiDAR image), 160 (br), 179 (b), 190: PACUNAM Foundation/Thomas Garrison

pp. cvr (cave map), 186 (inset), Rambles in the Mammoth Cave, During the Year 1844. Louiseville, KY: Morton & Griswold, 1845.

pp. cvr (woman running), 366: Lzf/ Dreamstime.com

pp. cvr (fox), 442: Michael Cummings/Alamy Stock Photo

pp. 3 (c), 84 (bc), 103 (b), 113, 114 (b), 150 (br): Greg Kahn

pp. 3 (tr), 84 (tl), 87 (t), 88 (inset), 150 (tl): eli_asenova/E+/Getty Images

pp. 3 (br), 85 (bl), 135 (b), 145 (t), 151 (br): Martingraf/Dreamstime.com

pp. 3 (tr), 110 (b): mauritius images GmbH/ Alamy Stock Photo

pp. 3 (bl), 110 (bl): Rares Pulbere/ Dreamstime.com

pp. 4 (br), 161 (bl, bc), 161 (r), 195 (bl, br), 214 (c), 215 (t, b), 216-217 (bg, cl, cr), 213 (br) Kirsten Carlson

pp. 4 (c), 189 (t): Iakov Filimonov/ Dreamstime.com

pp. 5 (t), 227: National Park Service

pp. 5 (bc), 235 (bg), 236 (bg): Nikolay Antonov/ Dreamstime.com

pp. 5 (bl), 235 (inset): Duane Braley/Star Tribune/ Getty Images

pp. 6 (c), 308: Jim Rogash/Getty Images

pp. 7 (br), 342 (cr), 361 (c), 368 (c), 392 (br): Skylynxdesign/Dreamstime.com

pp. 7 (cr), 342 (br), 361 (b), 371 (b), 393 (l): Kosin Sukhum/Dreamstime.com

pp. 7 (tl), 366 (airplane): Phive2015/ Dreamstime.com

pp. 7 (tr), 371 (t): Shubas/Dreamstime.com

pp. 26-27 (bg): Abhinav Jain/Dreamstime.com

pp. 32-34 (bg): Mila_ls/Shutterstock

pp. 42-43 (bg): Zakharchuk/Shutterstock

pp. 84 (bl), 87 (b), 98 (b), 150 (bl): Everett Collection Historical/Alamy Stock Photo

pp. 84 (cl), 94 (l), 150 (cl): Harold M. Lambert/ Archive Photos/Getty Images

pp. 84 (tc), 103 (t), 104, 119 (t), 150 (tc): Waterfront Partnership of Baltimore

pp. 84 (c), 103 (c), 109, 150 (tr): Stephanie Kwolek Innovative Lives Presentation, Archives Center, National Museum of American History, Smithsonian Institution

pp. 84 (tc), 105 (moon surface): NASA/GSFC/ Arizona State University

pp. 84 (tc), 105 (lunar rover): Owen Egan

pp. 84 (cc), 109 (tl): YUEH HUNG SHIH/ Alamy Stock Photo

pp. 84 (tr), 119 (t), 120, 121 (t, b), 151 (tl): Courtesy of Bharathi Rao

pp. 84 (br), 119 (b), 129 (tr), 151 (bl): Bloomberg/ Getty Images

pp. 84 (cr), 126, 151 (cl): TODD ANDERSON/ The New York Times/Redux

pp. 85 (tl), 137 (c), 150 (tr): J'rg Carstensen/ picture-alliance/dpa/AP Images

pp. 85 (cl), 142 (inset), 151 (cr): simonkr/E+/ Getty Images

pp. 86-87 (bg): Aleks49011/Dreamstime.com

pp. 87 (c), 93 (l): Everett Collection/Shutterstock

pp. 88-89 (bg): Simbert Brause/Shutterstock

p. 89 (tl): SSPL/Getty Images

p. 89 (tc): Nick Scott - Cameras/ Alamy Stock Photo

p. 89 (tr): Daderot/Wikimedia/CC0 1.0

pp. 92-94 (bg): N1chEZ/Shutterstock

p. 92 (t): National Archives (111-SC-2432)

p. 92 (b): Anton Prohorov/Shutterstock

p. 93 (r): Mike Flippo/Shutterstock

p. 97 (t): Jintanatta/Shutterstock

pp. 97 (b), 230 (b): Chronicle/Alamy Stock Photo

p. 98 (t): Pogorelova Olga/Shutterstock

p. 114 (b): Felix Mizioznikov/Shutterstock

p. 105: Bruce Morser

pp. 108-110 (bg): Upl/Shutterstock.com

p. 114 (t): PA Images/Alamy Stock Photo

pp. 118-119 (bg): Mariia Sigova/Dreamstime.com

pp. 119 (c), 124 (inset), 125 (t): iCPooch/Purina/ Splash/Newscom

pp. 124-126 (t): 4zevar/Shutterstock

pp. 124-125 (bg): Elenamiv/Shutterstock

p. 125 (c): Tina Rencelj/Dreamstime.com

pp. 129 (b), 130 (bg): Trygve Finkelsen/ Dreamstime.com

pp. 129 (tl), 130 (c): Svitlana Unuchko/ Dreamstime.com

p. 130 (bl): Marcio Jose Sanchez/AP Photo

p. 130 (br): Tribune Content Agency LLC/Alamy Stock Photo

pp. 134-135 (bg): Artistdesign29/Shutterstock

pp. 135 (t), 136-137 (bg): Photographer/ Collection/Getty Images

pp. 135 (c), 140 (inset): DIY Girls

pp. 140-142 (bg): allakuz/Shutterstock

p. 141 (inset): Hello Lovely/Corbis/Getty Images

p. 146 (b): Natthapon Ngamnithiporn/ Dreamstime.com

pp. 160 (tr), 179 (t), 181 (l), 212 (tr): Lamont-Doherty Earth Observatory and the estate of Marie Tharp Maps

pp. 160 (cr), 179 (c), 184-185 (bg), 212 (cr): Old Images/Alamy Stock Photo

pp. 161 (tl), 197 (b), 213 (tl): AP Images

pp. 162 (inset), 164-165 (inset), 168-170 (inset), 173-174 (inset): Mtsaride/Dreamstime.com

pp. 162-163 (bg): Michael Kulmar/EyeEm/ Getty Images

pp. 164-165 (bg): Nadezda Rabtsevich/ Dreamstime.com

pp. 168-170 (bg): Mel Surdin/Dreamstime.com

pp. 173-174 (bg): dszc/E+/Getty Images

pp. 178-179 (bg): Bardocz Peter/Shutterstock

p. 184 (inset), 186 (cl, bl, br)): Library of Congress Prints and Photographs Division

p. 186 (bg): Andreykuzmin/Dreamstime

pp. 189 (b), 212 (br): VW Pics/Universal Images Group/Getty Images

pp. 194-195 (bg): Avigator Fortuner/Shutterstock

pp. 195 (bl), 205 (inset): University of Richmond

p. 200 (b): Carlos Carivan/Science Source

pp. 205-206 (bg): narvikk/E+/Getty Images

p. 214 (b): Elaine Hood/National Science Foundation

pp. 216-217 (t): Stone36/Shutterstock

pp. 222 (tl), 225 (t), 226, 272 (t): Robert Fried/ Alamy Stock Photo

pp. 222 (cl), 225 (c),231 (b), 272 (c): Amy E. Price/ Getty Images Entertainment/Getty Images

pp. 222 (bl), 236 (t), 272 (b): Minneapolis Institute of Art/Gift of funds from anonymous donors/ Bridgeman Images; ©Cy Thao

pp. 224-225 (bg): Stepanida Popozoglo/ Dreamstime.com

pp. 230-231 (t): Kran Kanthawong/ Dreamstime.com

pp. 230-231 (c): Robertosch/Dreamstime.com

p. 232: Michel RENAUDEAU/Gamma-Rapho/ Getty Images

p. 236 (b): Minneapolis Institute of Art/Gift of funds from anonymous donors/Bridgeman Images; ©Cy Thao

Credits (continued)

pp. 274 (t), 275 (t): Pattern Paper Print/ Shutterstock

pp. 275 (c), 277 (c): Picsfive/Shutterstock

pp. 282 (tl), 285 (t), 286 (r), 332 (t): Bettmann/ Getty Images

pp. 282 (bl), 285 (b), 295, 332 (b): Stephen Mcsweeny/Alamy Stock Photo

pp. 282 (cl), 290 (tr), 332 (c): Mark Waugh/ Alamy Stock Photo

pp. 282 (tr), 301 (tl), 303 (r), 333 (tl): Brian Zak/ NY Post/MEGA/Newscom

pp. 282 (br), 301 (b), 312 (b), 333 (bl): DON EMMERT/AFP/Getty Images

pp. 284-285 (bg): Torsak/Dreamstime.com

pp. 285 (c), 291 (r): Cal Sport Media/ Alamy Stock Photo

p. 286 (l): Oleksii Terpugo/Dreamstime.com

p. 290 (tl): Jerry Bergquist/Alamy Stock Photo

p. 290 (b): Ralph Crane/The LIFE Picture Collection/Getty Images

p. 291 (l): ZUMA Press Inc/Alamy Stock Photo

p. 292 (tl): Portland Press Herald/Getty Images

p. 292 (tr): MediaNews Group/Orange County Register/Getty Images

p. 292 (bl): Compassionate Eye Foundation/ Steven Errico/DigitalVision/Getty Images

p. 292 (br): zeljkosantrac/E+/Getty Images

p. 296 (bg): ninell/Dreamstime.com

p. 296 (baseball grips): Karen Huang/ Curriculum Associates

pp. 301 (tr), 307, 333 (cl): Tom DiPace/AP Photo

p. 302 (b): Tim Clayton/Corbis Sport/ Getty Images

p. 303 (l): Stephanie Pennington

p. 306 (tr): Mary Schwalm/AP Photo

p. 306 (cl): David L. Ryan/The Boston Globe/ Getty Images

pp. 311 (inset), 312 (tr): patrice6000/Shutterstock

p. 311 (bg): Andreas Altwein/picture alliance/ Getty Images

p. 312 (tl): Ozier Muhammad/The New York Times/Redux Pictures

pp. 334-335 (bg): kzww/Shutterstock

pp. 334-335 (inset): Kovalchuk Oleksandr/ Shutterstock

p. 334 (l): SDI Productions/E+/Getty Images

p. 334 (r): Sergey Novikov/Dreamstime.com

p. 335 (tr): Design Pics Inc/Alamy Stock Photo

p. 337 (t): pio3/Shutterstock

p. 337 (b): REUTERS/Paul Childs/ Alamy Stock Photo

pp. 344-345 (bg): Chick2view/Dreamstime.com

pp. 342 (tr), 361 (t), 362 (l), 392 (tr): Thomas Dutour/Shutterstock

pp. 343 (tl), 377 (t), 379 (b), 393 (tr): Visual China Group/Getty Images

pp. 343 (r), 394 (t): Tony Bennett

pp. 344 (cl), 377 (c), 383 (l, r), 384 (inset), 393 (cr): Courtesy, Sandia National Laboratories

p. 362 (cl): National Geographic Image Collection/Bridgeman Images

p. 362 (cr): Adam88x /Dreamstime.com

p. 362 (r): Classic Image/Alamy Stock Photo

p. 363 (l): World History Archive/ Alamy Stock Photo

p. 366 (orange and leaves): Sergey Kolesnikov/ Dreamstime.com

p. 366 (strawberries): Ovydyborets/ Dreamstime.com

p. 366 (pointy leaves), SlavkoSereda/ Dreamstime.com

p. 368 (b): Psychoshadowmaker/Dreamstime.com

p. 372 (l): Aquariagirrl1970/Dreamstime.com

p. 372 (cl): Martin Muránsky/Dreamstime.com

p. 372 (cr): Jochen Tack/Alamy Stock Photo

p. 372 (r): CulturalEyes - AusSoc2/ Alamy Stock Photo

pp. 378-379 (t), 368 (t): Airubon/Dreamstime.com

p. 378 (b): Roman Pilipey/ EPA/ Shutterstock

p. 379 (c): Easton Chen/Dreamstime.com

p. 382: Jose Luis Cruz-Campa

pp. 383 (bg), 384 (bg): Ivan Mikhaylov/ Dreamstime.com

p. 394 (b): Courtesy of the Library of Congress, LC-DIG-highsm-54736

p. 395 (tr): Nuttakit Sukjaroensuk/ Dreamstime.com

p. 395 (maps): The Geekery Store/Shutterstock

pp. 395 (b), 397 (l, r): Kelly Charley

pp. 432-433: Photographs of the Ferris Wheel from Official Views of The World's Columbian Exposition Issued by the Department of Photography by C. D. Arnold and H. D. Higinbotham, Official Photographers, published by Press Chicago Photo-Gravure Company (1893).

p. 438: Michael Cummings/Alamy Stock Photo

p. 439: Holly Kuchera/Dreamstime.com

pp. 442-443: Thomas Dutour/Dreamstime.com

p. 451: Pavel Chagochkin/Shutterstock

p. 452: HelenField/Shutterstock

p. 462 (t): Svetlana Foote/Dreamstime.com

p. 462 (b): Ad_hominem/Shutterstock

p. 463: Naches/Shutterstock